Jerry Kirk
Ps. 34:3
Luke 9:23

FOLLOWING JESUS TOGETHER

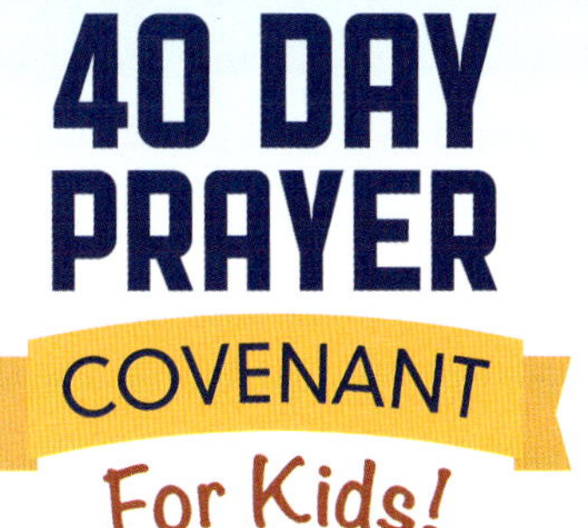

WWW.THEPRAYERCOVENANT.ORG

GRACE Dear heavenly Father, thank you for loving me and making me one of your children.

LOVE Help me love and obey you.

COMPASSION Help me love others the way you love me.

REPENTANCE I am sorry for my sins. Wash me clean.

WORSHIP I will praise you with all my heart!

COMMITMENT Jesus, I want to follow you as my Lord. Change me any way you want.

DEPENDENCE Fill me with your Holy Spirit.

INFLUENCE Make me an instrument of your grace, truth and justice.

DISCIPLESHIP Use me for your glory and to invite others to follow you.

AUTHORITY In Jesus' name I pray. Amen.

REFERENCES

I John 3:1
How great is the love the Father has lavished on us that we should be called children of God.

Matthew 22:37, 38
Love the Lord your God with all your heart and with all your soul and with all your mind. This is the first and greatest commandment.

John 15:12
My command is this, love one another as I have loved you.

Psalm 51:2
Wash me thoroughly from my iniquity and cleanse me from my sin.

Psalm 9:1
I will praise you, O Lord, with all my heart; I will tell of all your wonderful deeds.

John 13:13
You call me 'Teacher' and 'Lord.' You are right. That is what I am.

Ephesians 5:18b
Be filled with the Holy Spirit.

John 1:14
We have seen his glory, the glory of the one and only Son, who came from the Father, full of grace and truth.

Matthew 28:19
Go therefore and make disciples of all nations, baptizing them in the name of the Father, the Son and the Holy Spirit.

Philippians 2:9
Therefore, God exalted Him to the highest place and gave Him a name that is above every name.

The Power of THE PRAYER COVENANT For Kids

CANDY MARBALLI

With Stephen Eyre

Illustrations by **Luke Flowers** | Foreword by **Jerry Kirk**

40 Day Prayer Covenant Inc.
P.O. Box 40841
Cincinnati, OH 45240
www.theprayercovenant.org

Materials to supplement *The Power of the Prayer Covenant for Kids* are available at www.theprayercovenant.org, including free multiple-language versions of *The 40 Day Prayer Covenant Kids' Version* cards and full color Worksheets. Special discounts are available for bulk purchases.

Design by Sound Press

ISBN 978-0-9899525-1-4

Printed in the United States of America

Praying the adult version of The 40 Day Prayer Covenant is changing my life. Now, I can't wait to use this kids' version to encourage the children in my life to hide God's Word in their hearts and commit to daily prayer! What a wonderful tool to help us journey together.

– **BEKAH BOSWELL**, SIL International, InterMission Global Prayer Coordinator

The Power of the Prayer Covenant for Kids is a timely resource that will flame the fire already burning in the hearts of children in prayer.

– **IRMA CHON**, Children's Pastor, Director of Children in Prayer

The Power of the Prayer Covenant For Kids is a bold challenge to engage the hearts of children in the mission to advance the Kingdom of Christ through prayer. Thanks Candy for such an effective tool.

– **GARY L. FROST**, Vice President, Midwest Region and Prayer North American Mission Board

The Power of the Prayer Covenant for Kids is an amazing, one-of-a-kind book! Its power of focus, crystal clarity and profound simplicity make this a great gift to the body of Christ! I believe God will use this book to raise up a generation of passionate praying kids, rooted in the Word of God, and released into anointed ministry for the glory of Christ! As both a dad, and pastor of prayer, I highly recommend this book! Let's follow Jesus together in the place of prayer with our kids!

– **DR. JASON HUBBARD**, Director of Light of the World Prayer Center

This book is a beautifully illustrated and written prayer guide for children around the world and a must-have resource for churches, schools and families. It is both engaging and practical.

– **ROBERT A. MCDONALD**, Retired Chairman, President and Chief Executive Officer of The Procter & Gamble Company

The Power of the Prayer Covenant for Kids is going to ignite a fire that is already lit in my home on prayer. I cannot wait to watch the movement of this book in my family and others. The discipline of prayer and the discussions that will come through this book to many children has me inspired to share and invite many others.

– **SEAN MCKAY**, G.M./Director of Sales, Lynx Enterprises & Lynx Chemicals of Dayton, Father to four children: Stephen-14, Samantha-12, Skylar-9, Shayla-7

The most powerful tool we can give the next generation is prayer. This covenant allows our children to acknowledge the Lordship of Jesus Christ. Our congregation has been equipped. My children have been blessed and I know yours will be too.

– **REV. CURTUS MOAK**, Associate Pastor of Hamilton Christian Center

I am delighted that the prayer covenant is now prepared for children to use in their prayer life. I wonder if the most significant use of this prayer covenant will be in preparing children around the world to live a praying life. And so we loudly proclaim, "Come on children, learn to pray and worship God."

– **DR. LOU SHIREY**, Director of Clergy Development/Prayer Ministry, International Pentecostal Holiness Church

The Power of the Prayer Covenant for Kids masterfully develops Gods loving character and the children's identity as cherished sons and daughters who are fully able, by the Holy Spirit, to hear the heart of heaven and release it on earth, in unity, through the authority of Jesus' name.

– **KATIE STEELE**, Children's Director of Light of the World Prayer Center Member of 4/14 Movement

This book is not only a great tool for children to read to learn how to pray, it is simple, easy to understand and a great resource to help parents and leaders teach children to be disciples of prayer. With it tying so closely to the adult version of the prayer covenant, it makes it easy for families to engage in praying with and for each other, while learning how to expand that prayer into their local communities. Great job!

– **FORD TAYLOR**, FSH Group/Transformational Leadership

How life-changing for children to be taught the need for prayer, how to pray, and the power of prayer! In addition to the importance of prayer, the book also teaches children of God's love for them and the importance of obedience.

– **THOMAS E. TRASK**, Former General Superintendent of the Assemblies of God

God is raising up a generation of world-changer children and youth. The Power of the Prayer Covenant for Kids is an amazing resource for them to learn to pray Christ centered prayers for themselves and others every day. How cool is that! I'm a big fan! I plan to share it with all of my friends and colleagues, especially the younger ones. I encourage you to do the same.

– **TOM VICTOR**, President, The Great Commission Coalition, Facilitator, 4 to 14 Window North American Region

The Power of the Prayer Covenant for Kids is an awesome biblical tool to develop love and intimacy with and for the Almighty, in our children. I believe it will encourage all believers to pray, evangelize and disciple our kids to passionately pursue radical obedience to The Greatest Commandment and the Great Commission. Thank you for this great gift to the body of Christ!

– **K. MARSHALL WILLIAMS SR.**, Senior Pastor, Nazarene Baptist Church, Philadelphia PA and President, National African American Fellowship, SBC

Dedication

To all the children in the world; *may you grow to understand how much your heavenly Father dearly loves you.*

To my beloved husband Vik and our children, Jonathan and Maria, *for your love, support and encouragement.*

To Stephen Eyre, my co-author, *for graciously sharing his expertise, guidance and commitment to this project.*

To Jerry Kirk, *for his generosity and unwavering support in extending the vision of the 40 Day Prayer Covenant to the children of the world.*

To all the ladies that were on the team that helped develop the kids' prayer: *Amy Kirk, Sharon Mason, Stephanie Plankovitch, Sharon Schatz, and Katie Steele.*

To Irma Chon and Katie Steele of the 4/14 Movement, *for their input and guidance.*

I have been involved with the ministry of the adult Prayer Covenant for over 45 years. I am constantly delighted to see how God is blessing and expanding its ministry. However, the Kid's Prayer Covenant is one of the surprises of God. It never occurred to me, that is until Candy Marballi shared her vision. Candy was led by the Lord to create a team of specialists in Children's Ministry. Since Candy and her team have given their lives in ministry to children, they were eager to capture the Prayer Covenant in the language of children. After producing the kid's version of the Prayer Covenant, Candy and others saw the need for this book.

Like the adult version, the Kid's Prayer Covenant is a tool that guides and enriches prayer. And as the name implies, it is written for kids. It meets children where they are, but it doesn't leave them where they are. It is a beautiful, concise, direct, and challenging prayer that is just right for children's spiritual growth.

This book is written mainly for kids. But I believe it will bless and enrich parents too--so that they can be a channel of blessing to their children; it will also bless and enrich Sunday School teachers so they can bless their students; and it will bless and enrich pastors so that they can bless the entire Christian education process.

It is natural for children to pray; and it is natural for kids to pray with their parents whom they trust and love. What the Kid's Prayer Covenant provides parents and teachers with is a track on which to run. It is a prayer-shaped avenue that opens children to the love that God gives and the peace that every child needs.

Initially the Kid's Prayer Covenant seemed like a good idea. Now I believe producing the Kid's Prayer Covenant is one of the most important decisions our leadership team has made. It may be the match that ignites the flame of the Prayer Covenant around the world!

JERRY KIRK
Founder and President of The Prayer Covenant

We have an agenda, and we want you to know it!

We are writing to encourage and facilitate a spiritual awakening around the world!

We envision the Kids' Prayer Covenant and this book as a match in the hands of God's Spirit, igniting the church and transforming the world.

Said in another way, we have a big vision and a specific mission:

VISION:

To see children worldwide using the Kids' Prayer Covenant to deepen their intimacy with their heavenly Father and impact others for Christ.

MISSION:

To equip families, ministries, churches, and schools with the capabilities to use the Kids' Prayer Covenant to raise lifelong, committed disciples of Jesus Christ.

Introduction

In this twenty-first century, there is a new and exciting shift toward children within the Church around the world. The Church is discovering that children and youth make up the largest generational group in the world's population (Generation Z: born in the early 1990's to present). It follows that children should be a primary focus of mission and ministry. Not only is this perceptive, but it is also faithful to the Scriptures. Children have been a part of God's plan from the very beginning, and they still are.

The present Generation Z is a field ripe for mission. Research affirms that they want to impact the world—they are less interested in stuff and more interested in causes. They are tech savvy and connected 24/7, and they desire to make a positive difference. So it makes sense that now, more than ever, we need to engage, empower and equip children to be agents of Christ's kingdom to a lost and dying world: a world that needs the hope, love, and peace that only Jesus can bring. We believe that the Kids' Prayer Covenant will be a powerful tool to reach this generation of children and to equip them for the ministry to which God is calling them.

The Kids' Prayer Covenant was born out of Dr. Jerry Kirk's 40 Day Prayer Covenant for adults. What is the Prayer Covenant? It is a simple, yet comprehensive prayer designed to deepen and enrich discipleship, and it is a prayer especially intended to be used in a covenant relationship of mutual support for forty days. Countless thousands who have entered in the Prayer Covenant have discovered it to be powerful and life changing. It is a prayer of obedience and surrender. It keeps those who pray it sharpened, motivated, and in step with our Savior.

The adult Prayer Covenant inspired the simplified Kids' version. Simplified it may be, yet it is not lacking in depth and substance. Our heart's desire, our goal, and our reasoning behind offering a version for children is that this prayer deepens intimacy with their heavenly Father. We want kids to experience Jesus on such a personal level that it grips them and changes them forever. If children can pray a prayer daily that they can understand, it will unleash them to experience Jesus on a personal level, it will cause them to run to their heavenly Father daily, and it will enable and empower them to be filled with the Holy Spirit—the same Holy Spirit we possess as adults.

WHY FORTY DAYS?

Although this prayer can be used for a lifetime, forty days is the length of time the children can covenant with one another, whether it is with a teacher, parent, sibling, mentor, or friend. When forty days are complete, the child can invite someone new and begin another forty days of praying for that person, and so on. In this way prayer with and for other people becomes a way of life—the Prayer Covenant lifestyle.

WHY HAVE WE INCLUDED CORRESPONDING BIBLE REFERENCES FOR EACH LINE?

Our prayers are empowered and enriched by the Scriptures. Jesus said, "If you remain in me and my words remain in you, ask whatever you wish, and it will be done for you" (John 15:7). Memorizing Scripture is a powerful tool. It is something that, once learned, will stay with children all of their lives. The more Scripture memorized, the more strength and ability to face the challenges and temptations that will come.

THE FLOW OF THE PRAYER

The Prayer is more than a list or collection of individual requests. Each line builds on the one before it and leads naturally to the next. Through prayer the Father fashions children and youth to become more like his son Jesus Christ, children who will be:

- accepting his GRACE as a loving Father,
- LOVING others in obedience to him,
- showing COMPASSION the way he does,
- being truly REPENTANT of sin
- which results in true WORSHIP;
- while COMMITTING to follow Jesus daily,
- and living in DEPENDENCE upon the Holy Spirit.

The results will be:

- children who will INFLUENCE others in godliness,
- who are becoming mature DISCIPLES of Jesus Christ,
- who live and pray under the AUTHORITY of Jesus Christ.

THE LAYOUT OF THE BOOK

The first half of this book is just for kids. We want them to read it. We want adults to read it to them. We want the illustrations to inspire them, the Scriptures to capture their hearts, and the prayer to engage them. In reading the prayer this book can provide a form of worship by both meditating on God's Word and praying together. May it begin each day with joy and thankfulness, and close each day with comfort and peace.

The second half of the book is for kids, too; however, its primary purpose is to provide curriculum resources for teachers and parents to use in presenting *The 40 Day Prayer Covenant Kids' Version*. The second half provides additional Scripture references to allow for deeper study, discussion questions to encourage interaction, prayer breakout sessions, a Bible story, worksheets--including a Prayer Covenant Record for kids to use as they covenant with others--and last but not least, a rap allowing kids to express their creativity and excitement. The material in the second half may be read aloud as written or used as a guide in preparing your own curriculum—the choice is yours.

HI KIDS!

The Power of the 40 Day Prayer Covenant for kids is a book designed especially for you—to help strengthen and grow your prayer life. What's the first thing that comes to your mind when you think about power? Super heroes? Famous People? Money? God? If you guessed God, you are right! God IS powerful! "All power is given unto me in heaven and in earth." (Matt. 28:18 KJV) Uh, that's a LOT of power! The Bible also says, 'With God nothing is impossible!" Do you know that God's power is yours if you ask him? Jesus said, "If you ask anything in my name, I will do it." WOW! There is power in prayer and there is power in Jesus' name? Yes! And all you have to do is ask! Jesus said, "Ask so you can receive and you'll be happy." Prayer is not about asking for material things or wishes to be granted. It's asking God for things like love, faith, patience, healing, guidance and strength--it's asking him to make you more like himself. Asking Jesus to forgive your sins, to fill you with his Spirit, and to use you for his glory are all good things to ask for when you pray.

Jesus loves you personally and completely. Just as your parents enjoy hearing how your day went, what you are thankful for, or what might be troubling you, your heavenly Father also longs to hear from you.

Prayer is important, and it can be fun. You will find there is nothing more wonderful in the whole wide world than spending time with Jesus in prayer and reading his Word. We have included Bible verses for you to learn with each line of the prayer. Jesus said, "He who loves me will keep my words, and my Father will love him and dwell with him." That is a very special promise.

Prayer ***really*** is important. The more you pray, the more you will grow in his grace and knowledge, becoming more and more like Jesus and experiencing the fruit of his Spirit: "love, joy, peace, patience, gentleness, kindness, goodness, faithfulness, and self-control." This pleases Jesus.

We hope you find this book helpful and enjoy the time you spend reading and praying together with your mom, dad, sisters, brothers, grandparents, and friends.

Lastly, there is one thing that you must promise never to forget. It's that your heavenly Father loves you with an everlasting, never-ending, forever-and-always kind of love!

What's a prayer covenant?

You may be wondering, "What's a covenant?" A covenant is a promise between two or more people. You first start by praying this prayer every day by yourself or you can choose to pray this prayer with another person. If you start alone, be sure to choose someone soon to join you. You might choose to covenant with your mom, dad, grandma, grandpa, sister, brother or friend for 40 days. The number 40 is used a lot in the Bible—can you think of some Bible passages that use it? Check out these verses: Genesis 7:12; Exodus 34:28; Matthew 4:2. How it works is that you will pray for that person and that person will pray for you for 40 days. When 40 days is over you can invite someone new with whom to covenant.

Praying for others for 40 days is a neat way to show you love and care about them. And remember, Jesus loves hearing from you. He wants you to spend time with him every day. It's fun spending time with Jesus! And it's fun following Jesus together!

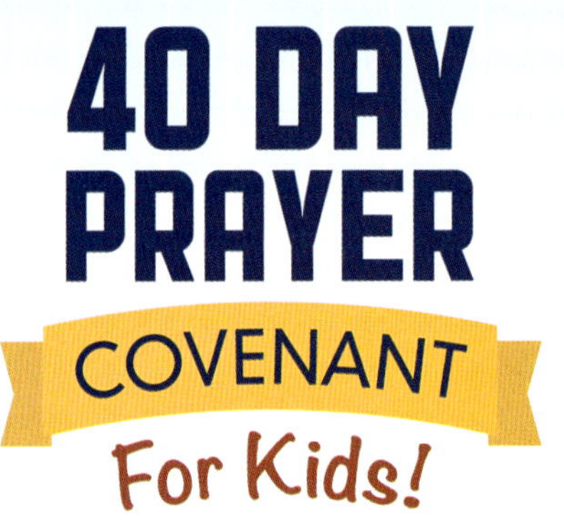

Dear heavenly Father,

Thank you for loving me and making me one of your children.

Help me love and obey you.

Help me love others the way you love me.

I am sorry for my sins. Wash me clean.

Jesus, I want to follow you as my Lord.

Change me any way you want.

Fill me with your Holy Spirit.

Make me an instrument of your grace,
truth and justice.

Use me for your glory and to invite
others to follow you.

In Jesus name I pray, Amen.

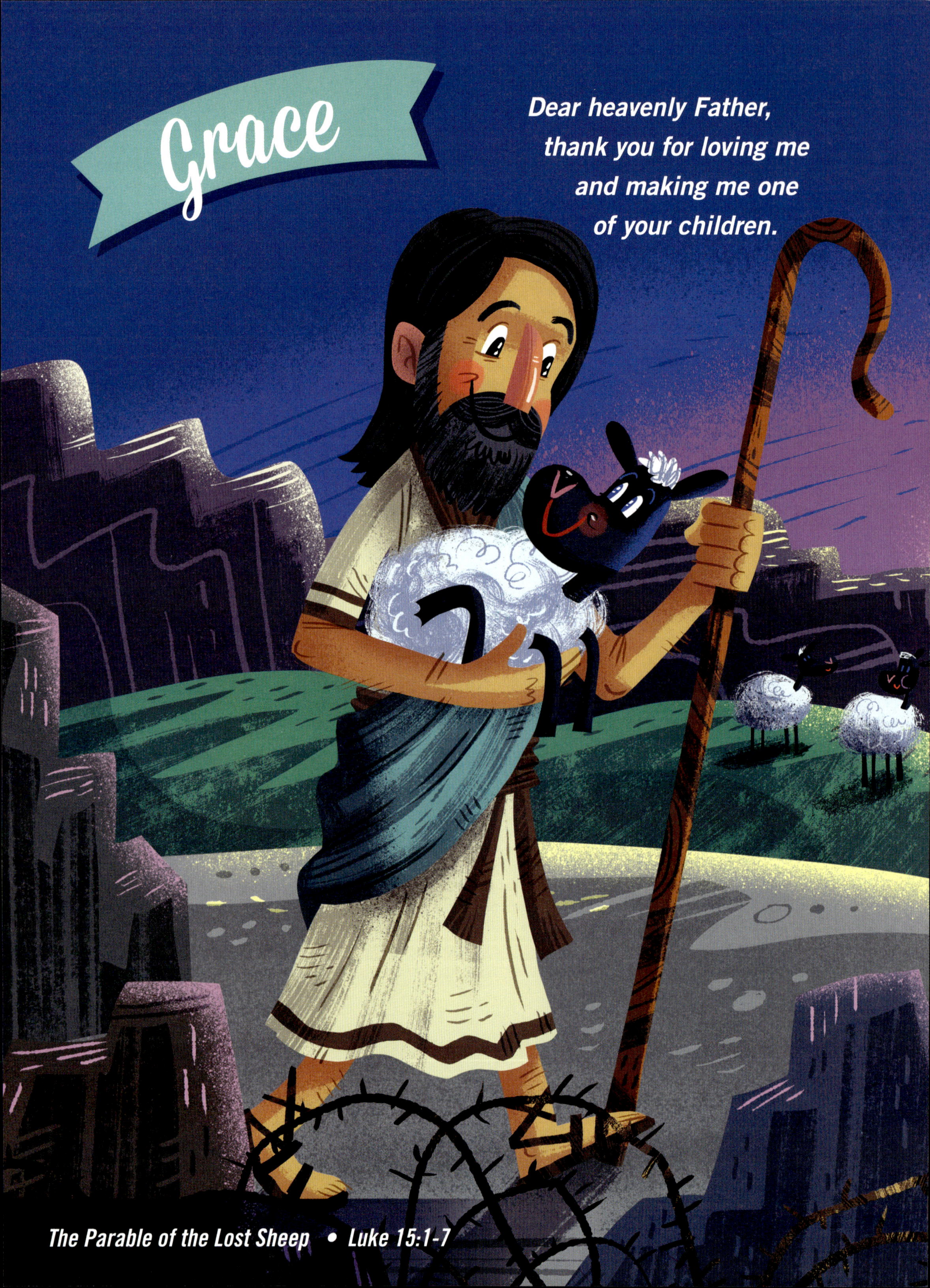
Grace
Dear heavenly Father,
thank you for loving me
and making me one
of your children.
The Parable of the Lost Sheep • Luke 15:1-7

And Jesus replied:
"You are my precious child, and
I love you with an everlasting love."

1 JOHN 3:1

How great is the love the Father has lavished on us, that we should be called children of God!

Love
Help me love and obey you.
The Story of Abraham • Genesis 12:1-5

And Jesus replied:
"I desire you to obey my words.
If you love me you will obey me
by keeping my commandments."
MATTHEW 22:37,38
Love the Lord your God with all your heart and
with all your soul and with all your mind. This is
the first and greatest commandment.

Compassion
Help me love others
the way you love me.
The Good Samaritan • Luke 10:25-37

And Jesus replied:

"As you begin to understand how much I love you, you will be able to love others. Show my love by praying for those who are sick and by helping and comforting those who are struggling and in need."

JOHN 15:12

My command is this: love one another as I have loved you.

Repentance

I am sorry for my sins.
Wash me clean.

Parable of the Unforgiving Servant • Matthew 18:21-35

And Jesus replied:

"Have no fear. I will forgive your sins. I will make you whiter than snow. But it is important to remember that I want you always to forgive others just as I forgive you."

PSALM 51:2

Wash me thoroughly from my iniquity, and cleanse me from my sins.

Worship
I will praise you with all my heart!
The Christmas Story • Luke 1 and 2

And Jesus replied:

"I love hearing you sing praises to me and worshiping me. This is what you should always do. Your thankful heart brings me so much joy."

PSALM 9:1

I will praise you, O Lord, with all my heart;
I will tell of all your wonderful deeds.

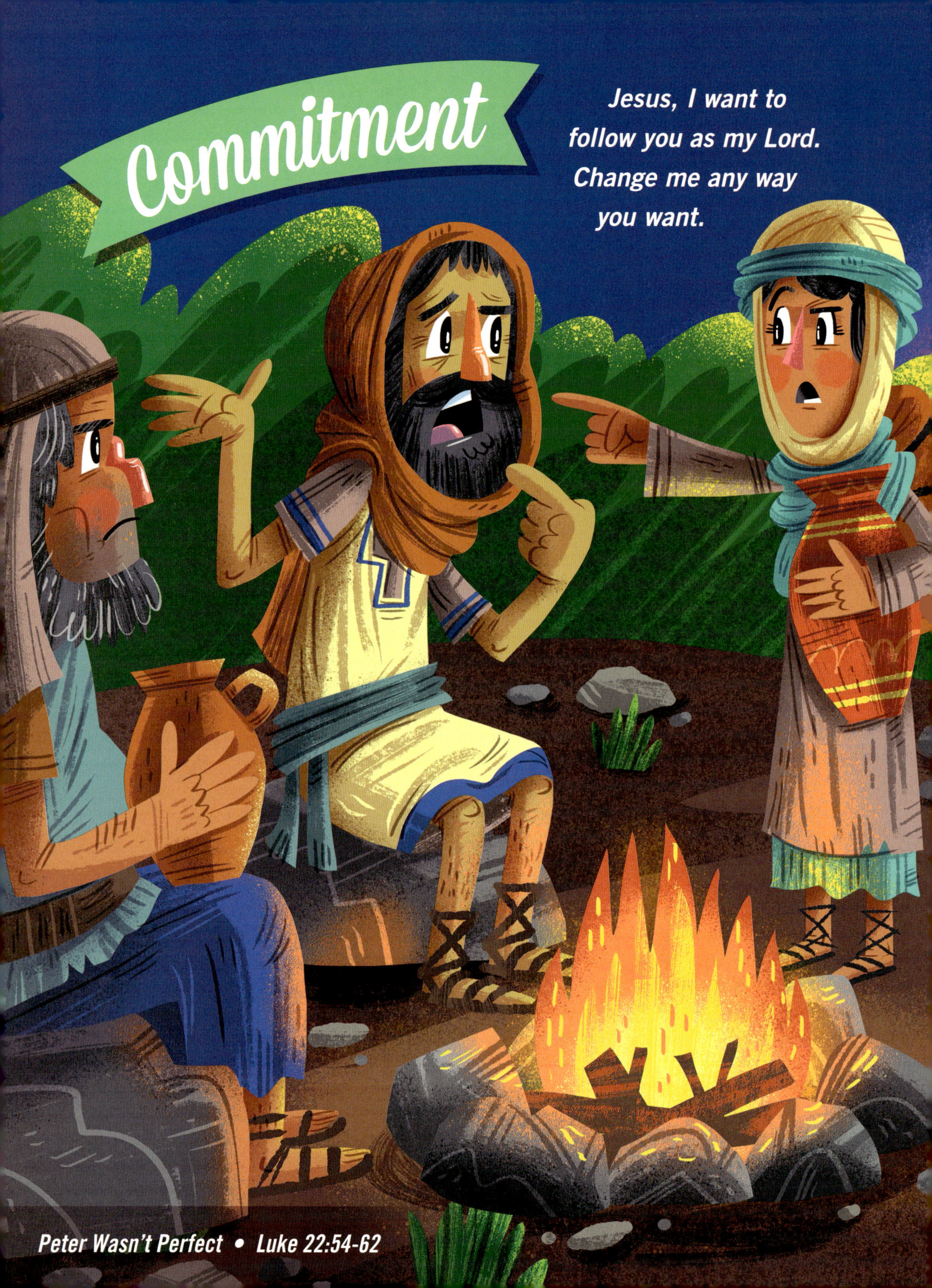
Commitment
Jesus, I want to
follow you as my Lord.
Change me any way
you want.
Peter Wasn't Perfect • Luke 22:54-62

And Jesus replied:

"I am your Teacher. I long for your obedient heart to follow me. The way may not always appear clear, but trust me—I will guide you every step of the way."

JOHN 13:13

You call me 'Teacher' and 'Lord'.' You are right, that is what I am.

Dependence
Fill me with
your Holy Spirit.
The Comforter • John 14:15-31

And Jesus replied:
“Remember, you are not alone. I am with you always and forever. I am your Comforter, your Teacher, and your Guide.”

EPHESIANS 5:18b
Be filled with the Spirit.

Influence
Make me an instrument of
your grace, truth, and justice.
Jesus and the Children • Matthew 18:1-6

And Jesus replied:
"Speak often of me to those I place in your path. Tell them of my saving grace, my words of truth, and my love for justice. I came to heal the sick, to help the poor, and comfort those who are hurting. I can use you to do these very same things."

JOHN 1:14

We have seen his glory, the glory of the one and only Son, who came from the Father, full of grace and truth.

Discipleship
Use me for your glory
and to invite others
to follow you.
Saul of Tarsus Becomes Paul, an Apostle of Jesus Christ • Acts 9:1-22

And Jesus replied:
"I want you to tell your family and friends about me. I want you to tell them about my wonderful, loving-kindness. Invite them to follow me! You will find following me together is exciting and fun."

MATTHEW 28:19

Go therefore and make disciples of all nations, baptizing them in the name of the Father, the Son and the Holy Spirit.

Authority
In Jesus' name I pray. Amen.
Blind Bartimaeus • Mark 10:46-52

And Jesus replied:
"In my name is power and authority. In me you will find joy, peace, forgiveness, hope, and safety."

PHILIPPIANS 2:9
Therefore God exalted him to the highest place and gave him a name that is above every name."

The Power of
THE PRAYER COVENANT
For Kids
Teachers' Section

Getting Started

The Kids' 40 Day Prayer Covenant Curriculum is a line-by-line study guide of the prayer. The following categories are throughout the study guide:

CAN YOU SAY IT?

Here is where the prayer and corresponding memory verse are introduced to the children. Lead the children in both the prayer and the memory verse, allowing them to repeat it. Do this a couple of times.

2

CAN YOU FIND IT?

Additional Scripture references are provided for studying the topic further. The kids can look these up in class, taking turns reading the Scripture aloud and talking about what they think it's saying to them.

CAN YOU FEEL IT?

Kids love asking questions, and here's their opportunity! It's a place where they can openly share their concerns, fears, doubts, and beliefs on the topic.

4

POPCORN PRAYER BREAKOUT SESSION

This is to be a quiet time for the kids to experience prayer personally. For smaller classes, they can stand in a circle and pray "popcorn prayers," or one-line prayers, as they feel led. Begin the time by praying the line of the prayer and then letting others follow. This can be done in small groups around a table, on the floor, over maps of the world and/or globes! It's to help kids learn that praying is easy, fun, and great to do together.

Getting Started

5

TALK IT!

This section includes some in-depth discussion starters to encourage conversation and interaction.

6

CAN YOU HEAR IT?

Read the Bible story provided for the children, or share the story in your own words.

CAN YOU DO IT?

This is the application section of the session. Challenges and goals are presented for the kids to contemplate and discuss.

8

WORKSHEETS

With each lesson you will find colorful worksheets to enrich the classroom time and allow kids to review what they have learned. There is a Prayer Covenant Record Keeper at the back of the book that will allow kids to record the names of those they covenant with. You can order them in convenient packs online at **www.theprayercovenant.org**.

IT'S A RAP!

We saved the best for last. This is the activity portion of the session. The leader starts off with the words in black, and the kids read the words in blue. Allow them creative expression by having them write their own rap from what they learned from the lesson. Write their ideas on the board and listen as the energy builds as they rap to what they wrote. You can increase the speed the second time around. Have fun with this as you "rap" up the session.

Grace

CAN YOU SAY IT?

Dear heavenly Father, thank you for loving me and making me one of your children.

1 JOHN 3:1

How great is the love the Father has lavished on us that we should be called the children of God!

CAN YOU FIND IT?

John 3:16

1 John 4:10

Romans 8:38-39

CAN YOU FEEL IT?

How do you know God loves us?

How do you show your love ?

What makes us his child?

What makes you feel loved?

"POPCORN PRAYER" BREAKOUT SESSION

If your class is large, break up into small groups and lead with, ***"Heavenly Father, thank you for loving me and making me one of your children."*** Have the children repeat that line and then ask them one-by-one to pray one-sentence prayers telling God how they love being his child, what God's everlasting love means to them, and thanking him for his love. If your class is small, you can do this by forming a circle holding hands, and as each child feels led to pray, they can.

TALK IT!

- Grace means being loved even when we didn't do anything to deserve that love.
- We know God loves us because he created us, provides for us, and sent his only Son, Jesus, to die on the cross for us.
- Do you know what everlasting love means? It means love that will never end. Not even in a zillion years.
- It won't end if you do something wrong.
- It won't end if you feel scared.
- It won't end if someone you love dies.
- It won't end if your parent loses their job.
- It won't end if you get a bad grade at school.
- No matter what happens, Jesus' love will never ever end and will never, ever fail.

Have the children share openly their thoughts on the love of God: fears and concerns about losing God's love or happiness and joy experiencing and learning about his love.

CAN YOU HEAR IT?

The Parable of the Lost Sheep (Luke 15:1-7)

Jesus wanted everyone to know how much God loves them. He told a story about a shepherd and his lost sheep. The shepherd was so concerned about one that was lost that he left the rest of the flock and looked especially for that lost sheep. Sheep sometimes stray and go their own way. They are helpless animals that can easily be attacked and eaten by bears, wolves, or lions. A shepherd's job is to protect sheep from danger, and that's just what the shepherd did. He was so happy when he found the sheep that he carried it on his shoulders all the way home. Then he called all of his friends and neighbors to celebrate that he found the sheep. Jesus said this is how it is in heaven when one boy or girl, man or woman, accepts him as their Savior—they go from being lost to being found, and that brings great joy, happiness, and celebration in heaven! Zephaniah 3:17 helps us feel the joy our heavenly Father has for his children. "The Mighty One will save; He will rejoice over you with gladness, he will quiet you with his love, he will rejoice over you with singing." How does that make you feel?

CAN YOU DO IT?

- Believe Jesus died for your sins and lives within your heart, and share it with others.
- Believe that his grace made you his dearly loved child.
- Believe that his love for you will never end, no matter what.
- Believe that God can use you to share his message of grace with someone today.

Grace

WORKSHEET

1. Can you remember the 1st line of the prayer, GRACE, and write it below?

2. Fill in the blanks.

   I John 3:1: "How _________ is the __________ the __________ has lavished on ______

   that ______ should be ___________ the ____________ of God."

3. In your own words can you share what you think makes you God's child forever?

4. Just like your parents, Jesus knows you by name and knows everything about you! Can you write a sentence or draw a picture describing how that makes you feel?

5. RESPONSE TIME:
   It is good to be thankful. This pleases Jesus. Can you write a thank you note to Jesus?

I'm a beloved child of the King of Kings!

I AM, I AM!

I'm his prized possession for all eternity!

I AM, I AM!

I'm saved by his grace and redeemed by his blood!

I AM, I AM!

I'm covered with his feathers and safe from harm!

I AM, I AM!

I'm thankful that his love for me will never, ever end!

I AM, I AM!

I'm a child of the most high God!

AMEN!

The teacher leads by reading the words in black, and the kids follow with the response in blue highlight. Afterward, encourage the class to write their own rap as a group, writing their suggestions on the board. Watch the excitement build as the kids rap what they have just written!

Love

CAN YOU SAY IT?

Help me love and obey you.

MATTHEW 22:37-38

Love the Lord your God with all your heart and with all your soul and with all your mind. This is the first and greatest commandment.

CAN YOU FIND IT?

Deuteronomy 7:9

John 14:15

2 John 1:6

Colossians 3:20

CAN YOU FEEL IT?

What is obedience?

Is love more important than obedience?

Why is love linked to obedience?

"POPCORN PRAYER" BREAKOUT SESSION

Lead the children in their prayer time once again by praying, ***"Help me love and obey you."*** Have the children repeat the prayer. Encourage them to pray one-sentence prayers asking God in their own words for his help in learning to love and obey him.

TALK IT!

- Jesus wants us to obey our parents.
- Jesus wants us to obey him. This makes him happy.
- We show our love for God by obeying him in all things.
- You will see in the story that blessing follows obedience.
- Obeying and following Jesus together is an exciting journey.

Here you can begin the discussion talking about obedience. When we obey our parents we are in fact obeying God, since he said we are to obey our parents in all things. Have kids share the challenges they find in being obedient but also the blessings they experience because of obedience. Finally, help them understand how love and obedience are linked.

CAN YOU HEAR IT?

The Story of Abraham (Genesis 12:1-5)

Abraham lived a very, very long time ago. When he was pretty old, God said to him, "Leave your country, your family, and your relatives and go to the land that I will show you. I will bless you and make your descendants into a great nation. You will become famous and be a blessing to others. Everyone on earth will be blessed because of you." Abraham obeyed God. He left with his wife, Sarah, his nephew Lot, and all of their belongings. They moved a long way from home, from a city called Heron to their new home, which they called the Promised Land. Can you think of why Abraham did what God asked him to do? Yep, you got it! He was learning to love and obey. His obedience was just the beginning of his lifelong adventure of growing in obedience, love, and faith.

CAN YOU DO IT?

- Show your love and devotion to God by being obedient to what he asks.
- Obey your parents because this honors God.
- Trust and obey God even when it doesn't make sense.

Love

WORKSHEET

1. Can you remember the 2nd line of the prayer, LOVE, and write it below?

2. Fill in the blanks.

   Matthew 22:37,38: " _______ the Lord _____ ______ with all your _________ and with all your __________ and with all your ___________. This is the _________ and greatest __________________."

3. What does it mean to obey?

4. What do you think is the hardest thing about being obedient?

5. RESPONSE TIME:

   On a piece of lined writing paper, use your best handwriting to write today's memory verse and then tape it onto your favorite colored paper – the colored paper should be larger so it looks like a frame. You can hang this on the wall of your bedroom or on your desk to remind you of God's greatest commandment.

What should you do at the start of every day?

TRUST, OBEY & PRAY!

What should you do when you read God's Holy Word?

TRUST, OBEY & PRAY!

What should you do when you're tempted to do wrong?

TRUST, OBEY & PRAY!

What should you do when you've had a bad, bad day?

TRUST, OBEY & PRAY!

What should you do when you're scared in the night?

TRUST, OBEY & PRAY!

What should you do that is pleasing in God's sight?

TRUST, OBEY & PRAY!

The teacher leads by reading the words in black, and the kids follow with the response in blue highlight. Afterward, encourage the class to write their own rap as a group, writing their suggestions on the board. Watch the excitement build as the kids rap what they have just written!

Compassion

CAN YOU SAY IT?

Help me love others the way you love me.

JOHN 15:12

My command is this, love one another as I have loved you.

CAN YOU FIND IT?

Matthew 5:44-48

1 Corinthians 13:4-7

1 John 4:7-11

1 John 3:18

CAN YOU FEEL IT?

Who are we commanded to love?

How are we to love?

When do you really feel the love of your family?

When do you feel loved by God?

"POPCORN PRAYER" BREAKOUT SESSION

Lead the children in prayer time once again by praying, ***"Help me love others the way you love me."*** Have the children repeat the prayer. Encourage them to pray one-sentence prayers asking God in their own words for ways to show his love to others.

TALK IT!

- Loving others is so important that it's up there with loving God with all of your heart, soul and mind.
- Loving others means loving your friends and your enemies. Ouch! That's a tough one.
- Loving others means loving as Jesus loved, sacrificially. That means putting others before yourself.

Encourage children to share and discuss openly their concerns and challenges in loving others the way Jesus requires. Refer to the passage in Matthew 5. Kids may wish to share their struggles in relationships and why it is difficult to love those who may not like them. Talk about the characteristics of love as laid out in 1 Corinthians 13. Which are more difficult to follow, which are easier?

CAN YOU HEAR IT?

The Good Samaritan (Luke 10:25-37)

What does it mean to love others the way God loves us? Let's find out. Someone asked Jesus, "Who is my neighbor?" Jesus explained by telling a story. He did that a lot. Jesus was a good storyteller. He said, "A man was traveling down the road from Jerusalem to Jericho and was attacked by a gang of bad men who beat him, stole his money and everything he owned, and left him half-dead on the side of the road. A priest walked by, and seeing the man went to the other side of the street." Between you and me, he wasn't very compassionate, was he? Jesus continued, "A Levite, a religious leader, also passed by the man, and he too crossed to the other side." Wow, really? Do you know what happened next? A Samaritan (someone looked down upon by the Jews) saw the injured man, and guess what he did? He showed God's love by helping to care for him. He cleaned and bandaged his wounds, put the man on his own donkey, took him to an inn (like a hotel), and asked the innkeeper to continue caring for him until he was better. The Samaritan said, 'Here are some silver coins to cover the expenses, and if it costs more, I will pay you back when I return this way.'" Do you know how Jesus finished the story? He said, "Now go and do the same."

CAN YOU DO IT?

- Love like Jesus loves, sacrificially.
- Love with our actions, not only our words. When you care for others you are showing compassion.
- Love Jesus with all your heart and ask his Holy Spirit to love others through you.

Compassion

WORKSHEET

1. Can you remember the 3rd line of the prayer, COMPASSION, and write it below?

2. Fill in the blanks.

   John 15:12: "My ____________________ is this, __________ one ____________________ as I have ________ you."

3. Why is Jesus' death on the cross an example of his perfect love for you?

4. Name one way you can show sacrificial love to someone you know.

5. RESPONSE TIME:

   Using construction paper, crayons and markers, make a card for someone you want to show love to. You may want to write the memory verse for today some place on the card!

IT'S A RAP!

I love you, God, with all my heart!

I DO, I DO!

I love you, God, with all my soul!

I DO, I DO!

I love you, God, with all my mind!

I DO, I DO!

I love you, God, with all my strength!

I DO, I DO!

Your love is something I want to see and feel!

I DO, I DO!

I want to show others your love is real!

I DO, I DO!

Give me a heart of compassion to change the world!

The teacher leads by reading the words in black, and the kids follow with the response in blue highlight. Afterward, encourage the class to write their own rap as a group, writing their suggestions on the board. Watch the excitement build as the kids rap what they have just written!

Repentance

CAN YOU SAY IT?

I am sorry for my sins. Wash me clean.

PSALM 51:2

Wash me thoroughly from my iniquity, and cleanse me from my sin.

CAN YOU FIND IT?

Matthew 6:9-15

Romans 10:9-10

1 John 1:9

CAN YOU FEEL IT?

How do you feel after you've done something wrong?

How do you feel after you've been forgiven?

What might prevent you from saying, "I'm sorry"?

"POPCORN PRAYER" BREAKOUT SESSION

Lead the children in prayer time once again by praying, ***"I am sorry for my sins. Wash me clean."*** Have the children repeat the prayer. Encourage them to pray one-sentence prayers asking God in their own words to forgive them and/or help them to forgive others.

TALK IT!

- What is the hardest thing for you to understand about forgiveness?
- Why can it be difficult to forgive others who have hurt you?
- Why is it hard to say, "I'm sorry, please forgive me"?
- How do you feel after coming clean before God, your parents, your siblings, or friends?

Lead the discussion by talking about God's willingness to forgive all of our sins. He is our example, and because he forgives us we need to be willing to forgive others. You may want to read the Lord's Prayer together. Encourage the children to share openly about times they find it hard to forgive, and compare that to how they feel when they have been forgiven.

Repentance

CAN YOU HEAR IT?

Parable of the Unforgiving Servant (Matthew 18:21-35)

Peter asked Jesus, "How many times should we forgive someone who sins against us, up to seven times?" Jesus replied, "Seventy times seven," and began to tell another story. There once was a king who called his servants to have them tell him what they owed him. One servant owed the king a huge amount of money that he would never be able to repay. The king said, "I am going to sell you and your family as slaves in order to pay the money you owe to me." The man cried, "No, please, please don't do that! I beg you. Please show mercy to my family and me." The king was a kind man and felt compassion and said, "I release you—you are free of all debt!" But guess what that very same man did? He went and found his servant that owed him a tiny amount of money and said, "If you don't pay me back every penny you owe I will throw you in jail" The servant begged, "Please be patient with me. I beg you for mercy!" But the man had a cruel heart and showed no mercy. Instead he put him in jail. It wasn't long before the king found out what his forgiven servant had done. He became very angry and said, "You wicked servant! I forgave you the huge debt because you begged me. Why didn't you show that same compassion to your servant?" And do you know what he did? He threw him into prison to be punished until the money he owed could be paid.

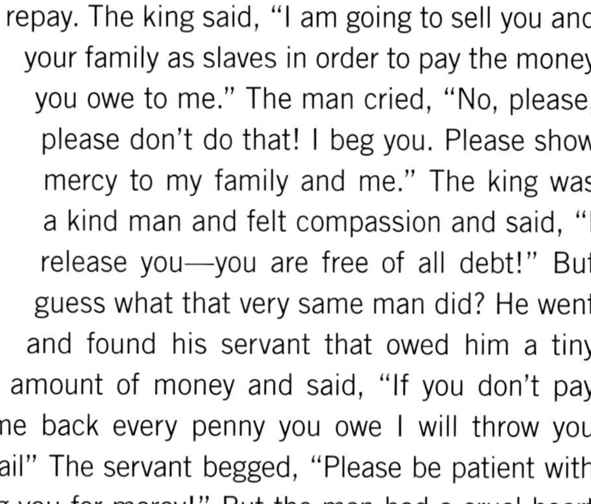

CAN YOU DO IT?

- Repent of your sins every day, asking God to wash you clean, making you white as snow.
- Believe that God washes away all your sin.
- Ask God to help you not to sin.
- Ask God to help you be forgiving and kind.
- Always be ready to forgive others and not hold a grudge against them.

Repentance

WORKSHEET

1. Can you remember the 4th line of the prayer, REPENTANCE, and write it below?

2. Fill in the blanks.

   Psalm 51:2: "Wash me ____________ from my ____________ and ____________ me from my ______________."

3. Why should we confess our sins to God every day?

4. Why is it so important that we forgive others?

5. RESPONSE TIME:

   Forgiveness Links – cut equal strips of paper. On one side of the paper write "God forgives me when….." On the back side write, "I forgive others when…." And staple or tape each link inside the next link. You can hang it in your room as a reminder to thank God for his unending forgiveness.

What should we do when we disobey?

REPENT, PRAY & TURN AWAY!

What should we do when we say something wrong?

REPENT, PRAY & TURN AWAY!

What should we do when we tell a lie?

REPENT, PRAY & TURN AWAY!

What should we do when we start a fight?

REPENT, PRAY & TURN AWAY!

What should we do when we don't forgive?

REPENT, PRAY & TURN AWAY!

What should we do when we are unkind?

REPENT, PRAY & TURN AWAY!

What should we do when we want our own way?

REPENT, PRAY & TURN AWAY!

The teacher leads by reading the words in black, and the kids follow with the response in blue highlight. Afterward, encourage the class to write their own rap as a group, writing their suggestions on the board. Watch the excitement build as the kids rap what they have just written!

Worship

CAN YOU SAY IT?

I will praise you with all my heart!

PSALM 91:1

I will praise you, O Lord, with all my heart; I will tell of all your wonderful deeds!

CAN YOU FIND IT?

Psalm 145

Matthew 21:16-17

1 Thessalonians 5:18

Revelation 4:8-11

CAN YOU FEEL IT?

What is praise?

How can I praise God?

When can I praise God?

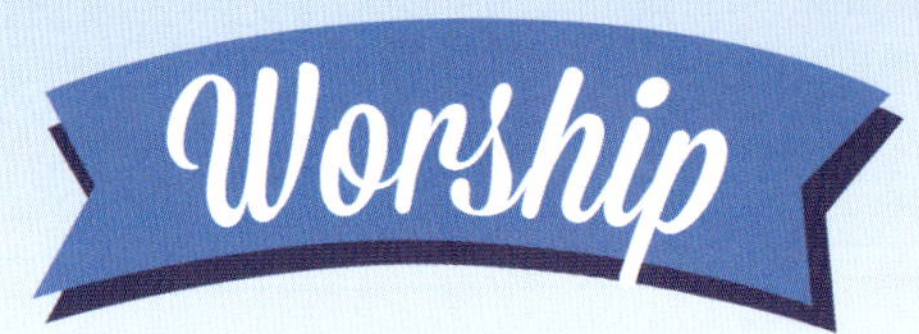

"POPCORN PRAYER" BREAKOUT SESSION

Lead the children in prayer time once again by praying, ***"I will praise you, O Lord, with all my heart!"*** Have the children repeat the prayer. Encourage them to pray one-sentence prayers of praise and worship—telling God how great, awesome, and wonderful he is. It can be a line from a worship song speaking of God's greatness or whatever they want to tell God.

TALK IT!

- Sometimes it is easier than others to praise God.
- Share when you feel it is easy to praise God.
- Share when you feel it is more difficult to praise God.
- Having a thankful heart not only pleases God but is part of praising him. Praise him when you wake up! Praise him when you eat! Praise him when you go to school and return home! Praise him before going to sleep!
- Developing a habit of praise will not only please your heavenly Father but will make you feel happy and blessed!

Kids know how to worship! They don't hold back in showing their love for Jesus, and it can be contagious. Have them share what style of worship they love best. Be sure to talk about thankfulness. It's hard to be thankful for everything all the time. It's never too late to start developing a habit of praise and thankfulness.

CAN YOU HEAR IT?

The Christmas Story (Luke 1 and 2)

A long, long time ago, more than two thousand years ago, a young girl named Mary was visited by an angel named Gabriel. He had a very special message for Mary. "Do not be afraid, Mary, you have found favor with God. You will be with child and give birth to a son, and you are to give him the name Jesus. He will be great and will be called the Son of the Most High." There was great rejoicing that followed Jesus' birth. "Suddenly many other angels came down from heaven and joined in praising God. They said: 'Praise God in heaven! Peace on earth to everyone who pleases God.'" (CEV) Shepherds soon came to visit and worship the newborn baby king. They were glorifying and praising God for the things they saw and heard. Wise men came from the east searching for baby Jesus. The beautiful bright shiny star that shone in the night sky led the way for them to come and worship their king. Just like Mary, Joseph, the shepherds, and the wise men honored and worshiped Jesus, we are to honor and worship him, too. And one day, when we are in heaven, we will be around his throne honoring and worshiping him forever and ever.

CAN YOU DO IT?

- Praise God every day throughout the day.
- Praise God in all circumstances. This is a choice!
- Have a thankful heart to God and for those God places around you: your family, your friends, and your teachers.
- Develop a habit of praise!

Worship

WORKSHEET

1. Can you remember the 5th line of the prayer, WORSHIP, and write it below?

2. Fill in the blanks.

   Psalm 91:1: "I will _______________ you with all my ____________; I will ____________ all of your ___________________ deeds."

3. Can you name different ways we can worship Jesus?

4. What is your most favorite form of worship?

5. RESPONSE TIME:

   Making a musical instrument (maraca) is simple and fun. Partially fill an emptied water bottle with rice or dried beans. Decorate the bottle with stickers or markers. Sing and dance for Jesus!

Jesus is worthy of all our praise!

AMEN, AMEN!

We should praise him every day throughout the day!

AMEN, AMEN!

It brings him great joy to hear his children sing!

AMEN, AMEN!

So all together now let his praises ring!

AMEN, AMEN!

Jesus came to save us from our sin!

AMEN, AMEN!

Forever we behold him as Christ our King!

AMEN, AMEN!

And we will sing his praises throughout eternity!

AMEN, AMEN!

The teacher leads by reading the words in black, and the kids follow with the response in blue highlight. Afterward, encourage the class to write their own rap as a group, writing their suggestions on the board. Watch the excitement build as the kids rap what they have just written!

Commitment

CAN YOU SAY IT?

Jesus, I want to follow you as my Lord. Change me any way you want.

JOHN 13:13

You call me 'Teacher' and 'Lord.' You are right. That is what I am.

CAN YOU FIND IT?

Matthew 4:18-22

Matthew 16:24

Galatians 2:20

CAN YOU FEEL IT?

What does it mean to follow Jesus?

How is God changing me?

Who or what are you committed to following?

What's it like to do what Jesus wants?

"POPCORN PRAYER" BREAKOUT SESSION

Lead the children in prayer time once again by praying, ***"Jesus, I want to follow you as my Lord. Change me any way you want."*** Have the children repeat the prayer. Encourage them to pray one-sentence prayers expressing their desire to follow Jesus as their Lord.

TALK IT!

- Commitment is a promise of loyalty to a person or a cause.
- Commitments involve time, money, and hard work. It's like being on a sports team—paying your fees, going to practices, and showing up for games.
- Jesus wants you to be committed to following him as Lord of your life.
- "Change me any way you want" is saying you are willing to live your life completely committed to Jesus Christ.
- Keeping commitments is not easy.

As you speak of commitments, have kids share commitments they are involved in (sports, music, etc.) and what is easy as well as difficult about keeping those commitments. Talk about what it means to be a committed follower of Jesus. In what ways are they different? In what ways are they similar? Encourage them to share openly and honestly.

Commitment

CAN YOU HEAR IT?

Peter Wasn't Perfect (Luke 22:54-62)

Peter once said to Jesus, "Even if all the others reject you, I never will!" Jesus knew differently and told Peter that before the rooster would crow, Peter would deny him three times in the courtyard of the high priest's house where Jesus was being questioned before his crucifixion. It happened just like Jesus said. A servant girl saw Peter and said, "You were with Jesus." "No, that's not true—I don't know what you are talking about!" Peter replied. Then another servant girl said to the people there, "This man was with Jesus," and again Peter denied it. Some time passed. Peter was scared and really nervous. He wanted people to stop recognizing him, but it happened again! "We know that you are one of them. You speak like someone from Galilee." Peter began cursing and swearing and said, "I do not know that man!" But then it happened just like Jesus said it would, "Cock-a-doodle-doo!" Uh oh, suddenly Peter remembered Jesus' words, and he ran away crying. He knew he had done exactly what Jesus had predicted and he felt awful. But do you know what? Jesus didn't give up on Peter. Later, after Jesus was resurrected, he was on the shore of Lake Tiberius having breakfast with some of his disciples. Jesus asked Peter three times, "Peter, do you love me?" Each time Peter answered, "Yes, Lord, you know that I love you," and each time Jesus said, "Feed my sheep." Jesus wanted Peter to be his disciple and make disciples. Even though Peter wasn't perfect, Jesus knew Peter really wanted to follow him as his Lord. Peter never denied Jesus again.

CAN YOU DO IT?

- Commit to following Jesus as Lord of your life.
- Commit to letting Jesus have full control of your thoughts, actions, and desires.
- Let Jesus know he means more than anything else in the world to you and that you want to follow him, obey him, and become more like him.

Commitment

WORKSHEET

1. Can you remember the 6th line of the prayer, COMMITMENT, and write it below?

2. Fill in the blanks.

   John 13:13: "You _________ me ____________ and _________. You are ____________.

   That is ___________ I _________."

3. Why is following Jesus a commitment?

4. What are some things you are committed to?

5. RESPONSE TIME:

   Close your eyes and ask Jesus, "What it would look like if I were a passionate committed follower of you?" What would you be doing? Draw a picture of what Jesus shows you and then share it with your class and your parents.

IT'S A 

You help your mom with chores throughout the day

THAT'S GOOD! THAT'S GOOD!

You sign up for a sports team but forget to go and play

THAT'S BAD! THAT'S BAD!

You help a friend who's struggling in English class

THAT'S GOOD! THAT'S GOOD!

You skip your piano lesson 'cause you'd rather take a pass

THAT'S BAD! THAT'S BAD!

You keep all the promises that you have made

THAT'S GOOD! THAT'S GOOD!

So keep your commitments and remember to pray!

The teacher leads by reading the words in black, and the kids follow with the response in blue highlight. Afterward, encourage the class to write their own rap as a group, writing their suggestions on the board. Watch the excitement build as the kids rap what they have just written!

Dependence

CAN YOU SAY IT?

Fill me with your Holy Spirit.

JOHN 5:18b
Be filled with the Holy Spirit.

CAN YOU FIND IT?

Acts 2:1-17

Romans 8:26,27

Romans 15:13

Galatians 5:22-26

CAN YOU FEEL IT?

What does it mean to be filled with the Spirit?

What does it mean to be dependent on God?

What are the fruit of the Spirit?

How can we be filled with the Spirit?

"POPCORN PRAYER" BREAKOUT SESSION

Lead the children in prayer time once again by praying, ***"Fill me with your Holy Spirit."*** Have the children repeat the prayer. Encourage them to pray one-sentence prayers asking for God to fill them with his Spirit and make them channels through which the Spirit can flow.

TALK IT!

- Being filled with the Spirit is not an easy concept to understand.
- You need to be dependent upon God's Holy Spirit so that he can use you for his glory.
- You need to be dependent on his Spirit to become more like Jesus.
- When you become more like Jesus and are filled with his Spirit, you will produce the fruit of his Spirit.
- Love, joy, peace, and patience are fruit of his Spirit living inside you.

Lead the discussion by talking about what it means to have a friend and a comforter that you can rely on to help guide you through each day. What does that relationship feel like? Discuss the various fruit of the spirit, and let the kids share which ones may be more of a struggle for them than others.

CAN YOU HEAR IT?

The Comforter (John 14:15-31)

Take a moment, close your eyes, and imagine a friend whom you really love. Do you see their face? Now imagine that person saying, "I'm leaving tomorrow and going away to a far, far-off place where you can't come. But don't you worry, I'm going to leave my spirit here to talk with you and to play." Now of course this would never happen outside of God, but this is what happened right before Jesus died on the cross and rose to the right hand of His Father in heaven. He did not leave us alone. Jesus said in John 14:16-17, "And I will ask the Father, and he will give you another Helper, to be with you forever, even the Spirit of truth."

Jesus sent his spirit to help the church begin their mission. It wasn't long after that on a very special day, called Pentecost, a strong wind blew, and he filled everyone with his Holy Spirit. His Spirit would be with them always as their comforter, helper, and friend.

CAN YOU DO IT?

- Become dependent on God's Spirit to guide, comfort, and teach you.
- Ask your heavenly Father each day to fill you with his Spirit.
- Pray that the fruit of the Spirit be reflected in you, which will then be a testimony, blessing, and encouragement to those around you.

1. It's getting more difficult, but you can do it! Can you remember the 7th line of the prayer, DEPENDENCE, and write it below?

2. Fill in the blanks.

   Ephesians 5:18b: "Be ________________ with the ____________ ________________."

3. Name the fruit of the Spirit below:

   ________________ ________________ ________________

   ________________ ________________ ________________

   ________________ ________________ ________________

4. What is the most challenging or difficult fruit for you to demonstrate?
   How can praying help you with that?

5. RESPONSE TIME:

   Draw a bowl on a piece of paper. Using construction paper cut out different fruits using different colors: orange, apple, banana, grapes—you choose. Then tape or glue them onto your basket and neatly print Galatians 5:22 and 23 at the very bottom. You can hang it up as a reminder to be filled with the Spirit.

Katie decided to invite her friend to church.

IN THE SPIRIT? YES, YES, YES!

Joe didn't study and cheated on a test.

IN THE SPIRIT? NO, NO, NO!

Suzie shared her testimony with the entire class.

IN THE SPIRIT? YES, YES, YES!

Luke disobeyed his parents when they asked him to be home.

IN THE SPIRIT? NO, NO, NO!

Brian prayed for healing for his mom, who's very sick.

IN THE SPIRIT? YES, YES, YES!

Peter took something that did not belong to him.

IN THE SPIRIT? NO, NO, NO!

Jesse wrote a letter to a missionary kid.

IN THE SPIRIT AND THAT'S A RAP!

The teacher leads by reading the words in black, and the kids follow with the response in blue highlight. Afterward, encourage the class to write their own rap as a group, writing their suggestions on the board. Watch the excitement build as the kids rap what they have just written!

Influence

CAN YOU SAY IT?

Make me an instrument of your grace, truth, and justice.

JOHN 1:14

We have seen his glory, the glory of the one and only Son, who came from the Father, full of grace and truth.

CAN YOU FIND IT?

Matthew 19:13-15

Acts 2:16,17

Luke 18:15-17

CAN YOU FEEL IT?

What are some gifts God has given me?

How can I show God's grace to others?

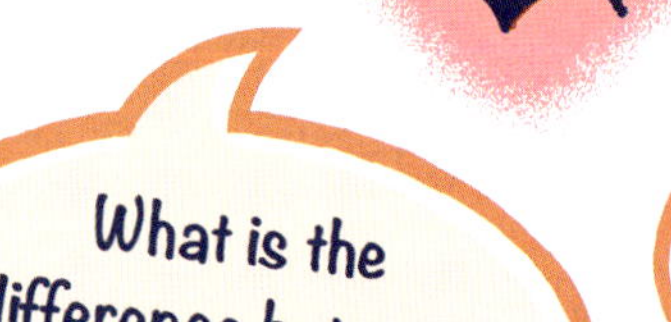

What is the difference between a truth and a lie?

What is wrong with lying?

"POPCORN PRAYER" BREAKOUT SESSION

Lead the children in prayer time by praying, ***"Make me an instrument of your grace, truth, and justice."*** Ask the children to pray one-sentence prayers asking God to use them to share his truth and show his grace to others around them.

TALK IT!

- Jesus showed justice every day when he was healing the sick and helping the poor.
- He did not care if they were old, young, rich, or poor.
- He treated everybody fairly.
- He was loving and gracious to everyone.
- He always spoke the truth. He did not ever lie.
- How can you help show justice with your friends, family, or community?

Have the children share ways they can be agents for justice. Discuss when it may be hard to tell the truth. How can hiding God's word in your heart help you speak truthfully?

CAN YOU HEAR IT?

Jesus and the Children (Matthew 18:1-6)

One afternoon on a bright and sunny day, the disciples were sitting around talking with Jesus. And just like we sometimes worry about who gets treated the best at home, at school, or on the playground, the disciples were wondering that very same thing. "Hmm, so, Jesus," they asked, scratching their heads, "who's the most important in the kingdom of heaven?" My guess is they were hoping Jesus would name one of them. Well, Jesus knew just what they were thinking, and called a child over. "Stand beside me," he said. Then he looked his disciples in the eyes and said the most amazing thing, "Whoever humbles himself like this child is the greatest in the kingdom of heaven." He said something even more amazing after that, "Whoever welcomes a little child like this in my name welcomes me." Whoa! And you know if Jesus said it, he meant it, because he only spoke the truth.

Jesus had a heart for justice. He always spent time with those whom most people wouldn't call famous, great, or important. He cared for the poor. He showed compassion for the sick. He brought peace to those who were hurting inside. And he always loved spending time with children, who were often ignored. Jesus said, "It will be terrible for any person who hurts a little child." Can you feel how much God loves and cares for you? Remember, God can use you, at any age, to be his agent of grace, truth and justice.

CAN YOU DO IT?

- Allow God to use you to share his message of grace, truth, and justice.
- Decide in your heart to always speak the truth.
- Memorize God's Word.

WORKSHEET

1. Can you remember the 8th line of the prayer, INFLUENCE, and write it below?

2. Fill in the blanks.

   John 1:14: "We have seen his _________, the glory of the _________ and only _________, who came from the _____________, full of ___________ and ___________."

3. Have you welcomed someone that was new to your school, church or neighborhood? If so, share a time when you welcomed that person. If not, how about giving it a try? The more you do it, the easier it gets!

4. Can you think of a time when you were able to influence or persuade someone to do the right thing in a difficult situation? If so, share how that person responded to your help.

5. RESPONSE TIME:

   Draw a picture of one way you can welcome a new student in your school, church or neighborhood.

I want to be your agent of truth!

I DO, I DO!

I want to speak your words of grace!

I DO, I DO!

I want to show your justice in my life every day!

I DO, I DO!

I want to help those who are lost and gone astray!

I DO, I DO!

I want to help those who don't have much!

I DO, I DO!

I want to help those whom others ignore!

I DO, I DO!

I want to be your agent of love!

The teacher leads by reading the words in black, and the kids follow with the response in blue highlight. Afterward, encourage the class to write their own rap as a group, writing their suggestions on the board. Watch the excitement build as the kids rap what they have just written!

Discipleship

CAN YOU SAY IT?

Use me for your glory and to invite others to follow you.

MATTHEW 28:19

Go therefore and make disciples of all nations, baptizing them in the name of the Father, the Son and the Holy Spirit.

CAN YOU FIND IT?

Mark 16:15

John 17:4-5

Romans 10:13-17

Colossians 3:17

CAN YOU FEEL IT?

What is a missionary?

What is a disciple?

What are some ways we can tell others about Jesus?

What does it mean to do something for the glory of God?

"POPCORN PRAYER" BREAKOUT SESSION

Lead the children in prayer time once again by praying, ***"Use me for your glory and to invite others to follow you."*** Have the children repeat the prayer. Encourage them to pray one-sentence prayers expressing their desire to be used for God's glory and boldness in inviting others to follow Jesus.

TALK IT!

- Missionaries are those who have been called by God to preach the gospel of Jesus Christ.
- Many times that means traveling to a faraway country and learning a new language and culture. It is a life of sacrifice and devotion to God.
- Jesus wants us all to be missionaries wherever we live and to be his light at school and at home.

You might want to begin by having the children share missionary stories from their church or from those they know around the world. Encourage them to talk about ways they can share Jesus with their family and friends.

CAN YOU HEAR IT?

Saul of Tarsus Becomes Paul, an Apostle of Jesus Christ (Acts 9:1-22)

Paul, once a hater and enemy of Christ and his followers, became one of the most important leaders of the early Church and a missionary of the gospel. It happened one day as Saul (before his name got changed to Paul) was walking on the road to Damascus. A very bright light from heaven caused him to fall to the ground. It made him blind. Saul heard a voice say, "Saul, why are you persecuting me?" "Who are you, Lord?" Saul asked. "I am Jesus, whom you are persecuting." Paul was scared and shaking. For three days he could not see. For three days he would not eat or drink. A godly man named Ananias was told by God to go and find Saul. "Ananias, I want you to restore Saul's sight. I have chosen him to be a missionary." This did not make sense to Ananias. He had heard all the terrible things Paul did to Christians, but Ananias obeyed God. God healed Saul, and Saul began preaching and teaching about Jesus everywhere he went. Many became Jesus' followers. Saul's name was later changed to Paul. The Bible is filled with Paul's teachings and letters to churches. He turned the world upside-down for Jesus, giving God all the glory and teaching others to do the same.

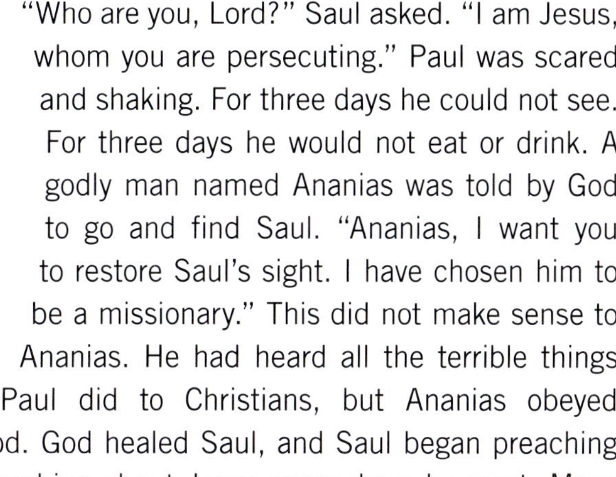

CAN YOU DO IT?

- Decide in your heart that whatever you do, you do to the glory of God.
- Recognize your talents and abilities come from God.
- Let all you do be a gift of love to Jesus.
- Ask God to help you grow in boldness in inviting others to follow him.
- Ask God for opportunities to share his love wherever you go.

Discipleship

WORKSHEET

1. You're almost done! Can you remember the 9th line of the prayer, DISCIPLESHIP, and write it below?

2. Fill in the blanks.

   Matthew 28:19: "Go ________________ and make ____________ of all ____________, baptizing them in the _________ of the _______________, the ____________ and the Holy ___________."

3. What is a missionary?

4. How can you or I be missionaries and make disciples even in our own neighborhoods?

5. RESPONSE TIME:

   Name one person you know who doesn't know Jesus. Write their name on a card and commit to praying for them every day. Remember God can use you to tell others about his love!

I really want to have God's heart to love

YES, YES!

I really want to have God's heart to serve

YES, YES!

I know God can use me as his little one

YES, YES!

To share the story of his unending love

YES, YES!

I want to go and make disciples in Jesus' name

YES, YES!

Will you help me do the same?

YES, YES!

Let's glorify our Father above!

The teacher leads by reading the words in black, and the kids follow with the response in blue highlight. Afterward, encourage the class to write their own rap as a group, writing their suggestions on the board. Watch the excitement build as the kids rap what they have just written!

Authority

CAN YOU SAY IT?

In Jesus' name I pray. Amen.

PHILIPPIANS 2:9

Therefore God exalted him and gave him a name that is above every name.

CAN YOU FIND IT?

Matthew 1:21

Matthew 28:18

John 14:13

Acts 4:12

CAN YOU FEEL IT?

What would happen if you were in charge of the world?

Why is there power in Jesus' name?

Why should we pray in Jesus' name?

"POPCORN PRAYER" BREAKOUT SESSION

Lead the children in prayer time by encouraging them to pray one-sentence prayers with a request in Jesus' name. This can be for healing for themselves or a loved one, or it may be to help them grow in love or to be used by God in a special way.

TALK IT!

- The Bible says, "All authority has been given to me in heaven and earth." When we pray in Jesus' name we have authority.
- This raises questions: Does God answer all of our prayers the way we want him to if we pray in Jesus' name? Does this mean God will give me everything I want?
- Our prayers must focus on things that would glorify our Father in heaven and that would advance his kingdom on earth.

Have the kids share openly about their prayer life. Have they experienced answer to prayers? Have they been frustrated because they have felt some prayers were not answered the way they hoped or not at all?

CAN YOU HEAR IT?

Blind Bartimaeus (Mark 10:46-52)

Bartimaeus was blind, and he was a beggar who lived in the streets of Jericho. He knew of Jesus and his wonderful deeds. He heard of how Jesus healed the sick, the blind, and those who could not walk. Bartimaeus wanted Jesus to heal him, too. He cried, "Jesus, Master, have pity on me! Have pity on me!" The people around Bartimaeus were not kind. They yelled, "Oh, be quiet!" but Bartimaeus ignored them and continued calling out to Jesus. Jesus heard him and said, "Bring him to me." The crowd said, "Cheer up! He is calling you!" Throwing his jacket, Bartimaeus jumped to his feet and went to Jesus. "What do you want?" Jesus asked. Bartimaeus replied, "I want to see!" Jesus answered, "Your faith has healed you." Bartimaeus believed that Jesus had the power to heal people. Well, you can imagine how happy Bartimaeus was when he could see. He followed Jesus, praising him for his wonderful deeds.

CAN YOU DO IT?

- Focus your prayers on things that will glorify your heavenly Father.
- Ask God, in Jesus' name, for wisdom and guidance.
- Ask God, in Jesus' name, for healing and strength.
- Believe in your heart that there is power in the name of Jesus.

WORKSHEET

1. Congratulations! You made it to the very last line of the prayer, AUTHORITY! Can you write it below?

2. Fill in the blanks.

   Philippians 2:9: "Therefore, God ___________________ him to the ________________ place and _____________ him a ________________ that is _____________ every _____________."

3. In thinking about today's Bible story, why do you think Bartimaeus was healed by Jesus? If Jesus heard Bartimaeus, can he also hear you? And if Jesus hears you, can he answer your prayers like he answered Bartimaeus'? The answer is, 'Yes'! You can ask God for healing, for strength, or for help for yourself and others, because God hears and answers prayer!

4. RESPONSE TIME:

   Make a Prayer Request Box. You can use any box: a shoe box, or a plain cardboard box of any size you choose. You can decorate the box with wrapping paper, or stickers or just simply write the words: MY PRAYER BOX. Write down your prayer requests and keep them in the box remembering to pray each day. As God answers your prayers be sure to write that down too and always thank him for hearing and answering your prayers!

Jesus is a name that is above every name!

AMEN! AMEN!

In the name of Jesus we find truth and power!

AMEN! AMEN!

In the name of Jesus we find healing and strength!

AMEN! AMEN!

In the name of Jesus we find hope and joy!

AMEN! AMEN!

In the name of Jesus we find grace and peace!

AMEN! AMEN!

In the name of Jesus we find perfect love!

AMEN! AMEN!

Let's all pray with one accord in Jesus' name!

AMEN! AMEN!

The teacher leads by reading the words in black, and the kids follow with the response in blue highlight. Afterward, encourage the class to write their own rap as a group, writing their suggestions on the board. Watch the excitement build as the kids rap what they have just written!

My Prayer Covenant Record

NAME	DATE

HOW CAN MY FAMILY OR CHURCH EXPERIENCE THE 40 DAY PRAYER COVENANT?

The best way to experience the Prayer Covenant is for the church and family together to begin a lifestyle of praying the Prayer Covenant.

FAMILY

For more reasons than we care to list, it can be difficult to get a family to pray together. However, the Prayer Covenant provides a simple and easy way to make praying together possible.

Imagine a family mealtime that concludes with the Kid's Prayer Covenant. Perhaps the family prays it together in unison; perhaps someone prays it out loud while the rest pray it silently; perhaps each line of the prayer is prayed around the table one by one. Be creative; pray it differently from night to night. It doesn't have to take a long time—keep it short, simple and limited.

Of course, the prayer might raise questions or stimulate reflections on ways that God is working in your family. Be sensitive to the spiritual curiosity of your children. As the conversation flows naturally, spiritual truths can be enjoyed together in extended time together. At bedtime mom and dad can read the kid's section of this book together; or you can listen to a child read it to you. Perhaps you might want to look up a different verse from the back of the Kid's Prayer Covenant each night. The resources for teachers in the second half of this book can provide creative and fresh ways to have bedtime discussions.

It is wise to have multiple copies of the Kid's Prayer Covenant cards available–have copies in the dinning room and bedroom. You can order plenty from our website **www.theprayercovenant.org**.

THE CHURCH

Our vision is to see entire churches embrace the Prayer Covenant. We have resources that could be used for a six, nine or twelve-week study series. While pastors preach about the Prayer Covenant on Sunday morning, small groups or classes can use the video series with brief presentations by Dr. Jerry Kirk and introductions and discussion questions by Stephen Eyre. While pastors are preaching on the Prayer Covenant and small groups are using it in adult education settings, the children's ministry of your church can be teaching the children the kid's version of the Prayer Covenant using the resources provided by this book, *The Power of the Prayer Covenant for Kids!* In addition, for your convenience, we have full-color Worksheets available for order for use in your Sunday School or VBS programs.

If your pastor is not familiar with the Prayer Covenant, a Launch Kit, which includes a copy of both the adult and children's Prayer Covenant books, 10 adult and children's Prayer Covenant cards and additional resources, are available at **www.theprayercovenant.org** website.

CONCLUSION

As fire burns brightest when many logs are ignited at the same time, so the Prayer Covenant's power is unleashed as many members begin to pray it for each other. Likewise, as an entire family enters into the Prayer Covenant together, mom and dad and the children, its power shines forth both within and beyond the family.

Resources are available at the website:
www.theprayercovenant.org

Your contributions can make a difference!

Let's keep the Kids' Prayer Covenant going—
Help us spread it to the 4 corners of the globe!

$325 will allow the kids' prayer covenant card to be translated into one new language.

Please go to www.theprayercovenant.org to donate now.
Your gift is fully tax-deductible and allows children all over the world to experience the power of the prayer covenant lifestyle.

THE VELVET UNDERGROUND EXPERIENCE

**U.S. edition of the monograph for *The Velvet Underground Experience* exhibition presented at 718 Broadway, New York.
October 10th—December 30th, 2018**

ISBN: 978-1-7320561-3-8 Hat & Beard Press
First North American Edition,
originally published in French in 2016 by Éditions La Découverte,
Cité de la musique-Philharmonie de Paris, 2016,
Dominique Carré éditeur, a label of Éditions La Découverte.
ISBN: 978-2-37368-015-7

Editorial Coordination
Christian Fevret
Carole Mirabello

Editors
J.C. Gabel
Margot Ross

Copy Editor
Sybil Perez

Translation
Margot Ross

Graphic Design
Change is Good, Paris
Rik Bas Backer & José Albergaria

Researchers
Madeleine Olive
Cécile Niesseron

Typefaces
Velvet67
by Martijn Oostra
Maison Mono and Maison Neue
by Milieu Grotesque

Paper
Astrobrights Eclipse Black
Lynx Opaque Smooth
Flo Gloss

Lithography
Fotimprim, Paris

Print
Print is Art Team
GLS Companies, St. Paul, MN

Cover: The Velvet Underground and Nico in Connecticut, 1966, Photographer Unknown. Division of Rare and Manuscript Collections, Cornell University Library. Back cover: Lou Reed & John Cale with The Exploding Plastic Inevitable at the Open Stage, 23 St. Marks Place, New York, April 1966. Photograph by Adam Ritchie. © Adam Ritchie Photography. Endpapers front: The Velvet Underground at Cafe Bizarre, December 1965. Photography: Adam Ritchie. © Adam Ritchie Photography. Page 1: Performance of the Velvet Underground at Dom, New York, April 1966. Photograph: Fred W. McDarrah. © Estate of Fred W. McDarrah. Pages 2-3: The Velvet Underground on stage at the Film-Makers' Cinematheque, New York, with Edie Sedgwick and Gerard Malanga, January 1966. Photograph by Adam Ritchie. © Adam Ritchie Photography.Pages 4-5: Sterling Morrison and John Cale at the Delmonico, New York, February 1966. Photograph by Adam Ritchie. © Adam Ritchie Photography. Pages 6-7: Andy Warhol and Lou Reed on the bus to Ann Arbor, Michigan, March 1966. Photograph by Nat Finkelstein. Page 8: Moe Tucker playing drums at the Factory, 1966. Photograph by Stephen Shore. © Stephen Shore, courtesy of 303 Gallery, New York.

TABLE OF CONTENTS

CURATORS' FOREWORD

How did this group, which was overlooked by success during their brief existence (1965-1970), despite a colorful collaboration with Andy Warhol, gradually evolve into preeminent rock legends? The trajectory of the Velvet Underground is unique. Too radical, too transgressive, and too uninhibited for their time, they became an inexhaustible source of inspiration for musicians in the decades that followed.

The Velvet Underground was born in New York, the product of a songwriter from Long Island, and a violinist from Wales. As a teenager, Lou Reed fed on rock 'n' roll and found sustenance in the writing of Allen Ginsberg and William S. Burroughs. John Cale, with his remarkable musical background, rubbed shoulders with elite avant-garde composers. Together, Reed and Cale rehearsed with literature-loving guitarist Sterling Morrison, and then hired drummer and Bo Diddley devotee, Moe Tucker. In December 1965, the group inspired Warhol to open the doors of his Factory, which led to the introduction of the golden-haired chanteuse, Nico, to the group.

At the beginning of 1966, Warhol's performances attracted painters, poets, musicians, filmmakers, and choreographers to the East Village of Manhattan, and these audiences were soon enraptured by the Velvet Underground. Debuting in 1967, *The Velvet Underground & Nico* began an aesthetic revolution—an underground revolution—the effects of which would take several years to be fully grasped. In the meantime, the Velvet Underground expanded its influence (David Bowie was an early fan) and separated from one of its founding members. In the wake of their second album, *White Light/ White Heat* (1968), the group ousted John Cale and changed their image. Electric eruptions, a descent into a maelstrom of drugs, and the quest for identity are meticulously surveyed in their third album entitled *The Velvet Underground* (1969). Their critical success was not reflected in record sales. To survive, the Velvets performed a series of concerts outside of New York—in Boston, Philadelphia, and San Francisco. Although the group was at the peak of its artistic oeuvre, its days were numbered: on August 23, 1970, Lou Reed unexpectedly announced his departure. A month later, the posthumous album *Loaded* offered hymns to the streets of New York that would influence the punk music that resonated from the city a few years later, in 1976-1977.

Despite the brevity of its career, the Velvet Underground bequeathed to music and the arts a beautiful heritage: half a century after its birth in a flat on the Lower East Side, its underground spirit, sound, and refrains shine through today in the firmament of contemporary culture.

—Christian Fevret and Carole Mirabello

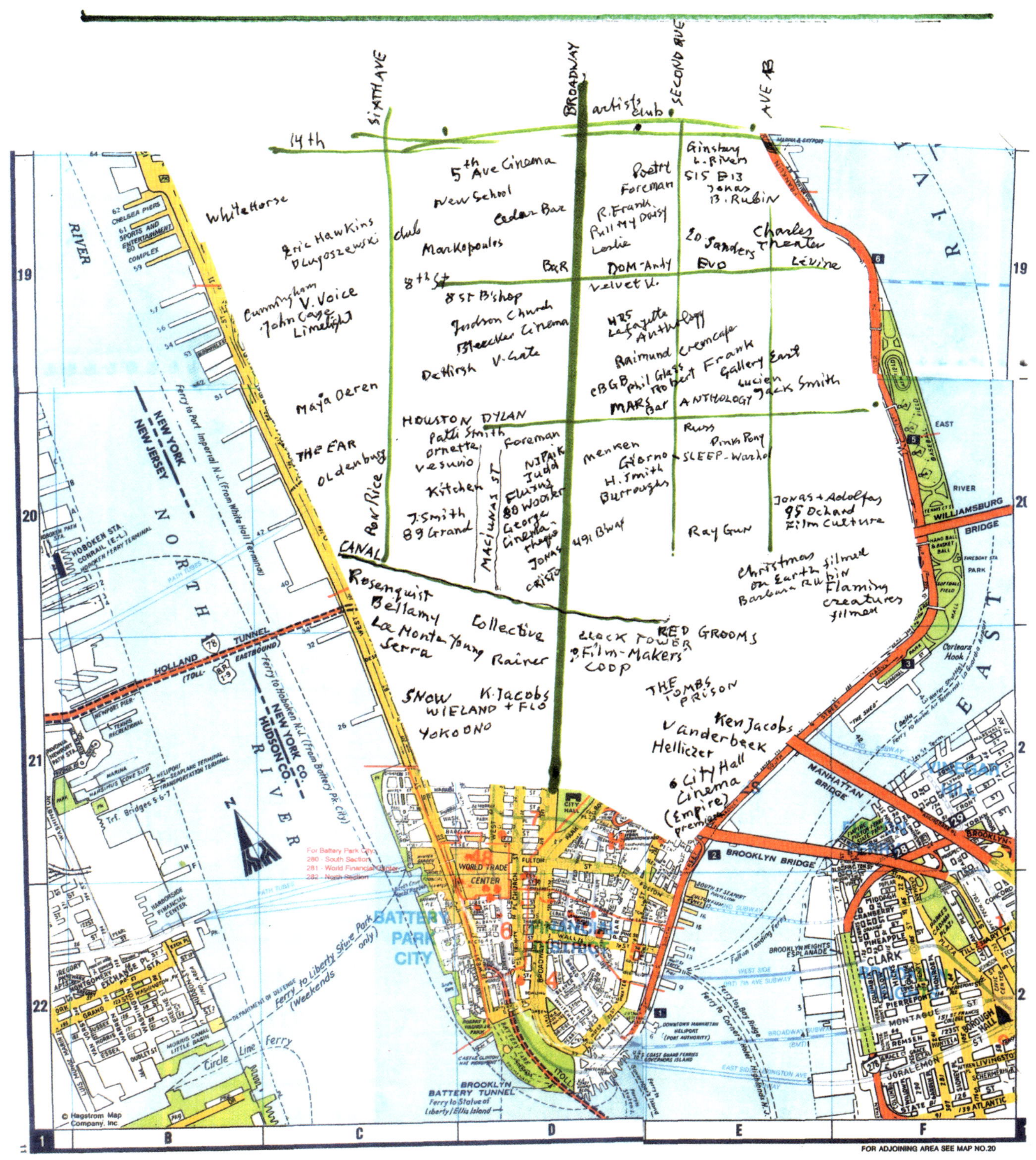

Map of Manhattan drawn by Jonas Mekas in 2010. Jonas Mekas Collection.

"The whole change of man's mind and heart is happening underground (in the lower, not very much respected regions). High above ground there is too much unnecessary noise going on."

—Jonas Mekas

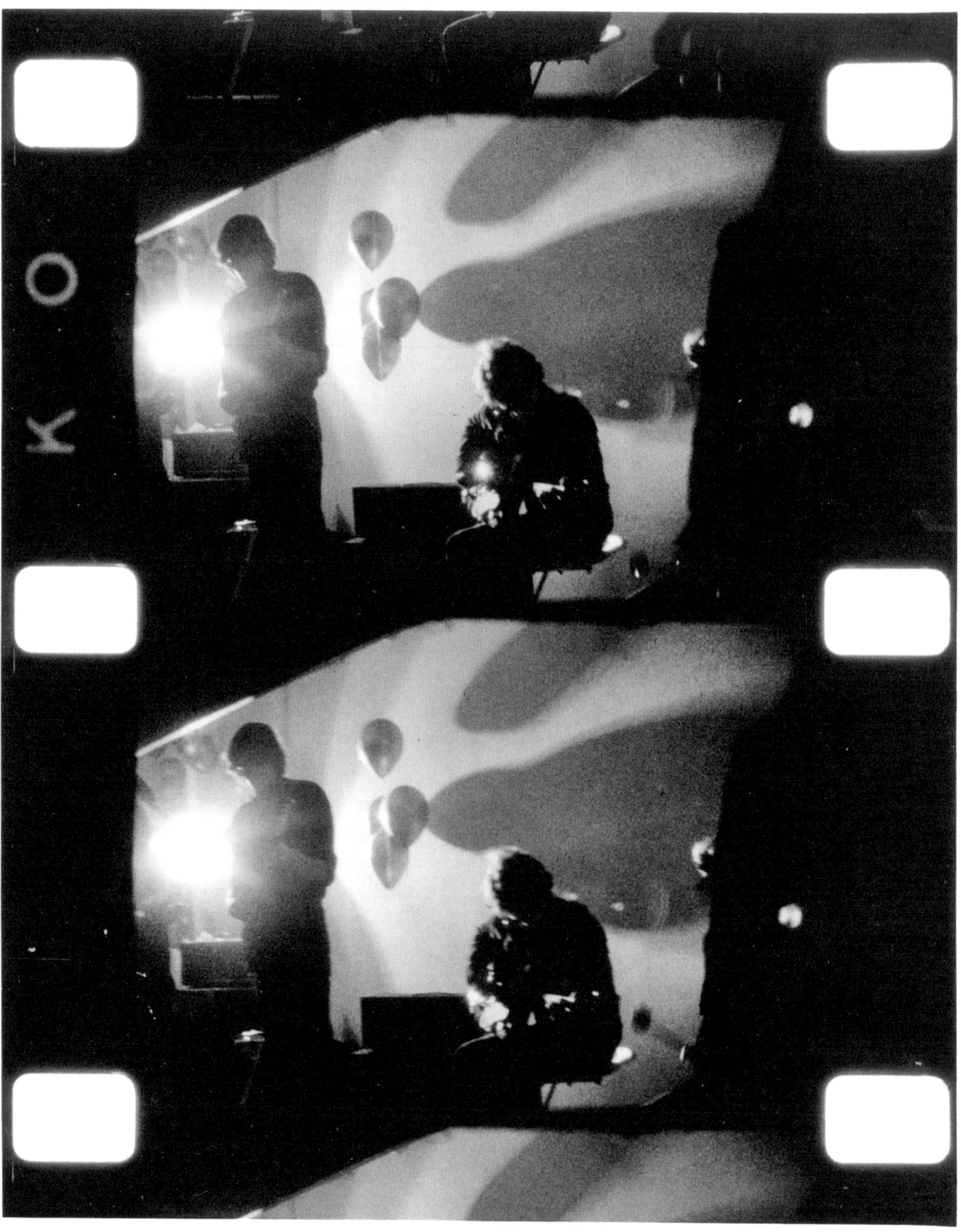
K O

THE VELVET UNDERGROUND CHRONOLOGY

1928

August 6: Andy Warhol (Andrew Warhola) is born in Pittsburgh, Pennsylvania.

1938

March 14: Angus MacLise is born in Bridgeport, Connecticut.

October 16: Nico (Christa Päffgen) is born in Cologne, Germany, or in Budapest, Hungary. There is some mystery surrounding Nico with the possibility that she was born in 1939, 1940, or even 1943.

1942

March 2: Lou Reed (Lewis Allan Reed) is born in Brooklyn, New York.

March 9: John Cale is born in Garnant, Wales.

August 29: Holmes Sterling Morrison is born in Westbury, New York.

1944

August 26: Maureen "Moe" Tucker is born in Levittown, Long Island, New York.

1947

Lou begins to play the piano at age five.

February 25: Doug Yule is born in Mineola, New York.

1949

John begins to play the piano at age seven and Sterling begins to play the trumpet, also age seven (he'll switch to guitar at age 12).

Andy Warhol moves to New York at age 21.

1957

In Paris, with the help of his friend Piero Heliczer, Angus MacLise founds *Dead Language Press*, a literary fanzine, which is also an independent poetry publishing company. These avant-garde, multidisciplinary artists will have an important influence on Lou and John a few years later in the New York underground scene.

1958

Release of seven-inch single "So Blue" by the Jades, written and performed by Lewis "Lou" Reed. The Jades played in public on a few occasions.

1959

In Rome, Nico played a part in Federico Fellini's *La Dolce Vita*.

At the age of 17, Lou receives electroshock therapy in New York.

1960

John Cale begins studying music at Goldsmiths College in London and starts a written correspondence with John Cage.

In the Spring, Lou begins his studies at Syracuse University, where he meets his teacher, the famous poet Delmore Schwartz, who becomes both his mentor and friend.

1962

Nico has the starring role in the French film *Sweet Skin* (originally *Strip Tease*) and records the title song written by Serge Gainsbourg, which is then replaced by a version sung by Juliette Gréco.

Christian Aaron "Ari" Boulogne, son of Nico and Alain Delon, is born on August 11th.

1963

After a summer session at Tanglewood, studying with Leonard Bernstein and Aaron Copland, John arrives in New York and plays with Angus MacLise, La Monte Young, and Tony Conrad and participates in Piero Heliczer's happenings.

Lou Reed tries heroin for the first time, foreshadowing the song.

In November, Andy Warhol opens his first Factory on 47th Street.

1964

In June, Lou receives his Bachelor of Arts from Syracuse University.

In September, Lou is hired by the small Long Island Pickwick label as a staff songwriter. Lou wrote and recorded a dozen songs under various names, released on cheap, trendy compilations on the label.

Nico auditions for the Blue Angel Club in New York.

In November, John Cale, along with Tony Conrad and Walter De Maria, is hired by Pickwick to promote Lou's single "The Ostrich" as the Primitives.

The Velvets at Paraphernalia, 1966. Film still by Gerard Malanga. Gerard Malanga Collection.

1965

Lou and John rehearse together at John's apartment on Ludlow Street, and perform as a duo in Harlem, mainly in front of the Baby Grand Bar on 125th Street.

Nico records her first single in London, "I'm Not Sayin'", with Jimmy Page and Rolling Stones manager Andrew Loog Oldham.

Angus MacLise, John's friend and roommate, becomes John and Lou's first percussionist in a band called the Falling Spikes, then the Warlocks. They are joined on guitar by Lou's friend Sterling Morrison, who is studying medieval literature. They compose and rehearse at their shared apartment on Ludlow Street, and provide live soundtracks for screenings at Jonas Mekas' Cinematheque.

In July, Lou, John, and Sterling record their first demo tapes at Ludlow Street.

In November, after Tony Conrad or Angus MacLise, (depending on the version) brings home a "book from the gutter" called, *The Velvet Underground*, the band immediately adopts it as their permanent name. Angus MacLise is replaced by Maureen "Moe" Tucker on drums for the first VU concert on December 11th, when they play three songs at Summit High School, New Jersey.

On December 15th, the VU begins a residency at Cafe Bizarre in Greenwich Village, where artists Barbara Rubin and Gerard Malanga bring Andy Warhol and he discovers them. He asks the VU to join the Factory to rehearse and becomes their manager.

1966

At the beginning of January, Warhol suggests Nico should join the band as a singer.

On January 13th, at the New York Society for Clinical Psychiatry banquet, Warhol is the special guest and asks the band, performing with Nico for the first time, to play for the psychiatrists, which creates a scandal.

Warhol films *The Velvet Underground & Nico: A Symphony of Sounds* while the band is rehearsing at the Factory. The movie is supposed to be projected on the band while they are playing live at future Warhol Exploding Plastic Inevitable shows.

From February 8th to 13th, Warhol hosts the "Up-Tight" happening at the Cinematheque on 41st Street, with the VU & Nico, showcasing films and light projections. Malanga and Edie Sedgwick dance and improvise.

In April, the Velvet Underground & Nico begin a residency for Warhol's multimedia Exploding Plastic Inevitable show (EPI) at the Dom, on St. Marks Place.

The first recording session for the first Velvet album is at Scepter Studios on April 25th, paid for by Warhol.

On May 3rd, the California tour of the EPI begins at Trip, in Los Angeles, for a month-long residency. Reviews are bad and the club is closed by the sheriff on the third night due to drug issues. The EPI "family" is trapped in The Castle, in Hollywood.

Poster for The Velvet Underground and Nico at Dom, New York, 1966.

Poster for the performance of EPI at the Chrysler Museum, Provincetown, Massachusetts, September 1966. Poster design: Glaisek.

Meanwhile, the band is still recording their first album with producer Tom Wilson in Los Angeles.

From May 27th to 29th, the EPI performs at the Fillmore in San Francisco.

From June 21st until July 3rd, the EPI has a residency at Poor Richard's in Chicago, without Warhol, Nico, and Lou Reed, who is in the hospital with hepatitis. MacLise joins on the drums, Moe plays the bass, and John is on lead vocals. Due to popular demand, the residency is extended. The show is filmed by Ronald Nameth, for an 18-minute movie, entitled *Andy Warhol's Exploding Plastic Inevitable*.

In July, the first single *All Tomorrow's Parties/ I'll Be Your Mirror* is released.

On July 11th, Lou's teacher and friend Delmore Schwartz dies of a heart attack at the age of 53.

In September, Warhol's eight-hour movie *Chelsea Girls* premieres at the Film-Makers' Cinematheque.

From September to December, the EPI show tours Massachusetts, Pennsylvania, the Midwest, Ohio, Michigan, the East Coast, New York, and Canada.

In December, the VU's second single *Sunday Morning/Femme Fatale* is released.

1967

In January, the VU plays a two-week residency in New York at The Scene on 46th Street.

At the beginning of February, Nico performs solo at the New Mod-Dom on St. Marks Place.

On March 12th, the first album, *The Velvet Underground & Nico*, is released. Andy Warhol "produces" the album and designs the artwork: a 3D peelable banana that unveils pink flesh.

The first album is delayed, badly promoted, and distributed, which leads to the demise of EPI "hype." Sales are poor and some critics are harsh.

In February, March, and April, the VU plays in Massachusetts, in New York at Jonas Mekas' Film-Maker's Cinematheque, at the Gymnasium on 71st Street, at the Cheetah Club on 53rd Street, in Providence at the Rhode Island School of Design, and in Ann Arbor, Michigan.

In May, the EPI returns without Nico to The Scene in New York for its last shows.

On June 3rd, the VU plays a benefit for Merce Cunningham at Philip Johnson Glass House in New Canaan, Connecticut.

Poster for The Velvet Underground and Nico and The Mothers of Invention, at the Fillmore Auditorium, San Francisco, May 1966. Poster design: Wes Wilson. Martha Morrison Collection.

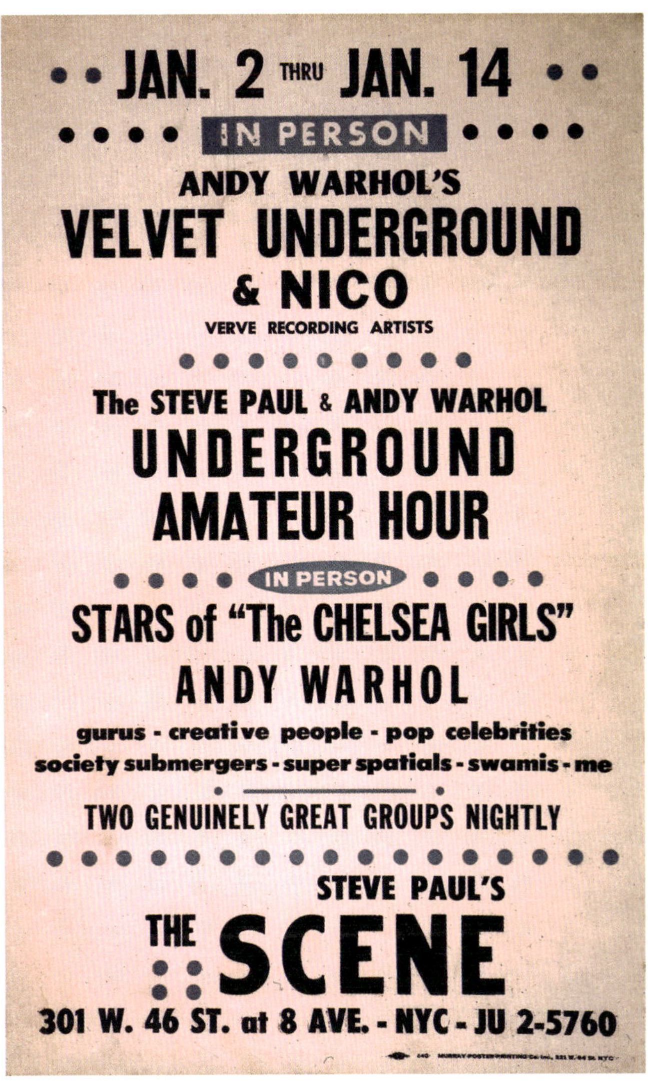

Poster for The Velvet Underground and Nico at Steve Paul's The Scene, New York, January, 1967.

In June and July, the VU performs at the Boston Tea Party in Boston, Massachusetts, at La Cave in Cleveland, Ohio, etc.

On August 11-12th, Warhol is at the Boston Tea Party to shoot the VU. The 34-minute short film will be shown for the first time in 2010.

In September, *White Light/White Heat*, produced by Tom Wilson, is recorded within two days. That same month, VU plays in Boston.

In October, Nico releases her first solo album, *Chelsea Girl*, with five songs written and played by the Velvet Underground members.

1968

On January 30th, *White Light/White Heat* is released.

In February, the VU plays Chicago, Boston, and Cleveland.

In March, the VU plays Chicago, Philadelphia, and Boston.

Andy Warhol's Factory leaves 47th Street and moves to Union Square.

In April, John Cale marries fashion designer Betsey Johnson. The Velvets had performed at the opening of her boutique, Paraphernalia, two years before. Betsey Johnson designs unique costumes for each member of the band for the release of *White Light/White Heat*.

On May 26th or 27th, 1968, Warhol and Nico arrive late at a VU show at the Boston Tea Party, and Lou refuses to let Nico sing and kicks her out of the band. A few months later, Lou fires Warhol and replaces him with Steve Sesnick.

On June 3rd, the feminist activist Valerie Solanas nearly murders Warhol.

The album cover of *White Light/White Heat* is a faint image of Joe Spencer's tattoo of a skull. He played the lead role in Warhol's 1967 film *Bike Boy*. It was Warhol's idea to use a black-on-black picture of the tattoo. Lou Reed chose the image from negatives from the film, and it was enlarged and distorted by Billy Name.

On September 28th, the VU performs their final concert with John Cale, who had been fired by Lou Reed at the Boston Tea Party.

On October 2nd, the VU performs at La Cave in Cleveland, their first concert with Doug Yule who has replaced John Cale.

In November, Nico releases her second solo album, *The Marble Index*. The songs are written by Nico and the album is produced by John Cale.

In November and December, the VU records its third album.

1969

From January to July, the VU tours Boston, Texas, Ohio, Pennsylvania, Massachusetts, Michigan, Missouri, and Canada.

In April, the VU releases its eponymous third album.

In May, the band starts recording their fourth unfinished "lost" album at Record Plant Studios in New York. In conflict with its record Company, MGM, the band quits and signs with Atlantic.

On June 21st, the VU plays a Pop Festival in Toronto, Canada, on the same night as Sly & the Family Stone.

On August 2, the VU plays the Hilltop Pop Festival in Mason, New Hampshire.

On August 5th, the first Stooges album is released, produced by John Cale.

From July 1969 to February 1970, the VU tours Massachusetts, Pennsylvania, Maryland, Minnesota, Texas, California, Oregon, and Illinois.

1970

From April to August, the VU plays a few dates outside of New York, while they continue to record their fourth album for their new label Atlantic, with entirely new songs—none of which were recorded for the previously planned "fourth album" with their former record company.

Moe Tucker is pregnant; Doug's brother Billy Yule plays the drums.

In March, John Cale releases his first solo album, *Vintage Violence*.

In June, the Velvet Underground is back in New York, playing in their hometown for the first time since 1967. During the summer, they have a residency at Max's Kansas City in Union Square for two sets a night, with Billy Yule on drums.

On August 23rd, after a gig at Max's, Lou Reed suddenly quits the band, going back to his parents' home.

Warhol's confidante, Brigid Berlin, records the show at Max's on a cassette. It was officially released in 1972 as, *Live at Max's Kansas City*. *Loaded* is released in September, without Lou participating on the final mixes.

1971

Since the original albums are difficult to find, MGM releases the double-LP, *Andy Warhol's Velvet Underground featuring Nico*, a compilation of the first three albums with a fake Warhol cover.

This compilation, along with the soon to be released *1969: Velvet Underground Live with Lou Reed*, is a way for many to discover and listen to the Velvet Underground in the 1970s.

1972

On January 29th, Lou Reed, John Cale, and Nico reunite for a one-off concert at the Bataclan, Paris.

In April, Lou Reed releases his first solo album, with eight then-unreleased Velvet songs, recorded in London with session musicians, including Steve Howe and Rick Wakeman from the band Yes.

Until 1973, with Doug Yule and manager Steve Sesnick, first with Moe and Sterling, then with different musicians, the Velvets keep a very low profile alive.

1974

A double live album, made from bootlegged recordings, is released under the name, *1969: Velvet Underground Live with Lou Reed*.

1980s

In 1985 and 1986, the albums, *VU* and *Another View*, are released, consisting of unreleased songs; two are with John Cale, the other ones are mainly from the "fourth lost album", which was recorded in 1969.

On July 18th, 1988, Nico dies from a brain hemorrhage in Ibiza, Spain, after falling from her bike.

1989 & beyond

On January 7th and 8th, 1989, Cale and Reed reunite for the first time in 17 years at the Church of St. Anne's, in Brooklyn, performing duets from *Songs for Drella*, in homage to Andy Warhol, who died two years earlier.

The Cale and Reed album, *Songs for Drella*, is released in April 1990.

In June, 1990, at the Fondation Cartier Warhol exhibition in Jouy-en-Josas near Paris, the four original members of the Velvet Underground—Lou Reed, John Cale, Sterling Morrison, and Moe Tucker—reunite for the first time since 1968 and improvise an unrehearsed, *Heroin*, in front of a few hundred attendees.

From June to July 1993, the original Velvet Underground reunites for a successful 22-date European tour, but disbands again before the American leg of the tour and plans of recording new material, due to disagreements between Lou and John. They will never play together again.

Apart from their time with the Velvet Underground, each member of the band had their own creative life, in the shadow or under the spotlight.

On August 30th, 1995, Sterling Morrison dies in Poughkeepsie, New York.

On October 27th, 2013, Lou Reed dies in Southampton, New York.

For now, the rest is history.

"MODERN MUSIC BEGINS WITH THE VELVETS"

I belong to the generation for whom the Velvet Underground was our Beatles and Dylan combined. I don't care who did feedback first, or if Lou Reed "sang like Dylan"—modern music begins with the Velvets, and the implications and influence of what they did seem to go on forever. "Black Angel's Death Song" alone is still ahead of its time, and of course all the other stuff sounds right up to date over a decade later. Who else has created a body of work of which this can be said? Almost all the artists and albums since, which have mattered the most to me (us?), have been blatantly influenced by them: the Stooges, *Sticky Fingers* and probably *Exile* even, Roxy Music and Eno's work, Patti Smith, Richard Hell and the Voidoids, David Bowie, if you like. The only thing I think would be a mistake in thanking them for this precious gift, would be romanticizing them too much.

—Lester Bangs
published in *NY Rocker*, July/August, 1980.

Lester Bangs, June 1977. Photograph: Stephanie Chernikowski

In the aftermath of the Second World War, a consumerist America is reborn as a seemingly more perfect version of itself bolstered by images propagated by the media. Rebelling against false pretenses, intellectuals and artists acrimoniously attack the rigidities of a society that claims to be liberal, yet is threatened by any deviations. Initially marginalized, these "outsiders" adopt, invent, and experiment with new forms of creativity. They radically defend different concepts of existence, pushing rules and taboos in the manner of Allen Ginsberg, tireless spokesperson for the Beat Generation poets. Above all, they confront a civilization with its moral turpitudes and suggest alternative paths.

Still from the film *America/America* (2016), by Jonathan Caouette. January 2016.

WELCOME
TO
AMERICA

AMERICA

Allen Ginsberg

America I've given you all and now I'm nothing.
America two dollars and twenty-seven cents January 17, 1956.
I can't stand my own mind.
America when will we end the human war?
Go fuck yourself with your atom bomb.
I don't feel good don't bother me.
I won't write my poem till I'm in my right mind.
America when will you be angelic?
When will you take off your clothes?
When will you look at yourself through the grave?
When will you be worthy of your million Trotskyites?
America why are your libraries full of tears?
America when will you send your eggs to India?
I'm sick of your insane demands.
When can I go into the supermarket and buy what I
    need with my good looks?
America after all it is you and I who are perfect not
    the next world.
Your machinery is too much for me.
You made me want to be a saint.
There must be some other way to settle this argument.
Burroughs is in Tangiers I don't think he'll come back
    it's sinister.
Are you being sinister or is this some form of practical
    joke?
I'm trying to come to the point.
I refuse to give up my obsession.
America stop pushing I know what I'm doing.
America the plum blossoms are falling.
I haven't read the newspapers for months, everyday
    somebody goes on trial for murder.
America I feel sentimental about the Wobblies.
America I used to be a communist when I was a kid
    I'm not sorry.
I smoke marijuana every chance I get.
I sit in my house for days on end and stare at the roses
    in the closet.
When I go to Chinatown I get drunk and never get laid.
My mind is made up there's going to be trouble.
You should have seen me reading Marx.
My psychoanalyst thinks I'm perfectly right.
I won't say the Lord's Prayer.
I have mystical visions and cosmic vibrations.
America I still haven't told you what you did to Uncle
    Max after he came over from Russia.

I'm addressing you.
Are you going to let your emotional life be run by
    Time Magazine?
I'm obsessed by *Time Magazine*.
I read it every week.
Its cover stares at me every time I slink past the corner
    candystore.
I read it in the basement of the Berkeley Public Library.
It's always telling me about responsibility. Business-
    men are serious. Movie producers are serious.
    Everybody's serious but me.
It occurs to me that I am America.

I am talking to myself again.

Asia is rising against me.
I haven't got a chinaman's chance.
I'd better consider my national resources.
My national resources consist of two joints of
marijuana millions of genitals an unpublishable
private literature that jetplanes 1400 miles an hour
and twentyfive-thousand mental institutions.
I say nothing about my prisons nor the millions of
underprivileged who live in my flowerpots
under the light of five hundred suns.
I have abolished the whorehouses of France, Tangiers
is the next to go.
My ambition is to be President despite the fact that
I'm a Catholic.

America how can I write a holy litany in your silly
mood?
I will continue like Henry Ford my strophes are as
individual as his automobiles more so they're
all different sexes.
America I will sell you strophes $2500 a piece $500
down on your old strophe
America free Tom Mooney
America save the Spanish Loyalists
America Sacco & Vanzetti must not die
America I am the Scottsboro boys.
America when I was seven momma took me to
Communist Cell meetings they sold us garbanzos a
handful per ticket a ticket costs a nickel and the
speeches were free everybody was angelic and
sentimental about the workers it was all so
sincere you have no idea what a good thing the
party was in 1835 Scott Nearing was a grand
old man a real mensch Mother Bloor the
Silk-Strikers' Ewig-Weibliche made me
cry I once saw the Yiddish orator Israel Amter plain.
Everybody must have been a spy.
America you don't really want to go to war.
America it's them bad Russians.
Them Russians them Russians and them Chinamen.
And them Russians.
The Russia wants to eat us alive. The Russia's power
mad. She wants to take our cars from out our
garages.
Her wants to grab Chicago. Her needs a Red *Reader's
Digest*. Her wants our auto plants in Siberia.
Him big bureaucracy running our fillingstations.
That no good. Ugh. Him make Indians learn read.
Him need big black niggers. Hah. Her make us
all work sixteen hours a day. Help.
America this is quite serious.
America this is the impression I get from looking in
the television set.
America is this correct?
I'd better get right down to the job.
It's true I don't want to join the Army or turn lathes
in precision parts factories, I'm nearsighted and
psychopathic anyway.
America I'm putting my queer shoulder to the wheel.

ALLEN GINSBERG

(1926–1997)

Allen Ginsberg in his apartment at 170 East 2nd Street, seated beside Peter Orlovsky and his brother Lafcadio, New York, January 1960. Photograph: Fred W. McDarrah. © Estate of Fred W. McDarrah.

Born in New Jersey, Allen Ginsberg discovered New York at the age of 17. Very quickly, he became the central figure of the Beat Generation. One of the founding texts of this literary and cultural movement was his collection of poetry, *Howl and Other Poems*, which was published in 1956 by City Lights in San Francisco. The poem caused a scandal as conservative circles called it obscene.

The following year, Ginsberg was the inspiration behind the Carlo Marx character in *On the Road* by Jack Kerouac. Heir to Walt Whitman, a militant defender of homosexuality, recreational drug user, Buddhist, and spokesperson for the marginalized, Ginsberg was both a pacifist and an anti-racist. Close to Bob Dylan and Lou Reed, he was both revered by hippies and celebrated by the precursors of punk.

Above left: Invitation to Ted Joans' birthday party, June 1959. Photograph: Fred W. McDarrah. © Estate of Fred W. McDarrah.

Above right: Advertisement for *Evergreen* magazine. Jonas Mekas Collection.

Below: Peter Orlovsky and Paul Bowles (seated); behind them (left to right) William S. Burroughs, Allen Ginsberg, Alan Ansen, Gregory Corso, and Ian Sommerville in Tangier, Morocco, July 1961. Photographer unknown.

AMERICA / AMERICA

Jonathan Caouette

Born in 1973, independent filmmaker Jonathan Caouette's multimedia video and sound installation, *America/America* (2016), produced for the exhibition, was inspired by the poem "America" by Allen Ginsberg.

"America", more than anything else, is a quintessential poem, a timeless political testimonial of the American experience. Allen Ginsberg's words are as relevant today as they were at the time of their publication, in 1956. The events that the poet identifies with resonate with the flow of consciousness of our time. My film *America/America* is an echo: a visual mythology, at the crossroads of political life and pop artistic expression, which unveils the mainstream culture and the counterculture of 1955-1965, while diving into the America that preceded the Velvet Underground. This period has always fascinated me, especially since 1965, as it carried with it the decline of the 60s. I wanted to produce a feverish mosaic of pop culture by simultaneously presenting the political, social, and musical facets of it.

J.C.

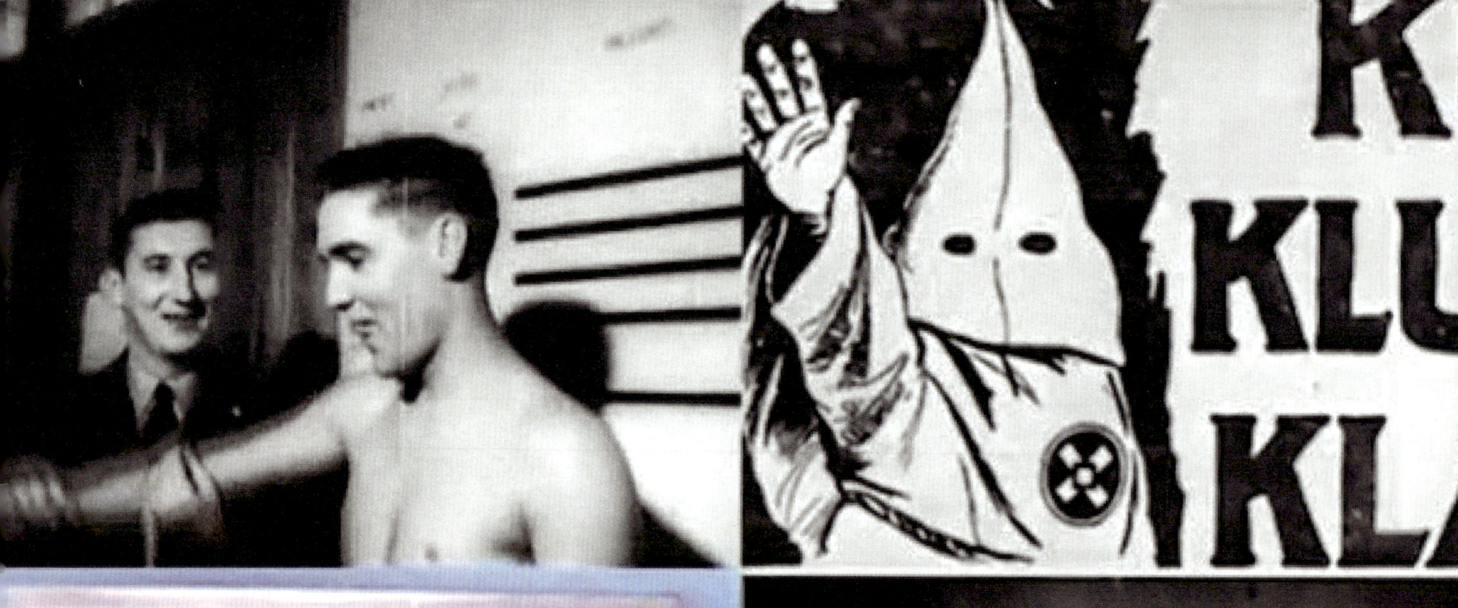

NBC

THIS PROGRAM WAS
REPRODUCED BY THE
KINEPHOTO PROCESS

ATOM AGE
VAMPIR

PLANTERS
PEANUTS
EMBASSY
DEM CONVENTION
JAP EARTHQUAKE

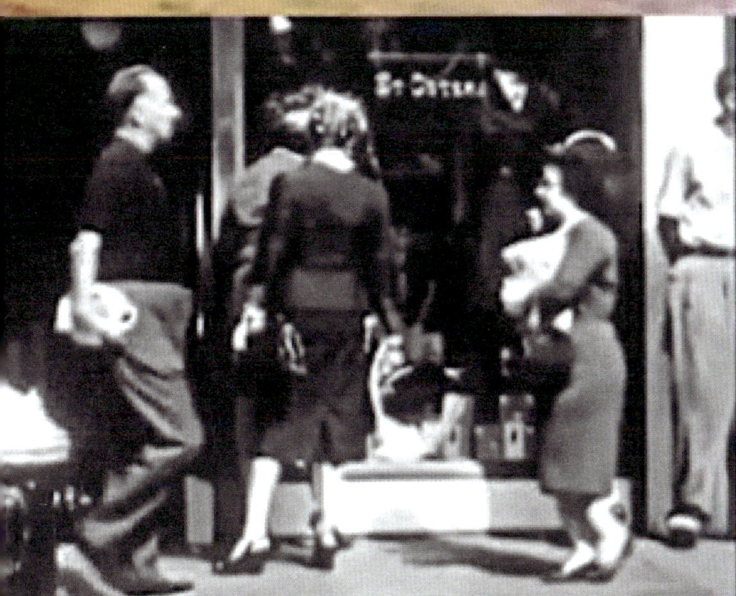

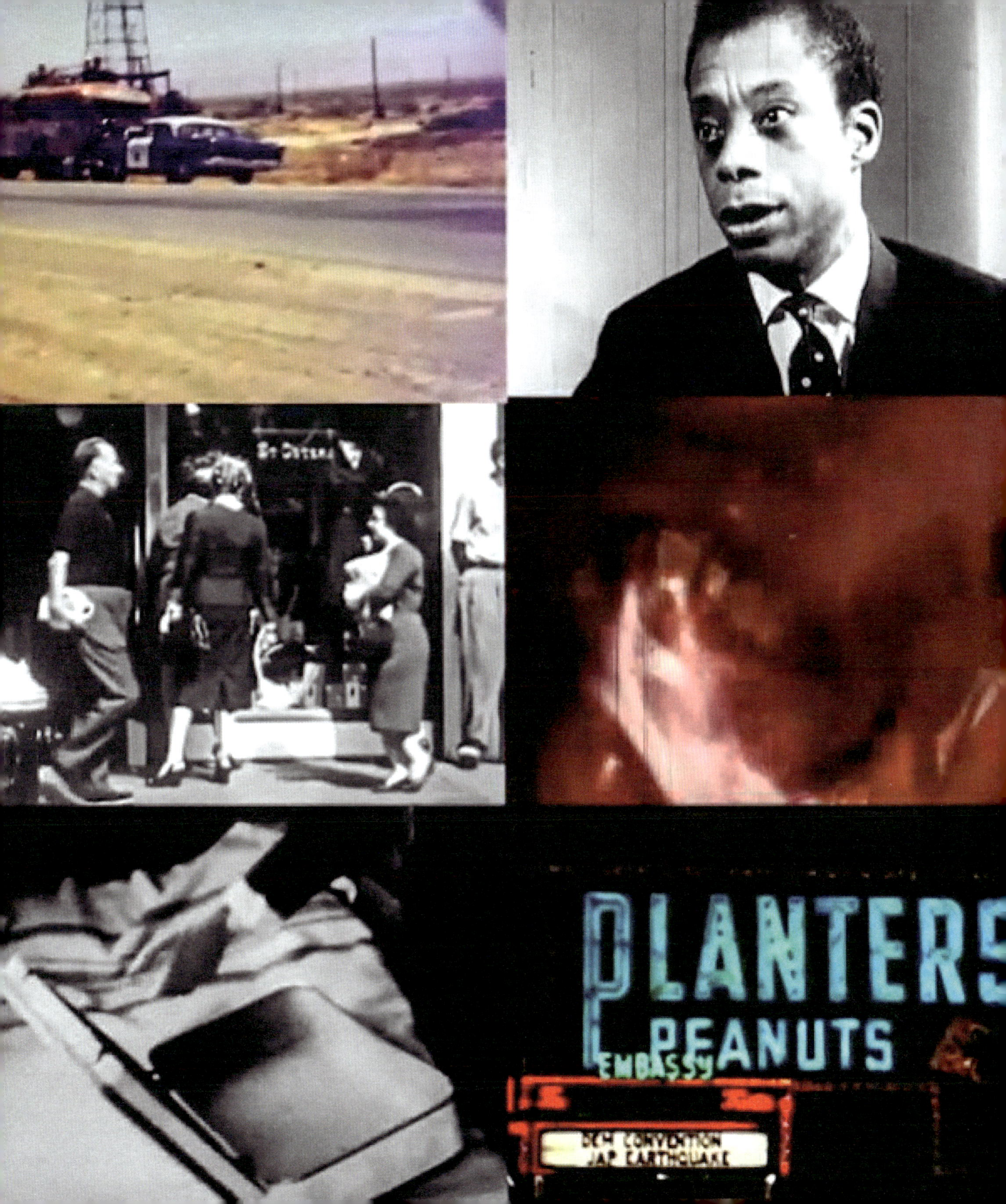

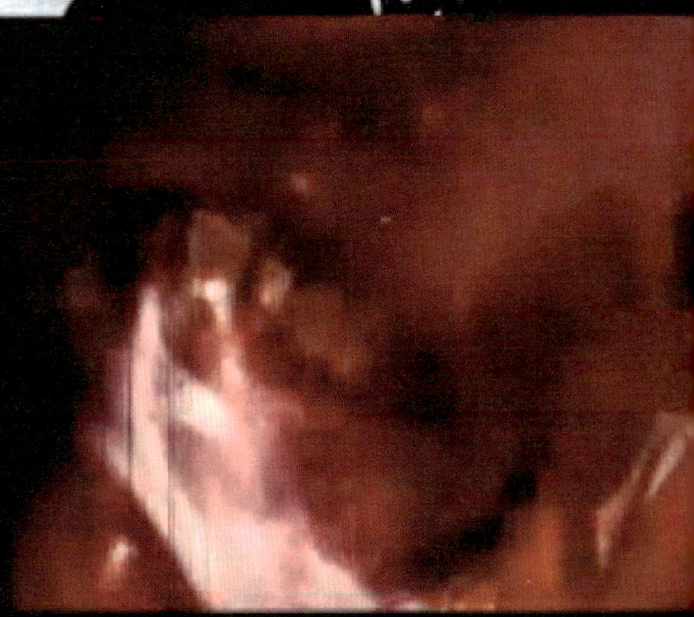

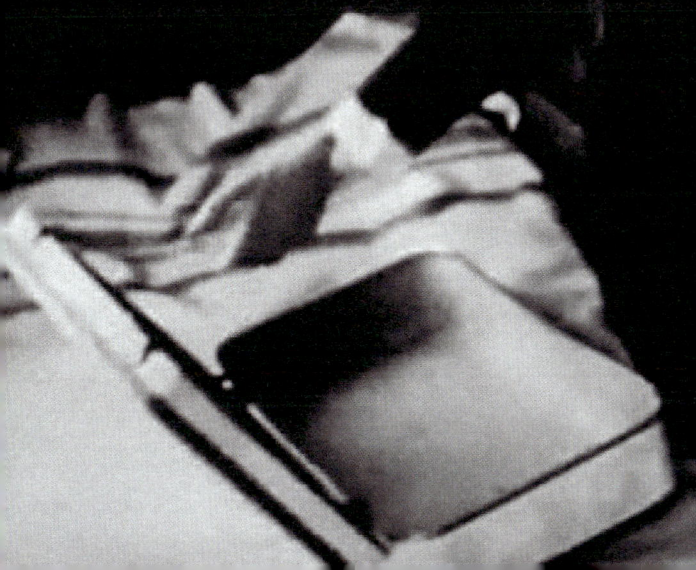

REED & THE ART OF

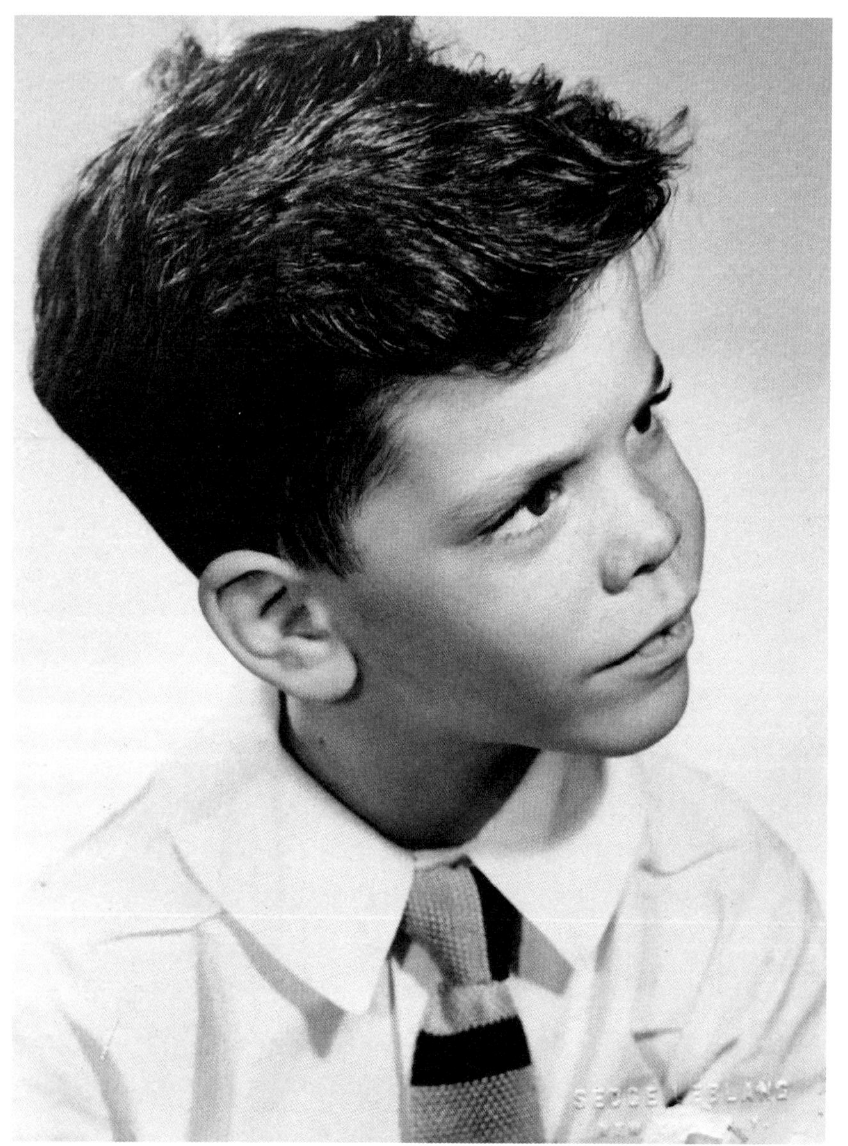

Lou Reed as a child. Merrill Reed Weiner Collection.

CALE

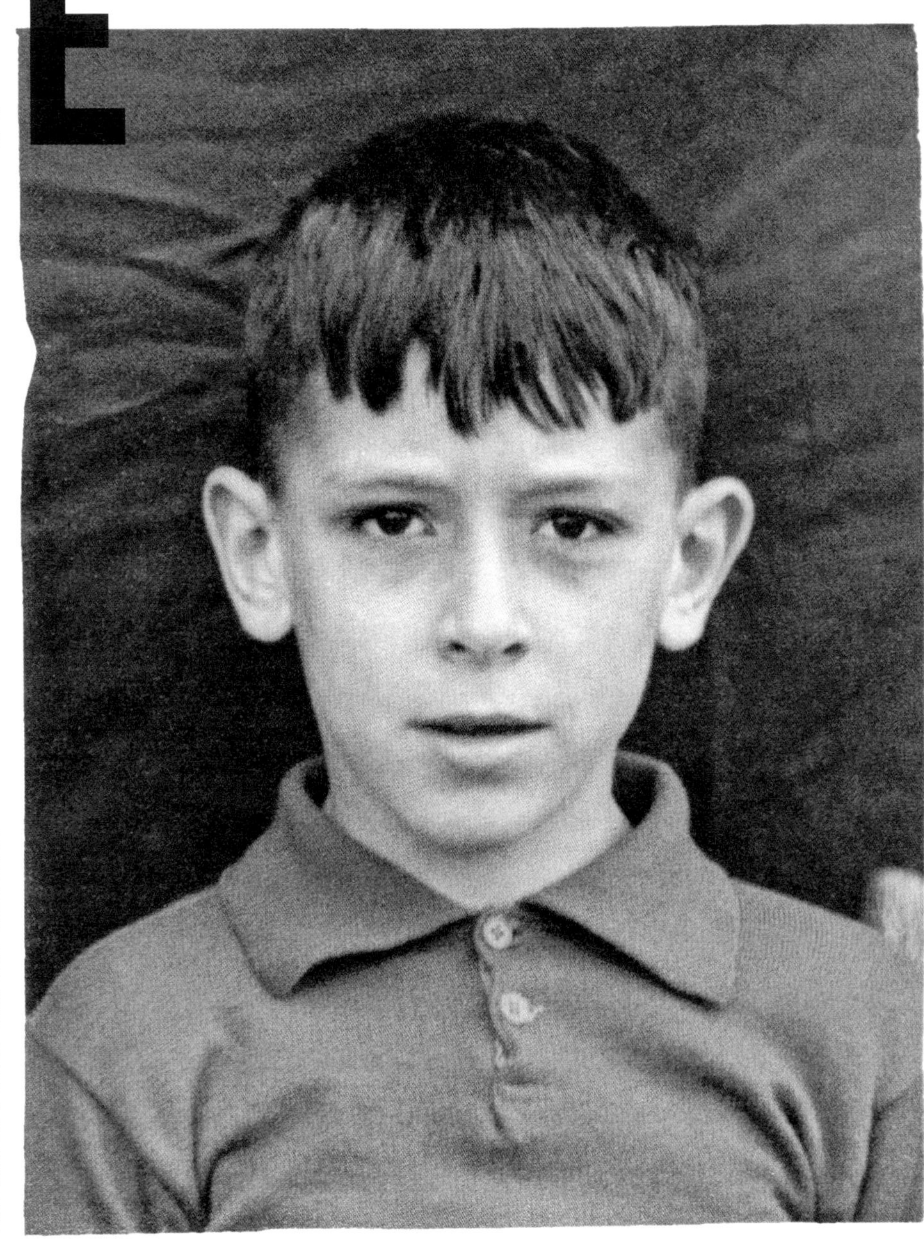

John Cale as a child. John Cale Collection.

CHILDHOOD

John Cale in Wales in 1959. John Cale Collection.

Lou Reed as a teenager. Merrill Reed Weiner Collection.

It is difficult to imagine two personalities and trajectories as divergent as the founders of the Velvet Underground. Before they met, John Cale and Lou Reed barely shared any similarities. The former was born on March 9th, 1942, into a working class family in Wales. Encouraged by his mother, he followed an academic path in music, with the intention of becoming a conductor. Lou Reed, born a week earlier in Brooklyn, came from a middle class, Jewish, New York family. From the outset, his temperament clashed with the rigidity of the Freeport suburb in which he grew up. The only thing that they had in common was a fascination with rock'n'roll and a desire to push its experiential boundaries.

John Cale holding his father's hand. John Cale Collection.

John Cale (bottom row left) at the Amman Valley Grammar School, Ammanford, South Wales. John Cale Collection.

John Cale on the piano. John Cale Collection.

John Cale

In his autobiography, *What's Welsh for Zen?* (Bloomsbury, 1999), John Cale revisits the course of his life, from his childhood in Wales to his New York adventure with the Velvet Underground.

I was born on March 9th, 1942, in Garnant, South Wales. Some 3,000 miles away in Brooklyn, New York, Lewis Reed had been born one week earlier, on the 2nd. I always knew he had an edge on me! After the Second World War, my family suffered from coupon rationing and the black market, which kept the poor downtrodden in Britain for the next 20 years.

I spent my first 18 years in a rural mining village. This was a strange, remote, some said mystical land. My father worked in the mine. He was bitter and exhausted. My mother, that was a different matter. She had married my father at age 36, after a brilliant career in the Welsh education system. She was full of life, passion, and joy. She loved playing the piano. I was her only child and she devoted herself to me for 20 years.

When I was seven years old, she signed me up for classical piano lessons and before long I could play very well. I realized that playing music helped me forge my own identity. I was so inspired and relaxed when my mother was there that I began to consider her presence to be crucial. This is how a lifelong dependency was born; the need to collaborate in order to complete my work and feel complete in myself.

Around that time, I began to suffer from asthma attacks. I was prescribed a cough mixture, the famous Dr Brown's, which contained opium. Maybe that was the start of the close connection between music and drugs for me. Lying in bed, gently rocked by hallucinations, I would watch the flowers on the wallpaper blossom and breathe.

At age 13, I joined the Welsh Youth Orchestra. I felt confident when I played concertos in public as part of the orchestra. I knew how to behave on stage. It required a certain control and I knew that it would pay off one day.

I began composing when I was in high school. One day in class, two very smart Londoners from BBC Wales turned up. They were looking for talented children. They interviewed me. I had just written a piece. I gave them the manuscript after playing it. Later they came to record it. But they had lost my score. Sitting in front of the grand piano, I thought, I have to find a second half. So I did. It only lasted two and a half minutes but it changed my life. Creatively, it liberated me; I started to take chances. From then on I knew what I wanted to do; I wanted to play music and improvise, compose music and conduct it.

Imagine me aged 15, 16, 17, lying in my little bedroom with the covers piled up to keep me warm and to bury the sound coming from around the world, from Radio Luxembourg and the Voice of America, where the pill-popping alcoholic genius Alan Freed, who made up the very term "rock and roll," turned on a million teens and changed the history of the world.

I had decided to go to university in London as a first step towards going to New York. I studied music at Goldsmiths, and I was interested in experimental composition (like Pierre Boulez and Luigi Nono), and concrete music. I met Cornelius Cardew, who introduced me to the London set of the art movement, Fluxus. In New York, John Cage and La Monte Young gravitated around this movement. I would soon meet them.

As I was about to set off to university across the Atlantic, I was terrified. I felt and still feel a complete lack of self-confidence. Once I arrived at the Berkshire Music Center, Tanglewood, in Massachusetts, I was welcomed by the composer Aaron Copland. I went to classes given by the Franco-Greek composer Yannis Xenakis.

I discovered New York through the elegant world of European classical music, when in fact what I was seeking was that revolution that was quietly rumbling inside me. New York was the place I had dreamt of my entire childhood, where I could achieve everything in full view. A city that never slept!

I was just as enamored with everything that was available to everyone as with what was hidden and would become my milieu for the years to come—the underground. In the Lower East Side scene, everyone was connected, by work or by love affairs.

I was one of the pianists who relayed to play Erik Satie's "Vexations" conducted by John Cage, during 18 hours and 40 minutes at the Pocket

National Youth Orchestra of Wales, Llandrindod Wells, 1961.
John Cale standing third row from the back, fifth from the left.
National Youth Orchestra of Wales Collection.

Theatre. The 180 notes of this 80-second long work were played 840 times. I lived in a ghetto apartment on Ludlow Street, in the Lower East Side with Tony Conrad. Angus MacLise was our neighbor. The street was lined with trash from the neighborhood and most of these buildings didn't have heating, hot water, or electricity. But the creative energy at work in Ludlow Street was stimulating. At that time, we were hanging around La Monte Young, who was dealing drugs. I helped him out in order to make some extra cash at the end of the month.

When I met Lou Reed for the first time, at the start of 1965, he was a young 22-year-old songwriter working for Pickwick Records in Long Island City, and I was a young 22-year-old classical musician who played in La Monte Young's Theatre of Eternal Music. Lou played me a few songs he had written on his acoustic guitar, as if they were folk songs, "Heroin" and "Waiting for the Man". His texts were an erudite vision of life, well written, hard, like those of a novelist. Lou was a high-strung, intelligent, fragile college kid, in a polo neck sweater, rumpled jeans, and loafers. He had been around and was bruised and trembling, quiet and insecure.

Lou was determined, and we began to play his songs together for fun. He could play lots of different kinds of music.

I had never rubbed shoulders with anyone who knew blues and picking country. He sat down and composed songs. All of a sudden, he would sing. It was fascinating. For Lou, words came as easily as musical composition came to me. I wanted to learn from him. You could even say that that is what I really wanted, more than success. Lou Reed was the first person my age in America with whom I connected.

It was a spiritual meeting around literature and other aspects of art. Before I met him, I had snorted, smoked, and swallowed the best drugs in New York, thanks to La Monte, but I had never injected myself. He introduced me to heroin, and it opened up a channel between us and created this us-against-them attitude, which would become characteristic of the band. We were called Falling Spikes. We also got hepatitis.

Lou and I had one of those rapports where you think the other guy is thinking what you're thinking, but he's not. He couldn't figure me out and I couldn't figure him out. The only things we had in common were drugs and an obsession with risk-taking. We attacked everything that got in our way; we thought evil was better than doing nothing. Lou made me come alive in New York, like nobody else ever had.

We both really wanted to go far, to be the best band in the world. As people, our image was that we were weird, sadistic, aloof, unfriendly, and nasty and that was how we always came across. Our aim was to upset people, make them feel uncomfortable, make them vomit. We never smiled and would turn our backs on the audience or give them the finger.

Sterling Morrison, a school friend of Lou's, arrived in 1965, as lead guitarist. Angus MacLise played the drums for us from time to time. We called ourselves the Warlocks.

One day, Tony Conrad dropped in to see us while we were playing. He had a battered paperback about sex with him, which he had found in the gutter and it was called *The Velvet Underground*. We immediately adopted that as our definitive name.

Program from the Little Festival of New Music in which John Cale participated, held at Goldsmiths College, London, 1963. John Cale Collection.

John Cale and Harry Kraut, administrator of Tanglewood, Massachusetts, 1963. John Cale Collection.

John Cale and his friend David Griffiths. John Cale Collection.

Lou and his sister Merrill. Merrill Reed Weiner Collection.

Merrill Reed Weiner

An excerpt from "A Family in Peril: Lou Reed's Sister Sets the Record Straight About His Childhood."

Lou Reed's sister Merrill describes growing up with her older brother Lou, and the difficulties he faced during his teenage years.

We were an average middle-class Jewish family. My mother, Toby, was a housewife and a doting mother. My father, Sidney, had dreamed of becoming an author or lawyer, but instead became a certified public accountant, as his mother wished.

My parents bought a small, three-bedroom ranch house for $10,000 in the blue-collar community of Freeport, on the south shore of Long Island. They settled there in 1952 to raise Lou and myself. For nine-year-old Lou, the move from Brooklyn to Freeport was a difficult transition. During those first years in our Freeport home, we were quite isolated. We knew no one and my mother didn't work.

During Lou's teenage years, it became obvious that he was becoming increasingly anxious, withdrawn, and resistant to most socializing, unless it was on his terms. He would withdraw, lock himself in his room, and refuse to meet people. At times, he would hide under his desk. He possessed a fragile temperament. His hyper-focus on the things he liked led him to music and it was there that he found himself. Self-taught, he began playing the guitar, absorbing every musical influence he could. In high school, he formed bands and played in the school variety shows. His band began to get bookings at small local clubs, which led to playing gigs in New York City.

By the age of 16, he was experimenting with drugs and closing the door on any communication with our parents. Verbal fights between Lou and my parents erupted, about going into the city to play band dates, about the dangers he might confront. My parents were frightened, upset, and bewildered. Lou's behavior terrified them and they were ill-equipped to respond effectively. Meanwhile, Lou continued to self-medicate with drugs and alcohol.

The following year, my parents sent Lou to New York University, with pride and possibly some trepidation. They were about to encounter some very difficult issues with their son and the "help" they received from the medical community set into motion the dissolution of my family of origin for the rest of our lives. The 1960s were marked with psychiatric theories that would ultimately harm families and do irreparable damage. During his freshman year at NYU, when I was 12, my parents went to the city and returned with Lou, limp and unresponsive. They said he'd had a "nervous breakdown."

My parents finally sought professional help for Lou. I heard only the superficial pieces of what was going on. My mother came into my room and told me that they thought he might have schizophrenia. She said that the doctors told her it was because she had not picked him up enough as an infant, but had let him cry in his room. She sobbed. "The pediatrician told me to do that! He said that's how you teach a baby to go to sleep." Lou was not able to function at that time. He was depressed, anxious, and socially unresponsive. If people came into our home, he hid in his room. He might sit with us, but he looked dead eyed, non-communicative.

Despite their misgivings, my parents brought Lou to a psychiatrist. Who knows what happened in the therapy sessions? I only know that the treating psychiatrist recommended electroshock therapy. My parents were like lambs being led to the slaughter, confused, terrified, and conditioned to follow the advice of doctors. Told by doctors that they were to blame and that their son suffered from severe mental illness, they thought they had no choice.

I watched my brother as my parents assisted him coming back into our home afterwards, unable to walk, stupor-like. I assume that Lou could not have been in any shape to understand the treatment or side effects. It may well be that he was fearful he would be committed to a psychiatric hospital and not allowed to remain home if he did not agree to treatment. But Lou did get better. After he recovered, he and my parents decided he should go off to Syracuse University and begin again. That's what he did.

The members of the Primitives—Tony Conrad, Lou Reed, Walter De Maria, and John Cale with Terry Phillips from Pickwick Records, during the promotional tour of "The Ostrich" in 1965. John Cale Collection.

TO DELMORE SCHWARTZ FROM LOU REED

In 1962, Lou Reed took courses under Delmore Schwartz (1913-1966), a poet and literature professor at Syracuse University, who ultimately became Reed's mentor and friend. This letter was written by Lou Reed in 1965.

Dear Delmore- it has been a veryllong summer and winter. I got out of school just in time to have hepatitis. it wasn't a bad case though and after 2 odd months i was out of bed. then i became involved with a record company and worked at a job as a songwriter a performer and a musician. I helped make one of those cheap $!.98 albums that you see in supermarkets. We wrote 33 songs and sang, played and recorded them in 2 days. I commuted from the city to home from home to the city. worked 6-7 days a week from9 or 10 to anywhere from 11 to 3 in the morning not counting my lousy hour trips on the train to get to the studio. My first record came out. It was hysterically funny if you go for that kind of thing. We recruited a group to accompany me on promotional trips. One guy was from Wales. He got here on a Leonard Berstein scholorship, a starving viola player. the other was a violin player from harvard, who helped do the sound track for an "underground " film called Flaming Creatures by a gentleman named Jack Smith. The last showing drew the police of ny who arrested everyone insight, the projectionist, viewers, etc. -said the film was obscene. The third member of my tribe was an m.a. from u.c.l.a. who just had a showing at an art gallery that was a flop. There was trouble with the promo trips to say the least. We created quite a stir and the young girls in the audience loved us quite alot, autographs, people knew us in a diner and thought we were ENGLISH. But I wasn't up to it I'm afraid the way i would have been what seems like years ago. I quit my job (after first determining that i could work as long and as well as anyone there). But this bit wasn't for me. Then (I was still under contracts of various sorts, they possessed 25% of nothing) my manager brought in this guy with lots of money who wanted to buy us instruments (we were one of the few bands in existence that had no instruments, they rented them for us on occasion) and book us in his nightclubs. I said no and quit the group. Meanwhile I had a folk album going for me. They loved me and my stuff but thought the lyrics were offensive (not dirty, just offensive) and would I change the lyrics and i said no and that was that. Interestingly enough a new record just came out which i had a hand in writing which is quite good and might stand a chance. One song of mine is in hollywood, another is in england where a longhaired group is mulling it over, and my manager has dug up some smaller but more liberal (?) folk record companies. Plus the record company I'm affiliated with now is interested in my making another record even though i don't work there anymore and am not meant for promotion tours. So now I'm getting this job with the welfare department (because you don't have to dress and its kind of a usefull job- you try to help people with 6 children and rats in one room apartments, if that's possible). Its a kind of ny peace corp with pay.

My harvard application has been sitting for awhile now because i didn't know if i was ready to go to school anymore, or if i should anymore, at anytime. I was drafted and naturally ruled exempt, unacceptable for the obvious reasons. Thus I am free of the draft and slowly but surely people who depend on me for music or talent or advice or etc. I've had some strange experiences since returning to ny, sick but strange and fascinating and even, sometimes ultimately revealing, healing and helpful. The record industry is viscious as are most businesses, but this one a little more so. ny has so many sad, sick people and i have a knack for meeting them. they try to

Letter from Lou Reed to Delmore Schwartz, 1965. Delmore Schwartz Papers, Yale Collection of American Literature, Beinecke Rare Book and Manuscript Library.

drag you down with them. If you're weak ny has many outlets. Ican't resist peering, probing, sometimes participating, othertimes going right to the edge before sidestepping. Finding viscousness in yourself and that fantastic killer urge and worse yet having the opportunity presented before you is certainly interesting. Interesting is not the word. You have to wait a few days to use it, but often you are truely cold. The easy ways of making money, group bravado, the rich johns on park ave who dig watching fornicating couples enough to pay $250, $500, $&700 prices up for group perfomances of 3 or more or the more esoteric sexual art forms. fuck fuck fuck

I feel better myself. I am better. I needed no school. I have let 6 months go by without looking at anything I had written. I needed to be cool- I needed to be away from the writing so that I could look at it more coldly. I finally did that and I decided that I'm very very good and could be a good wri writer if i work and work. i know thatswhat ive got to do, no getting around it, but things had to get established. MAYBE i will go to school again. maybe i'll teach, maybe euope, who knows. But mainly it must be writing and I think I'm good enough to give it a run for its money. Hope my latest records a smash because I'll be needing the money to be sure. I'm lucky though. It doesn't take much of anything that has to do with money to keep me quiet or happy or mollified. Its the peripheral things round you that need bread. You'll notice my spelling hasn't improved.

HOW ARE YOU? I mean that, how are you? I hope very much that you are well. I also hope very much that you are my spiritual godfather, and I mean that quite a bit too.

Lou Reed

NEW YORK SPIRIT

Viewed from the heartland of the United States, New York has always been perceived as the great Babylon, a cosmopolitan center incompatible with the values of middle America. In the early 1960s, in a city divided by economic and social crisis, no neighborhood aroused more suspicion than the Village, located in the south end of Manhattan—a haunt for idle students, immoral artists, and intellectuals with pernicious ideas. Repulsion went hand in hand with a powerful attraction; a decadent hell in the eyes of the majority. For others the Village was a promised land, a fertile ground for creation. It was a point of convergence for experimental musicians and underground filmmakers, taboo-breaking poets and young people defying social and sexual norms. Freedom was the key word: "Everything is allowed." In this unique context, before giving birth to the Velvet Underground, Lou Reed and John Cale rubbed shoulders with beat poets, the daring harmony of La Monte Young, and the underground experimental film scene. They were at the confluence of pop culture and the avant-garde, conceptual art and rhythmic circles, juvenile antics and sophisticated theories.

Jack Kerouac reading Beatnik poetry in a Lower East Side loft, New York, February 1959. Photograph: Fred W. McDarrah.

WINE
LIQUOR
STORE
ST. MARKS
LIQUORS
SAVINGS

FRED W. MCDARRAH

(1926–2007)

Demolition in Greenwich Village at 10th and Greenwich Avenue.
Photograph: Fred W. McDarrah. © Estate of Fred W. McDarrah.

Born in Brooklyn, Fred W. McDarrah became the official *Village Voice* photographer in the mid-1950s. On behalf of this challenging New York weekly, he traveled the streets of New York day and night, with a preference for Greenwich Village and the Lower East Side. His lens captured political activists, actors and choreographers, painters and poets, avant-garde musicians and visual artists,

Above: The Living Theatre, New York, October 1965.
Photograph: Fred W. McDarrah. © Estate of Fred W. McDarrah.

Below: Birthday party of free jazz trumpet player, American poet, and painter Ted Joans, New York, June 1959.
Photograph: Fred W. McDarrah. © Estate of Fred W. McDarrah.

World Trade Center site, looking north from Liberty St., August 24, 1967.
Photograph: Fred W. McDarrah. © Estate of Fred W. McDarrah.

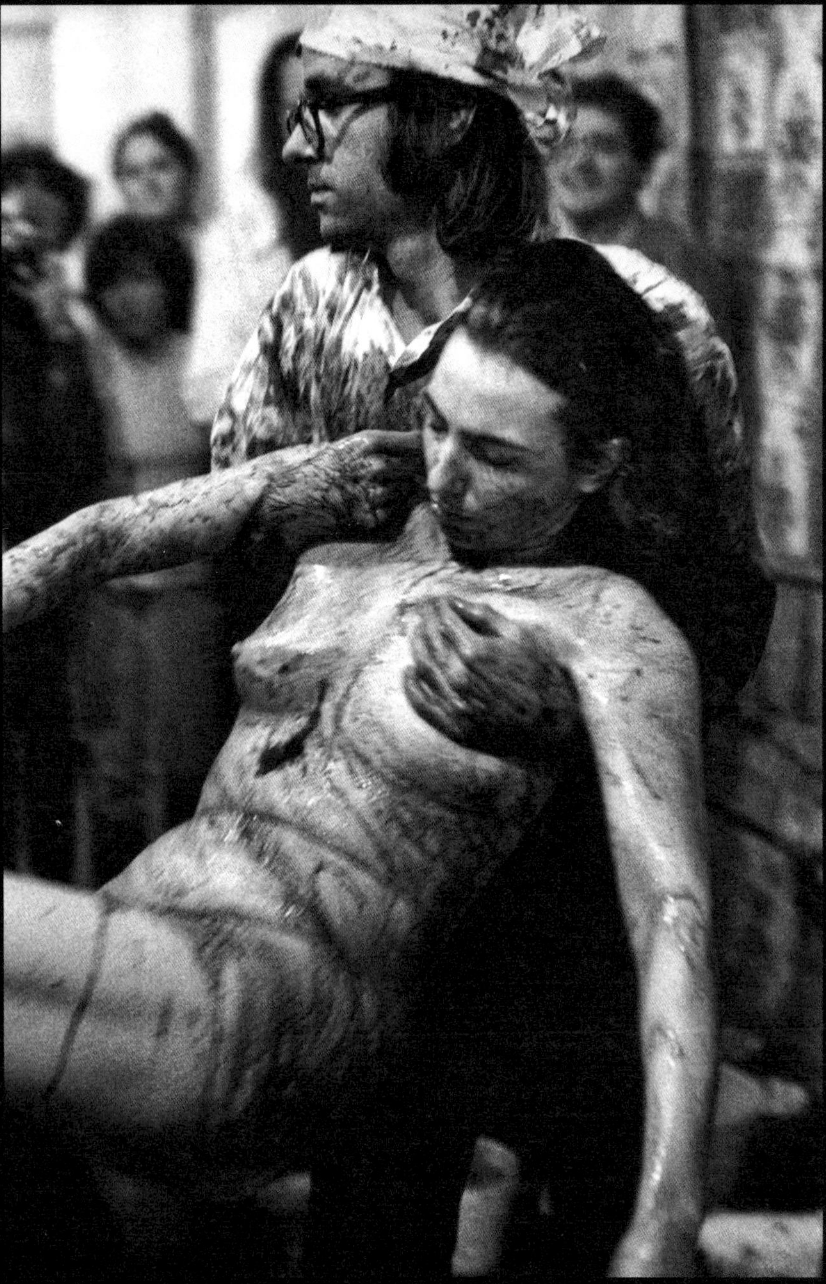

Above: Conversation between Hubert Selby Jr. and LeRoi Jones (also known as Amiri Baraka), November 1960, New York. Photograph: Fred W. McDarrah. © Estate of Fred W. McDarrah.

Below: Carolee Schneemann (R) in her performance art piece "Meat Joy" in the Judson Memorial Church auditorium, Thompson St. and Washington Square South, November 16, 1964. Photograph: Fred W. McDarrah. © Estate of Fred W. McDarrah.

Above: High-angle view of a large crowd of people gathered on the sidewalk in front of Nathan's Famous, at the corner of Surf and Stillwell Avenues in Coney Island, for a rally in support of John Lindsay's ultimately successful mayoral candidacy, July 1, 1965. Photograph: Fred W. McDarrah. © Estate of Fred W. McDarrah..

Below: Charles Mingus and his musicians at Five Spot Cafe, St. Marks Place, New York, August 1962. Photograph: Fred W. McDarrah. © Estate of Fred W. McDarrah.

Pages 54-55: California poet and painter Jack Micheline reading his poem, entitled "Warren Finnerty Riding a Bicycle on 4th Avenue at Midnight Dreaming of Love and Wine and Franz Kline," on the Hudson Pier at 13th Street, New York, June 1963. Photograph: Fred W. McDarrah. © Estate of Fred W. McDarrah.

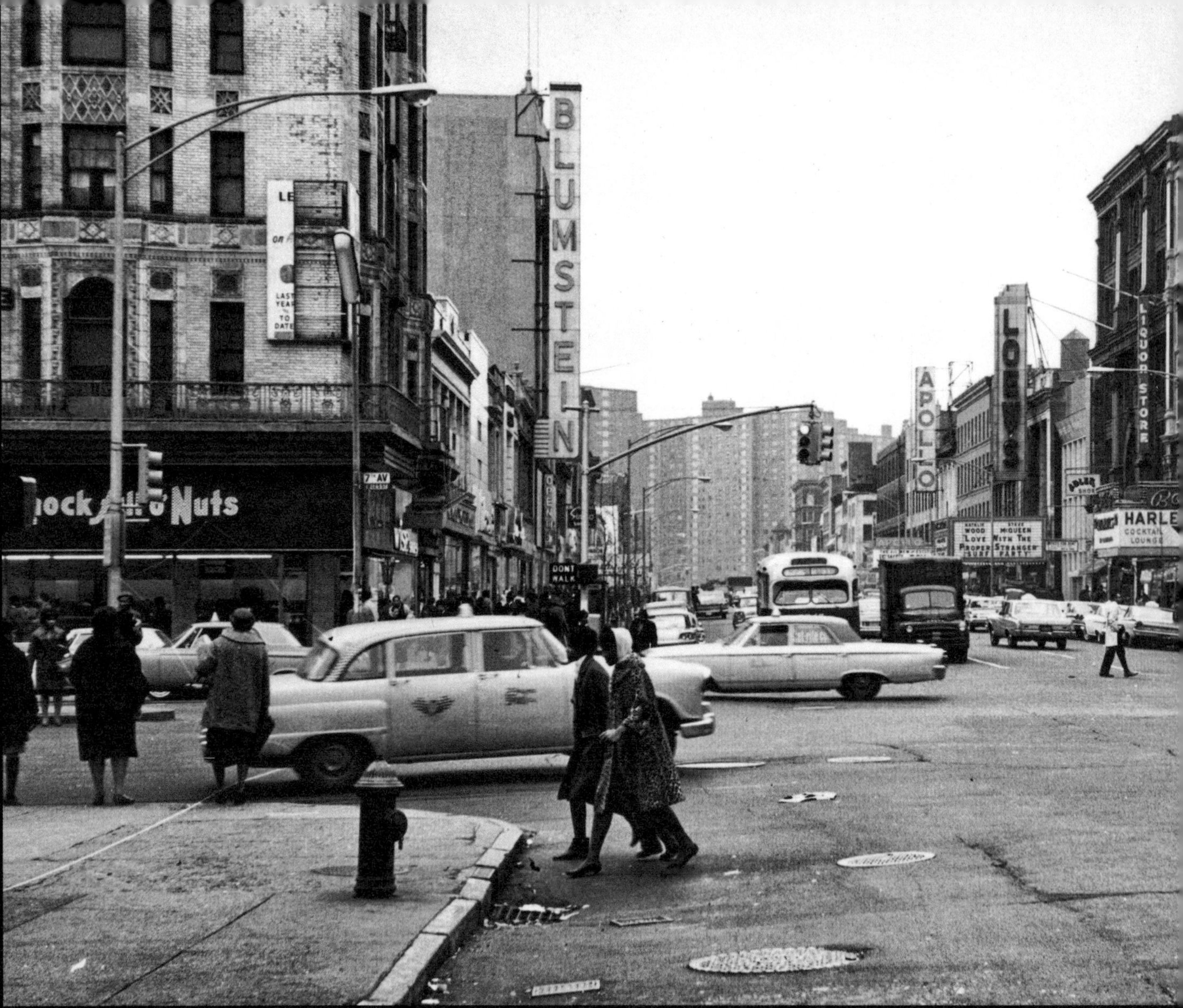
BLUMSTEIN
APOLLO
LOEW'S
LIQUOR STORE
DONT WALK
COCKTAIL LOUNGE

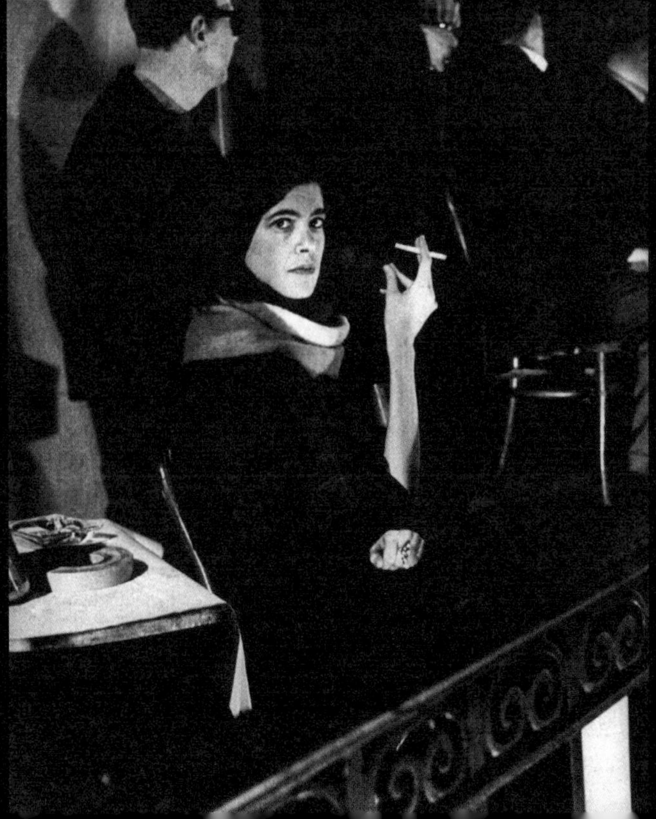

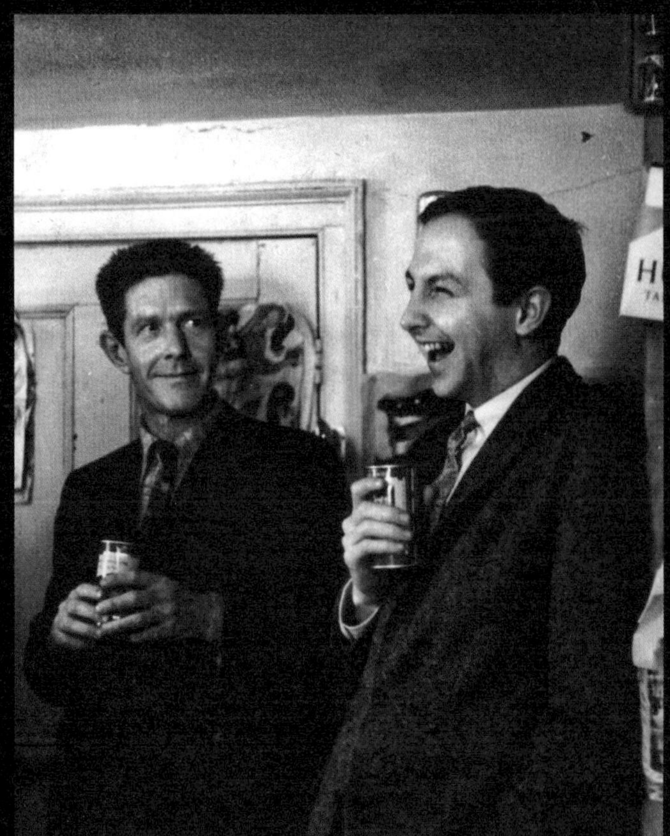

Pages 56-57:
Above left: 125th Street at 7th Avenue, New York, March 1964. The sidewalk to the right of the Apollo Theatre. Photograph: Fred W. McDarrah. © Estate of Fred W. McDarrah.

Above right: Martin Luther King at the Lincoln Memorial during the March on Washington for Jobs and Freedom, August 1963. Photograph: Fred W. McDarrah. © Estate of Fred W. McDarrah.

Bottom left: Susan Sontag attending a seminar about sex at the Mills Hotel, New York, December 1962. Photograph: Fred W. McDarrah. © Estate of Fred W. McDarrah.

Bottom middle: American composer John Cage (1912–1992) (left) and Pop artist Robert Rauschenberg (1925–2008) share a laugh at a party in Greenwich Village, April 26, 1959. Photograph: Fred W. McDarrah. © Estate of Fred W. McDarrah.

Bottom right: Bob Dylan, Karen Dalton, and Fred Neil at Cafe Wha?, MacDougal Street, New York, February 1961. Photograph: Fred W. McDarrah. © Estate of Fred W. McDarrah.

Above: James Baldwin and actor Marlon Brando hand in hand at the Lincoln Monument during the March on Washington, August 1963. Photograph: Fred W. McDarrah. © Estate of Fred W. McDarrah.

Below: Cassius Clay arrives at the Bitter End Club (147 Bleeker Street) for a lecture on poetry, New York, March 1963. Photograph: Fred W. McDarrah. © Estate of Fred W. McDarrah.

Above: Speech by Malcolm X during a rally in Harlem, New York, September 1963. Photograph: Fred W. McDarrah. © Estate of Fred W. McDarrah.

Below: Tom Wesselmann, Roy Lichtenstein, James Rosenquist, Andy Warhol, and Claes Oldenburg. The Pop Art Popes pose together at Andy Warhol's Factory, New York, 1964. Photograph: Fred W. McDarrah. © Estate of Fred W. McDarrah.

View of an enormous crowd of demonstrators as they sit on a hill that leads up to a statue of Union General John A. Logan astride a horse in Grant Park during protests at the Democratic National Convention, Chicago, Illinois, August 27, 1968. Photograph: Fred W. McDarrah. © Estate of Fred W. McDarrah.

EXPLOSIVE YEARS

Jonas Mekas

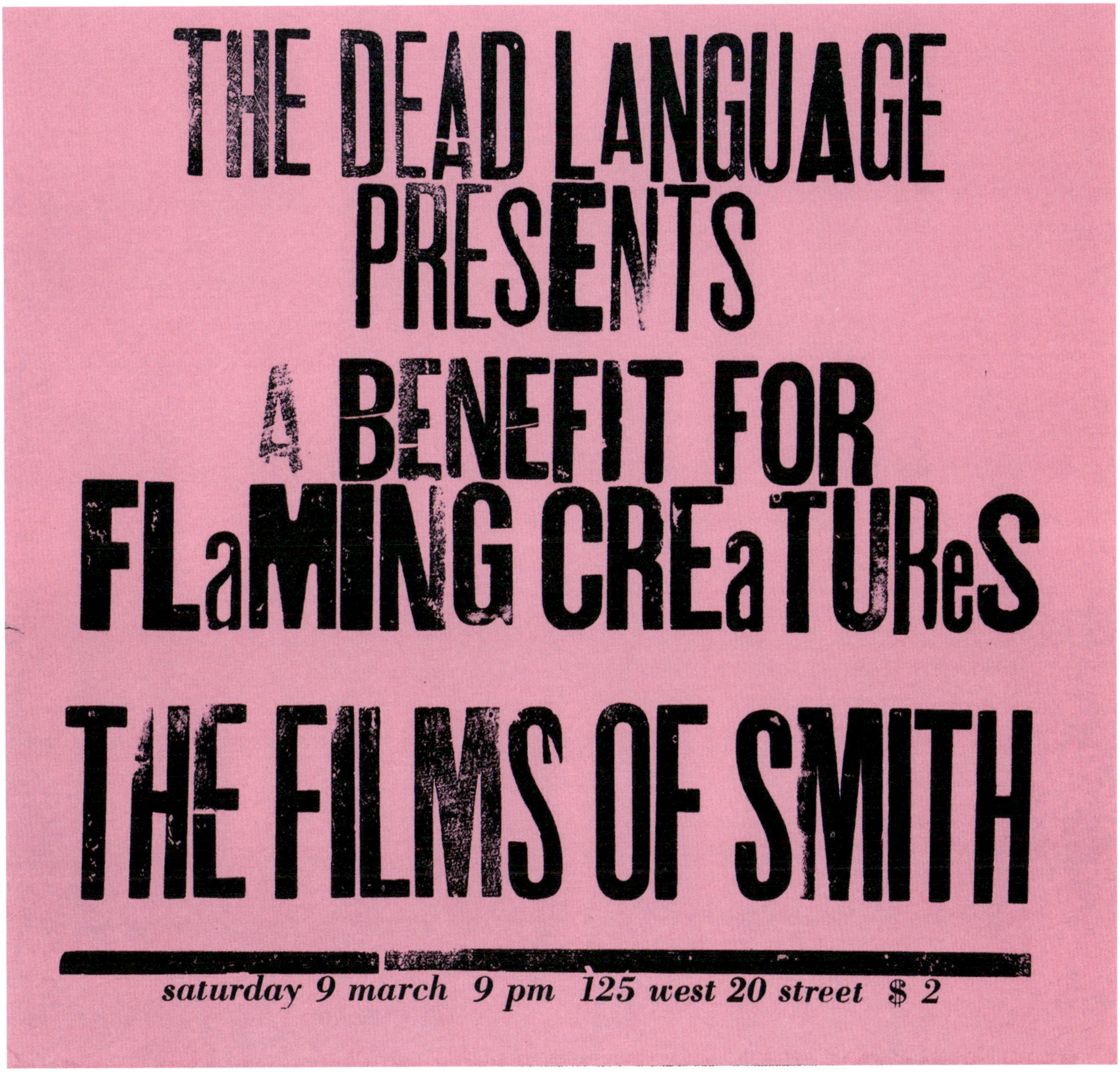

THE DEAD LANGUAGE
PRESENTS
A BENEFIT FOR
FLaMING CREaTUReS

THE FILMS OF SMITH

saturday 9 march 9 pm 125 west 20 street $ 2

Flyer for an event to support *Flaming Creatures*, a film by Jack Smith. Jonas Mekas Collection.

Jonas Mekas gives a testimonial of the New York underground, diving into the heart of the "explosive years" of the 1960s avant-garde.

John Cage performing *Suite for Toy Piano* (1948) beneath the projectors of the Living Theatre, New York, March 1960. Photograph: Fred W. McDarrah. © Estate of Fred W. McDarrah.

OK… This is almost an impossible task. But I will try. I will try to sum up the period from 1960 to 1966. The time when the Velvet Underground slowly emerged, the very busy time for the Film-Makers' Cinematheque. The period, really, when the classic, all the classic arts—theater, architecture, poetry, dance, music—had reached a certain point in the 50s, when things began drastically to change, like something new was emerging.

Music: there was John Cage. Theater: Foreman, the Theater of the Ridiculous. Dance: Yvonne Rainer, there was the Judson Dance Theater at the Judson Memorial Church, Carolee Schneemann's "Meat Joy" (1965), [Peter Schumann's] Bread and Puppet Theater….

There was La Monte Young emerging, AG Gallery, the beginning of Fluxus, there was Claes Oldenburg, and there were the filmmakers.
So much was happening already in cinema.
I mean when I came to New York in 1949 it was already beginning. There were already like a dozen film societies, something was already budding—the beginnings of the early American avant-garde that was united in the 60s already. San Francisco, New York, there was Kenneth Anger, there was Gregory Markopoulos, there was Stan Brakhage emerging somewhere in Colorado, and then the Living Theatre in New York, 100th Street and Broadway.

And then in 1966 it all reached a climax.

Suddenly, Andy appeared somewhere there, The Factory … And there was so much going on—the freedom, the emerging freedom, nobody wanted to be restricted in theater and films. I clashed, and I was arrested twice, for screening *Flaming Creatures* and Jean Genet's *Un Chant d'Amour*.
We created the New American Cinema Group in 1959 to help each other, then the practical hand of our own distribution center, the Film-Makers' Cooperative. We had complete control. That was on 414 Park Avenue South. It became very, very important.

That's where we met every day, every evening, screening films for each other. It was a meeting ground for poets, painters, filmmakers.
It was also like Andy's film school. And the muse, Barbara Rubin came to help me at the Film-Makers' Cooperative and became like a central figure, challenging, bringing people together. That was Barbara.

Here is a list—I made a little list of various places where activities were taking place.
It was so active, so intense, so intense.
Somewhere there was Angus MacLise, Lou Reed, John Cale, Tony Conrad. Something was beginning to happen in music. It was Barbara Rubin who brought them to the Cinematheque, which I brought into existence to get around the censorship. We opened in Midtown at Astor Playhouse, in 1965. That's where the first Expanded Cinema Festival took place. That's where Andy used to come, and

"Ironworks/Fotodeath" (1961), a performance by Claes Oldenburg, staged at Ruben Gallery, New York, February 1961. Photograph: Fred W. McDarrah. © Estate of Fred W. McDarrah.

20 Flux Films at the Anthology Film Archives, New York. Poster designed by George Maciunas. Jonas Mekas Collection.

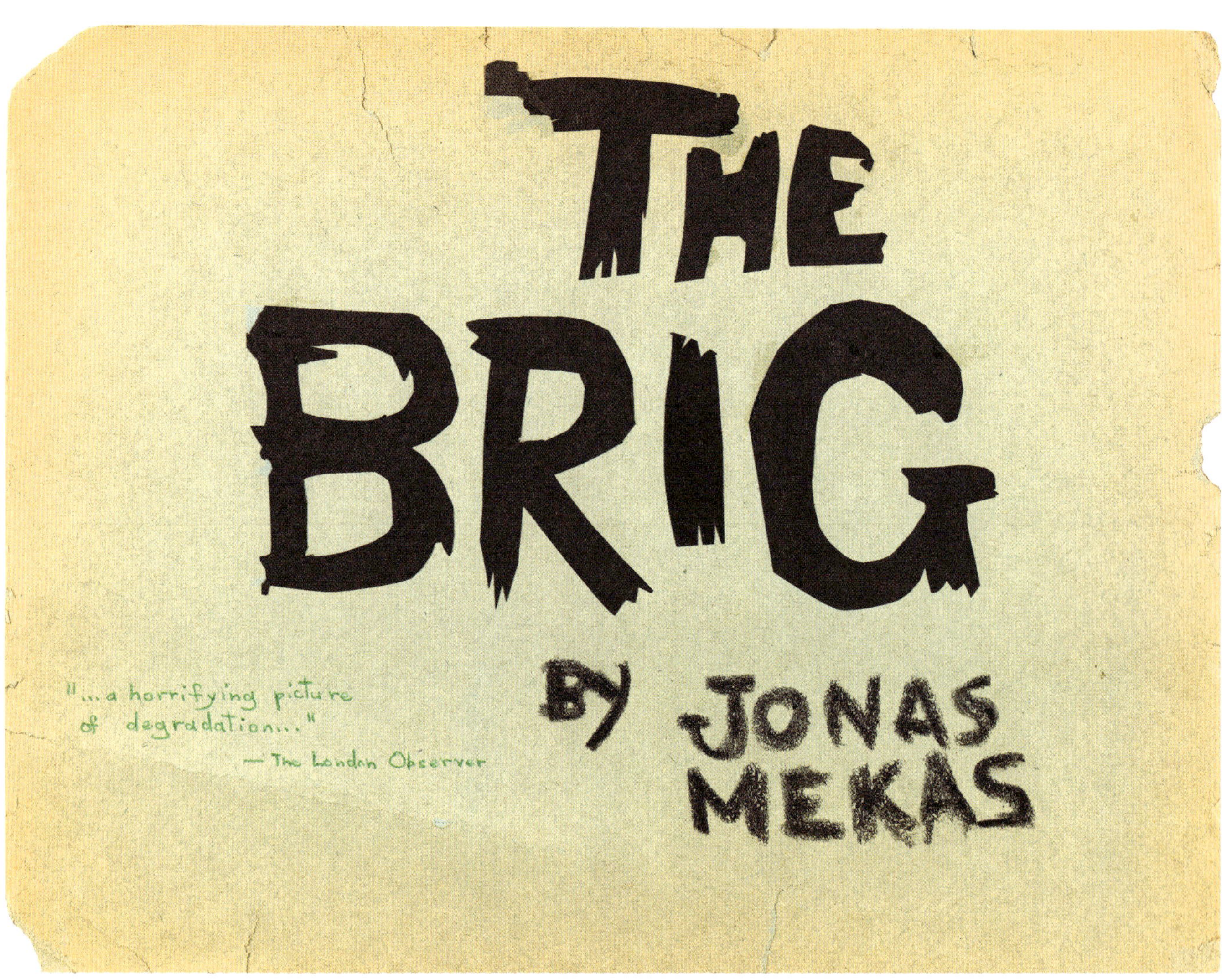

Flyer for *The Brig*, 1964. Jonas Mekas Collection.

bring his new sound period films. The early silent films were projected when Film-Makers' Cooperative was running a showcase on 27th Street—The Film Makers' Showcase. Moving from 1965 to 1966, there is Kenneth Anger, there is Jack Smith, then moving to the Astor Playhouse, then 31st Street in the heart of Times Square, that's where Barbara Rubin organized the first Caterpillar Changes Festival, where Lou Reed and the Velvet Underground first performed together. During that period, Barbara also introduced Andy to the Velvet Underground. February 1966 was also their first public performance at Hotel Delmonico, and then the premiere of *Chelsea Girls* which was alson on 41st Street.

It was so active, so busy, I don't know which angle to approach it from. Everybody was working together with everybody else. There were poets, Allen Ginsberg, there was Robert Frank, there was Ed Sanders …

It was like you could see them in almost all these places.

I mean it was quite incredible, that level of intensity, and it lasted, like burning electrical wires, high tension, for like a decade or so. There was Michael Snow's 1967 film, *Wavelength*. Minimalism was coming in, and structuralism had already arrived.

Of course La Monte Young was already there, Fluxus, George Maciunas. I took Andy Warhol in 1962 I think, or 1963, to one of La Monte Young's performances, one note extended to four or six hours. He wanted to see what was happening, he was very much in it, in all those aspects also.

So of course he immediately saw the possibilities of the Velvet Underground. There was also, of course, Gerard Malanga, and that's the next stand up: it came out from Expanded Cinema Festival, where about 30 artists, filmmakers, musicians, and dancers did performances that you couldn't really fit into any narrow form of art, that were branched, used, went across borders of their own and other's art.

Whitman, and of course, Snyder, Jacky Castle, Stan VanDerBeek, all these artists, they said some wonderful things, like Claes Oldenburg and Rauschenberg did at the Cinematheque and the

Ed Sanders at the Peace Eye Bookstore (383 East 10th Street), New York, January 1966. Photograph: Fred W. McDarrah.

Below: Advertisement in the *Village Voice* for "Andy Warhol, Up-Tight", February 10, 1966. Alfredo Garcia Collection.

Armory. The Cinematheque was one of the centers where they could meet, and from which they were shooting in different directions, and of course there was the Film-Makers' Cooperative headquarters. Many of these artists went downtown, where they used to walk to 28th Street, to the Belmore Cafeteria just across from the Film-makers' Cooperative. That was an all-night taxi drivers' place.

Amazing!

So …

You get the idea, the intensity of the activity, of the explosion that was taking place at that time, and some of the people, we can still feel it. How many decades past? We are still feeling it, it still reverberates, it still affects us, it's still there. Amazing.

Sun. 5:30, 8, 10; Mon. 8 10; Tues. 10 $1.50

The Bridge Film Society Members: Month (3 shows): $4;
Tues., Feb. 15 8 10 PM Season: $18
RENE CLAIR, Entr'Acte. MAN RAY, Emak Bakia. ARTAUD, Seashell and Clergyman. TV COMMERCIALS IN AMERICA.

4 ST. MARK'S PLACE OR 3-4600

". . .monuments of ________." — **East Village Other**
"Her eyes are the color of twice-frozen Hershey bars." —**NY Times**

ANDY WARHOL, UP-TIGHT

presents live

THE VELVET UNDERGROUND
EDIE SEDGWICK
GERARD MALANGA
DONALD LYONS
BARBARA RUBIN
BOB NEUWIRTH
PAUL MORRISSEY
NICO
DANIEL WILLIAMS
BILLY LINICH

Up-tight Rock 'n Roll, Whip Dancers, Film-maker Freaks, Tapers, Anchovies. Filming live episodes of the "Up-Tight" series and including Film Premiere for the first time anywhere: Andy Warhol's MORE MILK, YVETTE starring Mario Montez and The Velvet Underground.

Tues. thru Mon., Feb. 8 to Feb. 13th
Weekdays 8 pm, 10:30 pm
Sat. and Sun., 2:30 pm, 8 pm, 10:30 pm

Film-Makers' Cinematheque

41st St. THEATER

125 West 41st St. **564-3818**

"when

THE FILM-MAKERS' COOPERATIVE

At the end of the Second World War, an artistic renewal was needed in the United States, particularly in New York, where many artists who had arrived as refugees began to return to Europe. In film, the "system" symbolized by Hollywood and large studios was challenged by a handful of creatives who wanted to redefine the codes of conduct in the industry. Jonas Mekas and his acolytes in experimental film and poetry were open to the innovations and, in 1961, decided to create the Film-Makers' Cooperative: a communal structure that helped them to produce and distribute their work. It wasn't surprising that there was overlap and exchange with the Velvets and Underground Cinema — spearhead of the counterculture. Converging at the center of this nebula was everything that contravened the established values and pretense of the "official" America.

FILM-MAKERS'
CINEMATHEQUE
41st STREET THEATER
125 W. 41st ST. NYC 564-3818
ANDY WARHOL'S
MY HUSTLER
SIN IN THE SUMMER ON FIRE ISLAND
APRIL 3 thru 10
8 P.M. and 10 P.M.
UNDERGROUND · AVANT-GARDE SHOWCASE
OPEN 7 NIGHTS · $1.50
FOR DETAILS SEE OUR WEEKLY VILLAGE VOICE "AD"

Above left: Poster for the film *My Hustler* (1965) by Andy Warhol. Jonas Mekas Collection.

Above right: Logo for the Film-Makers' Cooperative.

Below: Three issues of *Film Culture* magazine, founded by Jonas and Adolfas Mekas. Issues from 1955, 1965, and 1970. Private Collection.

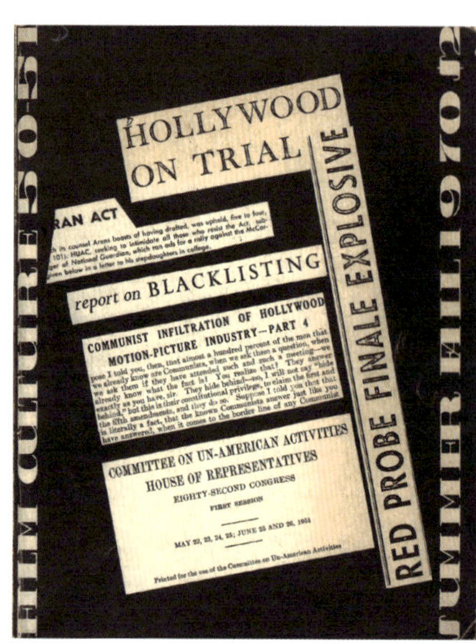

ANTI-100 YEARS OF CINEMA MANIFESTO

Some are talking about the End of History.
There are others who say that we are at the End of Cinema.

Do not believe any of it!

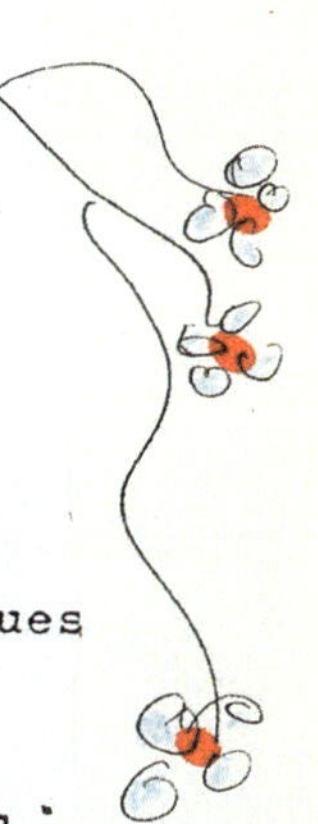

And the movie industries and the movie museums around the world are celebrating the 100th anniversary of cinema; and they talk about the millions of dollars their cinemas have made; they discuss their Hollywoods and their stars --

but there is no mention of the avantgarde, of the independents, of OUR CINEMA. I have seen the brochures, the programmes of the museums and archives and cinematheques around the world. I know what cinema they are talking about.

But I want to take this occasion to say this:

In the times of bigness, spectaculars, one hundred million movie productions, I want to speak for the small, invisible acts of human spirit, so subtle so small that they die when brought out under the Kleegue lights.

I want to celebrate the small forms of cinema, the lyrical forms, the poem, the watercolor, etude, sketch, postcard, arabesque, triolet, and bagatelle, and little 8-mm songs.

In the times when everybody wants to succeed and sell, I want to celebrate those who embrace social and daily failure to pursue the invisible, the personal, things that bring no money and no bre[illegible] contemporary history -- art history or any other history --

I am for art which we do for each other as friends, for ourselves.

I am standing in the middle of the Information Highway and laughing --

because a butterfly on a little flower somewhere, somewhere, just fluttered its wings and I know that the whole course of history will drastically change because of that flutter --

a super-8 camera just made a little soft buzz somewhere on New York's Lower East Side -- and the world will never be the same --

the real history of cinema is the invisible history --
history of friends getting together
doing the thing they love --
for us cinema is beginning
with every new buzz of the
projector,
with every new buzz of our cameras
our hearts
jump
forwards,
my friends!

Jonas

...A CAMERA FOR JONAS...

HOW I DISCOVERED THE UNDERGROUND

John Cale

As told to Christian Fevret for *Les Inrockuptibles*, 1990.

There is no futility in rock 'n' roll. There is futility in the avant-garde.

Rock 'n' roll is too urgent to be futile, that's how fantastic it is. It's the expression of someone who really wants to communicate with someone else. Of course, it was avant-garde, but it was not obvious, it was not explained. When people came to watch our band Dream Syndicate play, it was a form of psychotherapy. In the face of musicians who kept a note for a very long time and at a very loud, very corrosive volume, they found themselves alone in front of themselves, almost forced into introspection. There was no one to explain anything to them.

In the early 1960s, I lived in Soho and worked with La Monte Young in Tribeca.

I came from an extremely conservative environment. At the time, it was difficult for me to live in a city as cosmopolitan as New York, to be confronted with the aggressions and the disorder of the streets. Lou was already acclimatized and showed me how to react, how to do it.

He was smart. I learned a lot from him. We constantly discussed literature, topics like expression of risk in literature and in art. We made it a game: real risk or simulated risk? With him, I understood the value of words, which gained intensity under the influence of certain psychotropic substances. We often found ourselves in rather frightening situations, where the slightest word could be decisive … One day, in a restaurant, a drunk guy came to piss us off.

Instead of ignoring him or saying something to make him leave, Lou was friendly and asked him [*whispering*]: "Would you fuck your mother?" Such scenes were common. He was trying not to make things better, but to see how far they could go … to the worst possible outcome. And then we stopped this stupid game. Things happened … regrettable things, which ended tragically. Some guys who got their legs torn off by shotguns … We got so close to … [*he mimes slaughtering*]. The game was finished.

We lost a lot of time trying to understand the meaning of each term in these very special circumstances. It fascinated us. We fed on this with a lot of discussions about novels and poetry.

I guess for Lou, this whole period was linked to the horror of electroshock, the hatred of going to the doctor, the sight of waiting rooms full of vegetables. He could not stand to see them. I think that destroyed any sense of compassion in him.

My experience with Dream Syndicate allowed me to understand that hypnosis in music gives you a huge space. And the more you take that hypnosis out of the music, the more space you give to the song. The idea was that more space was gained by holding a single chord than by changing it. It was my way of doing Phil Spector.

We wanted to create an orchestral situation on stage, with Lou improvising. We went through different group compositions. It was Lou who forced me to continue to play the violin. I wanted to do rock 'n' roll, to be on bass.

Jonas Mekas Collection

He didn't stop telling me, "Play the violin, play the violin …" and thwarted my dreams of becoming a rock 'n' roll star.

Heroin was already written, but it was only when Sterling started to play the bass part, and me the violin on *Venus*, that I felt that we had discovered a style. When we found the arrangement for *Venus*, I knew that there was a really original, dirty, unhealthy, indecent style.

When I went to the Factory and saw what was going on, I realized that it had nothing to do with the idea of repetition. Contemporary art was like a mystery to me. I had been hanging out in London with a lot of artists, but I felt like they did not really pay attention to what they were doing. They were careless in their approach to the technique and did not work very hard. When I arrived at the Factory, I was impressed by the amount of work being done at all times. It took a great deal of work to produce these screenprints. It was obvious that they applied themselves. It was very professional, they worked very late every night.

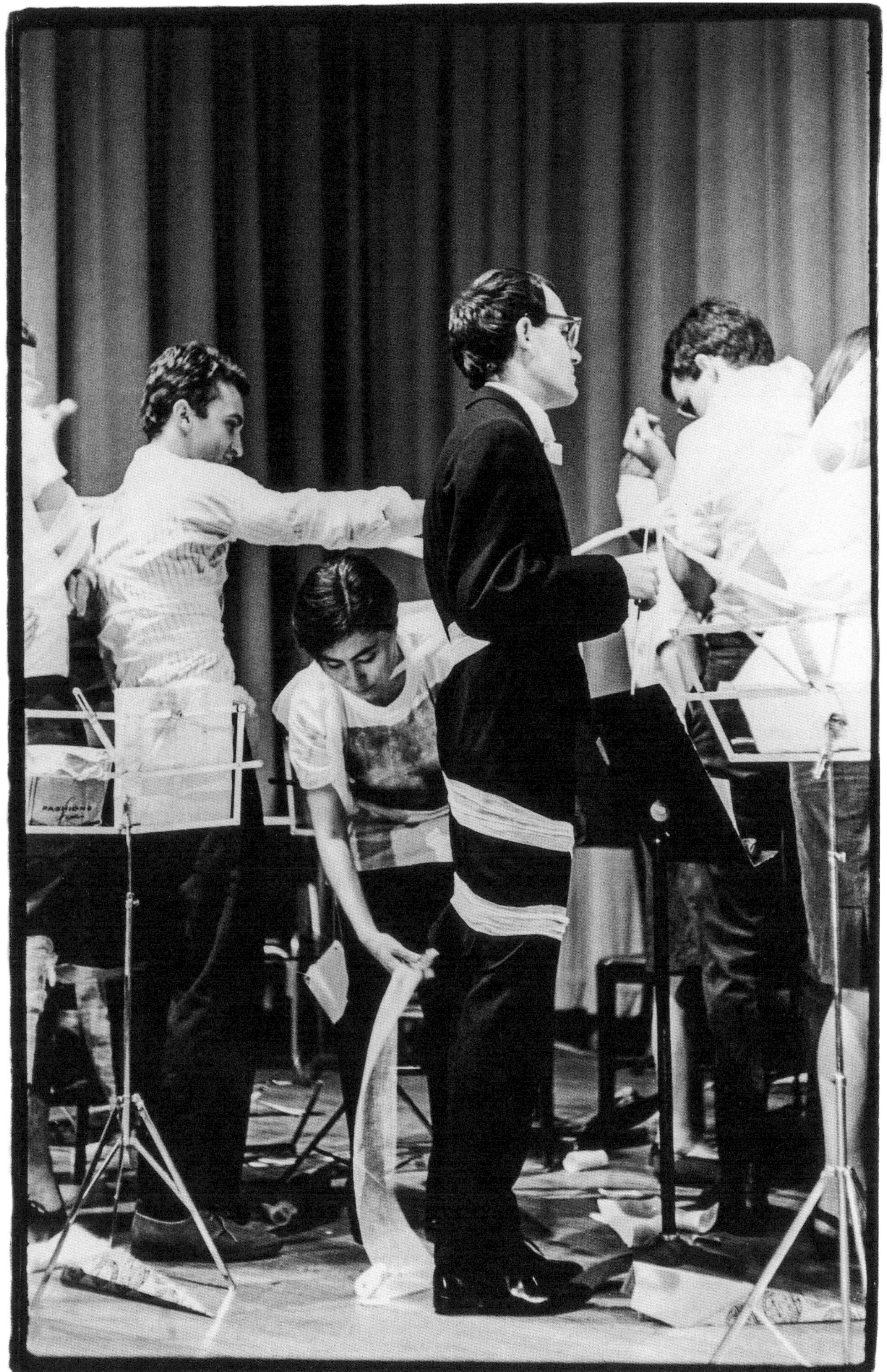

Yoko Ono wrapping La Monte Young during their Fluxus performance "Sky Piece to Jesus Christ" at Carnegie Hall, New York, September 1965. Photograph: Fred W. McDarrah. © Estate of Fred W. McDarrah.

LA MONTE YOUNG

Born in Idaho in 1935, La Monte Young owed his first musical experience to the droning of an electric transformer, located behind his grandfather's gas station. A passionate jazz musician, Young apprenticed in Los Angeles before relocating to Darmstadt, Germany, in 1959, where he attended a composition seminar under Karlheinz Stockhausen, who introduced Young to serialism, aleatoric performance, and musical happenings. The following year, Young moved to New York, where the ardor with which he defended the minimalist cause made him a pillar of underground culture and one of the initiators of the Fluxus art movement. Young's light and sound installation "The Four Dreams of China" (1962) was first presented in a setting reminiscent of a Buddhist temple, wherein a group of musicians called Theatre of Eternal Music (or Dream Syndicate) performed the same droning note for hours. Among the musicians in the group were Angus MacLise and John Cale, future members of the Velvet Underground. The arrangement of the first two Velvet albums illustrates the lasting influence that La Monte Young had on John Cale.

La Monte Young and Marian Zazeela on stage, 1965. Photograph: Steve Schapiro. © Steve Schapiro.

Peter Moore photo of Tony Conrad in Action Against Cultural Imperialism, 1964. © 2018 Barbara Moore/Licensed by VAGA at Artists Rights Society (ARS), NY. Courtesy Paula Cooper Gallery, New York.

I STARTED LIKING ROCK 'N' ROLL

Tony Conrad

(1940–2016)

Tony Conrad, a pioneer of minimalist composition, joined La Monte Young's Dream Syndicate in 1963, alongside Angus MacLise and John Cale.
As told to Christian Fevret in New York, November 2015.

I met La Monte Young in 1959, or was it in 1957? No, 1959. It was summer in California. We became friends, and I often saw him on the way to college. I learned a lot from La Monte, especially gagaku, and other traditional practices. We listened to many indigenous recordings from India and elsewhere. Thanks to the drugs too, he always had interesting drugs to test: mescaline … no, maybe not mescaline, but hashish, opium … different drugs. Many people stayed [at his home] for a while, taking drugs and listening to music.

I was very excited to discover all this, to meet the people who visited him, including Billy Name (Billy Linich), Bob Olivo (Ondine), and all the people who would later participate in the Factory. Then I went to Boston, where I read a lot about music, ancient music using the violin in different ways and with different chords, and I also read about contemporary music by John Cage and David Tudor, who influenced me a lot. I had long discussions with my friend Henry Flynt, conversations that really nurtured me.

Of course, when I moved to New York I reunited with La Monte, who had started doing improvised concerts with other musicians, including Marian Zazeela, Angus MacLise, and Billy Name. The emergence of drone music overtook me, as did the idea of creating it without a composer. We were experiencing the end of formal music and its structure, as everything dissolved and fell to the wayside. Cage used to say that the problem with music was not in learning how to produce it, but in understanding how to listen to it.

Listening intently in order to understand, this kind of project interested me, so I practiced and discovered that I liked it a lot. I even started liking rock 'n' roll, which I did not like at all until then. In short,

John Cale joined the group because he had studied avant-garde composition and he wanted to work in New York with experts in the field. We were not specialists, but we made the most exciting, original, and significant music of the moment. We also introduced a new idea, one that eschewed the role of composer, and emphasized a new approach to listening that focused on the performer's manipulation of sound rather than a kind of idealistic identification of a tone, melody, or any other criteria.

John moved into my place when my roommate left, and found that I was listening mostly to rock 'n' roll, instead of the cream of the crop of avant-garde music. Together, we explored this new way of listening. We procured and listened to lots of singles. It was in 1963, at the time when rock 'n' roll was at its lowest level: the airwaves played things like "The Gypsy Cried", do you know this song? [*He sings.*] Blues for teens, romantic clichés, atrociously stupid, with really crazy lyrics, like "Ahab the Arab", completely absurd stuff.

For a variety of reasons, Lou Christie interested me. Specifically, because he did "The Gypsy Cried". I was going to rock 'n' roll concerts in Brooklyn, taking drugs and attending shows where dozens of artists—The Shirelles, The Ronettes, Lou Christie, etc.—all came to sing their little pop songs, then they would play a movie, an Elvis Presley movie for example, and then the concert would start again. It fascinated me, this huge concert hall in Brooklyn. I stayed there for 10 hours and I went to see the same show two or three times in a row.

The Beatles arrived and with them all this frenzy about haircuts. (By the way, I see that you yourself have a Beatles haircut!) The hair did not come down under the ears, that's how ridiculous it was. But John, me and the others did not care about our haircuts. We let ours grow over our ears, etc. We did not have a specific haircut. One day, our neighbor said to us, "I know guys in Brooklyn looking for musicians to work on a record." We decided to meet them. We met at a party on the East Side, and these famous guys arrive, dressed in polyester trousers, with gelled hair and little mustaches. Skeptical, we still went to see them, but they had already recorded the album in question. They had set up a record label, Pickwick Records, which issued re-releases, but also signed local bands, which they would promote on their records next to big names. For example, Gene Vincent (in large print on the album cover), and with him (in smaller print), The Doodles. Gene Vincent would have one track on the album, and the local guys, 10. We decided to give it a try.

[The Pickwick guys] pulled up in a station wagon with this guy who was going to do vocals. We piled into the back with our friend the sculptor, Walter De Maria. They gave us guitars all tuned on one note! "Wow! That's exactly what we do! What is this craziness?" And the singer tells us, "Hey, man, all you have to do is [*he sings: dong dong dong*]". That's what we did. During our rehearsals, it became clear that Lou Reed was a pure rock 'n' roll animal. You gave him a microphone, and rock came out immediately. At the time, I left the scene. I left the apartment, and John stayed, so Lou settled there, and together they decided to set up a band, The Falling Spikes. But then they found this infamous book and finally chose "The Velvet Underground" as a band name.

I had come across the book some time before and I thought it was cool. I thought that this account of S&M was a really lame attempt to lure consumers into second-class pornography. The book was hanging out in the gutter, all dirty, which seemed fitting to me: it was a disgusting book. I left it in the apartment, and when I came to get my things, they had already spotted it and stolen the title.

Everything that happened after that point had nothing to do with me. They met Andy, who I also knew, and the crew with Ondine and all those other people. To be honest, this nostalgia for the 60s disgusts me. The Velvet Underground, blah blah blah. Sometimes I tell myself that I would have been better off not to have been involved in it at all. In fact, if this period was important to me, it was from a situationist perspective. At La Monte Young's, that was where the most cutting-edge music of the time was created. Since then, we have never known such growth and it could be considered the most sophisticated music era of all time.

In this environment, we spent hours doing nothing: smoking weed, meditating, and analyzing every conceivable concept. Then, at dusk, I would go home to the Lower East Side, past The Tombs prison. Crossing the city, I would pass from "high" culture to "low" culture. In my neighborhood, one found the dregs of society: the homeless, hippies (or, rather, proto-hippies because hippies did not yet exist), beat poets, and all kinds of imbeciles wearing sandals, street musicians, shady characters, struggling directors who could only afford to make half a film, and so on. If I lived there at that time, it was because it cost nothing. I navigated from one culture to another as I traveled through New York. The Velvet Underground was born when these "high" and "low" cultures were about to intersect. They sort of epitomized this moment.

Tony Conrad, La Monte Young, Marian Zazeela, and John Cale performing as the Theatre of Eternal Music, New York, December 1965.
Photograph: Fred W. McDarrah. © Estate of Fred W. McDarrah.

CHORDS AND WORDS

Lou Reed
(1942–2013)

As told to Christian Fevret
for *Les Inrockuptibles*, 1990.

"Take the sensibility of Raymond Chandler or Hubert Selby or Delmore Schwartz or Poe and put it to rock music."
— Lou Reed

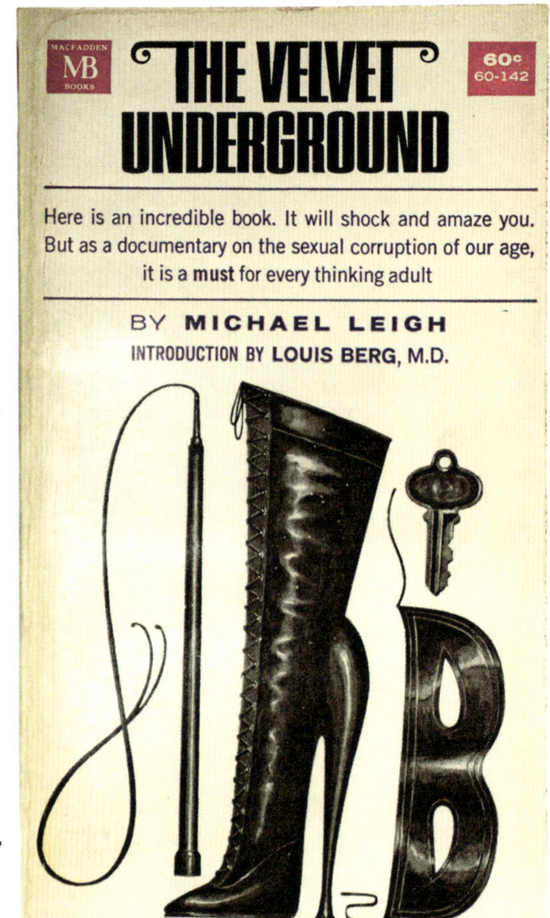

First edition paperback of *The Velvet Underground* by Michael Leigh, Macfadden Books, 1963.

I was a big fan of Ornette Coleman, Cecil Taylor, Don Cherry, Archie Shepp. I also liked rambling, free jazz and heavy funk, James Brown and rockabilly: Warren Smith, Bo Diddley.

I listened to a lot of the classics, but that didn't do much for me. I especially loved everything else since the day that I had, for the first time, heard something other than the classics. I have always wanted for my music to remain relatively simple, so that when people listen to the radio, they can say: "I can do that." And it's true, they can. When I was doing a guitar solo, I wanted it to sound like a saxophone, which is why I used distortion.

Sterling and I were big fans of Black music but we didn't want to imitate other music. We took some ideas from it, but then we played it our own way. I'm not Black, so I don't do soul. I'm not a hillbilly or a redneck, so I don't do Country and Western. I don't hang out on the corners doing Doo-wop. I didn't want to be a singer. All that remained was to say, "Let's see how we sound." I also brought a lot of vocabulary to the music, which I had not seen done at that point. But it seemed very natural to someone like me, who was studying English literature. I saw all those songwriters who only wrote about a very limited field of experience. It seemed obvious and easy to approach the songs as a novelist would, so much so that I didn't understand why nobody else was doing it. "Come on, let's take *Crime and Punishment* and make it a song!"

At university, I was interested in writing. My friend and teacher, Delmore Schwartz, had written some new pieces that impressed me so much that I thought I could play those chords that I loved so much, while satisfying that part of me that wanted to be a writer. It seemed easy. We could combine the two, and I would have everything that I really liked: the electric guitar, these chords and the words, these simple words. But I didn't want to sound like everyone else.

American writer Hubert Selby (*Last Exit to Brooklyn*, *Requiem for a Dream*) (1928-2004), on the Brooklyn Bridge, May 11, 1973

ANGUS MACLISE

(1938–1979)

In the spring of 1965, John Cale and Lou Reed shared an unheated apartment on Ludlow Street, neighboring with percussionist Angus MacLise. Invited to participate in rehearsal sessions with Sterling Morrison, MacLise showed an original sense of rhythm inspired by Eastern cultures; spontaneously and inventively playing the tambourine, bongos, or the tabla. In addition to being a drummer, MacLise was a composer, poet, calligrapher, underground film actor, and a regular at the happenings in the Village. Road trip companion to Piero Heliczer, MacLise followed whatever inspired him in the moment. His refusal to conform to societal norms earned him a reputation for being both marginal and mysterious.

He left the Velvet Underground before contributing to any of their recordings. John Cale described him as a "vagabond/wanderer in pursuit of his soul."

DAILY RECORD | YEAR

DESCRIPTION | RECEIVED | PAID OUT

— SOUNDS —

1. Slow, reflective drum pieces; silences
2. Harmonium
3. Tampura Tape
4. Poetry
5. 4-track
6. Loops (esp. of flute, gong, vox)
7. Sound-box
8. Synthesiser
9. Mix of waters: Ocean, Waterfall, Spring, Rain, etc.
10. Mix of Voices

Angus MacLise's handwritten note for one of his happenings.
Columbia University Rare Book & Manuscript Butler Library Collection.

Angus MacLise in front of the Bash Bish Falls, Massachusetts, 1969. Photograph: Don Snyder. Gerard Malanga Collection.

JONAS MEKAS

Handwritten document by Jonas Mekas. Jonas Mekas Collection.

Jonas and Adolfas Mekas in 1962. Jonas Mekas Collection.

Jonas Mekas had already lived a thousand lives by the time he co-founded the first association of independent and experimental filmmakers, known as the Film-Makers' Cooperative, in 1962. Son of a peasant, his passion for books saved him from a crumbling Lithuania. Mekas escaped from a German labor camp in 1944. With nowhere to go, he found his way to New York in 1949. The city allowed this writer, critic, activist, and filmmaking pioneer to immerse himself in its burgeoning underground art scene. Hosting the Velvet Underground's first show at his Cinematheque in 1966, Mekas also captured Nico's debut with the group as they performed before dumbfounded members of the New York Society for Clinical Psychiatry.

WHY WE AREN'T ANGRY YOUNG MEN

Jonas Mekas

The Village Voice, July 25, 1963

Film still from *Walden* (1969), a film by Jonas Mekas. Jonas Mekas Collection.

In the July 13 issue of *The New Yorker* magazine, we were presented as angry underground filmmakers, which was very nice. But the truth is, we love the world and we hate nobody.
If the Establishment understood this, it would see something of what's really happening:
That our new poets, filmmakers, painters differ from those of, say, England (even in England it may not be true any longer) in at least one quality, they have given up hating. They have learned that it really doesn't matter who rules, a king or a president, both are equally capable of evil and stupidity. Mailer was insistently and patiently silent at Carnegie Hall on all questions that were thrown mercilessly at him about the South and the Negro. There is a longing for a deeper, more essential (and more existential) change of man: the change of man's heart. The films of Ken Jacobs, Jack Smith, Ron Rice, Brakhage, etc., and the writings of the new poets have no anger similar to that of the British "angry young men." Ginsberg had some of it; but even he has given it up. He washed it down in the waters of the Ganges. "Anger is hopeless," was the message Allen brought back from India (November 16, 1962). And then, "Howl" was more sad than angry. There is a great sadness in "Howl" when you read it again.

Underground cinema, yes. But the truth is that the whole change of man's mind and heart is happening underground (in the lower, not very much respected, regions). High above ground there is too much unnecessary noise going on.

Film still from *Williamsburg*, filmed in 1951, edited by Jonas Mekas in 2002. Jonas Mekas Collection.

BARBARA RUBIN

(1945–1980)

Barbara Rubin was not yet 17 when Jonas Mekas invited her to the Film-Makers' Cooperative in 1963. Under the guidance of the filmmaker, the young runaway soon became his muse. She soon revealed an intellectual vigor, insatiable curiosity, and a capacity to bring spirits together, however diverse. A filmmaker in her own right, she created *Christmas on Earth* (1963), a 30-minute sexual poem inspired by Arthur Rimbaud, symbolizing the rebellious and libertarian spirit of her underground artist friends. Among them was a budding Velvet Underground, of which Rubin was a sole supporter—up until she convinced Andy Warhol to see them play in a dive bar called Cafe Bizarre.

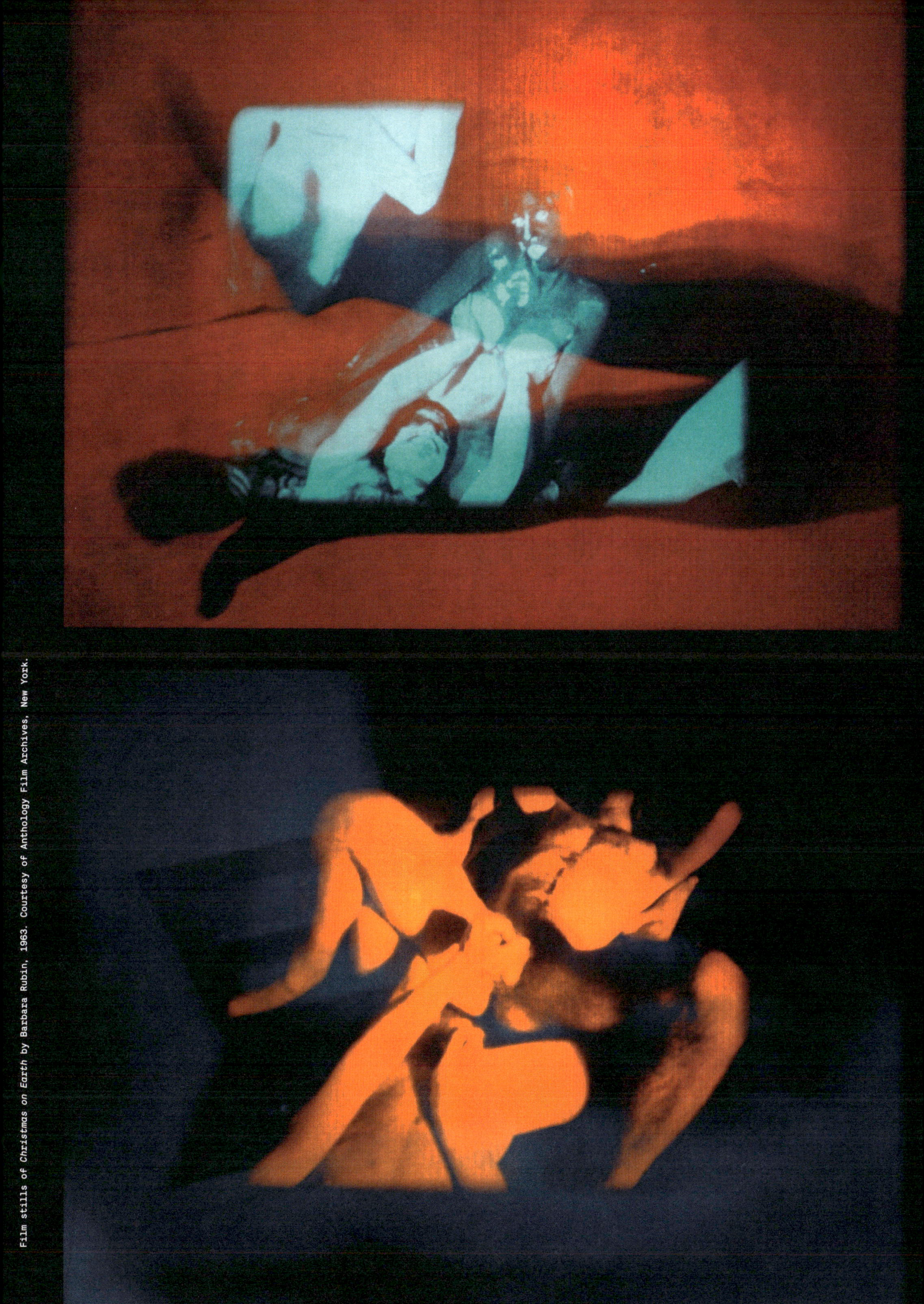

Film stills of *Christmas on Earth* by Barbara Rubin, 1963. Courtesy of Anthology Film Archives, New York.

From the Diaries: on Barbara Rubin

<u>December 18, 1980</u>

Gordon Ball called to confirm Barbara (Bracha, as she called herself during the last ten years) Rubin's death. Bracha Barsacon was her married name. The address & name was given to me in 1976 by Kassandra. Bracha Barsacon, E.S.T., 50 Monte Reigne de la Victoria, Aux Les Bain. This address was given to me in Kassandra's fancy illegible handwriting, so I may not have gotten all the letters straight. But it supposed to be somewhere in the South of France, and she was married, I was told, to some guy, member of some very tough religious cult or sect. Tougher, I was told, "than the upstate hassids" (to one of whom Barbara was married for a couple of years, then she split). I haven't met anybody who had received any real communication from her since 1974. Not even a rumor. But Harry (Smith) came the other day (two weeks ago) to tell me that Rosebud, an old friend of Barbara, had heard that Barbara (Bracha) had died. She died during the birth of her sixth child. The child lived. Supposedly, she was getting heavier with every childbirth, it's a disease for which there is a medical name -- and by the time she was giving birth to her sixth, she was something like 300 pounds. Which did her in.

So we talked with Harry a little about it, and we were both wondering, calmly, how unemotionally we were taking this news. Barbara had left us all so long ago, and had cut off all the ties with us so totally, with all her friends, that she was like dead to us, in a way, for years already, so that now it was like an old news to hear that she was really dead.

Yes, Gordon confirmed it. He had heard it from two or three other people who had come from Europe. They related it to him in about the same words as Rosebud had already related it to Harry. So that must be it.

Good-bye, Barbara. I owe you a lot.
And so do many other people. I can not imagine the New York film underground scene of the early Sixties without you. You breezed in like a mysterious agent. You urged us, you scolded us, you pushed us, you kept us together, you provoked us, and you argued and you argued and you argued. And you were everywhere. You moved from Jack Smith to Genet to the Beattles to Ginsberg to Bob Dylan to Burroughs to Harry Smith to Lenny Bruce to...

Your energy was inexaustible, your belief and faith in us and what we were doing was absolute.

\- - - - - -

When I met Barbara in the Spring of 1963, she was seventeen. She died seventeen years later, at the age of 34 or 35.

One evening, after a show at the Gramercy Arts Theater -- the screenings run by the Film-Makers' Cooperative -- films such as <u>Twice a Man</u>, <u>Scorpio Rising</u>, <u>Chumlum</u>, <u>Sleep</u>, <u>Flaming Creatures</u>, <u>Blue Moses</u>, <u>Fleming Faloon</u> were premiered there -- William Rubin, the art historian, approached me and asked whether I needed some assistance, at the Coop. He had a niece who loved movies and she was just sent home from -- I don't remember what place it was but it was one of those places where they used to place teenagers when their parents thought they had gone totally "wrong." But she was O.K. now, he said, and they are letting her home with the condition that she'd get a "regular" job to occupy her mind & time. I told him that she should come to the Coop on Monday.

She came. Thin, frail, very young, totally scared, and totally silent. She was still in a stupor. She did everything I asked her to do, but she said practically no word. Maybe she thought she was sent to some extension of the Correction House, I don't know... She only listened, nodded, and, sometimes, smiled weakly. She was very sensitive, and very responsive. But she said no word.

Several weeks passed like that. David Brooks, who was the secretary of the Coop at that time, kept asking me, wondering, why I was employing this simpleton. He thought she was a totally dumb suburb kid (from Cambria Heights, Queens or L.I.). He himself, at eighteen at that time, was a man of the world who knew all the jazz places, who played where and what,and what drugs were going around and who took what, etc. etc. When he smoked pot, he did it hiding, in order not to shock Barbara...

Excerpts "From the Diaries: On Barbara Rubin", Jonas Mekas. Sent in the form of letters to his friends after the death of Barbara Rubin. Jonas Mekas Collection.

This, as I said, went for weeks. The Cooperative in those days was a meeting ground for a lot of different people. You could bump into Warhol (if you knew how he looked, which I didn't until somebody told me -- it was Naomi Levine --"You must be joking -- he has been sitting in your place for months, watching movies.") Ginsberg, Jack Smith, Jerry Joffen, Ron Rice, Ken Jacobs, Brakhage, Naomi Levine, Taylor Mead,Bhob Kaufman, Robert Frank, Bill Burroughs -- and Andrew Sarris, Peter Bogdanovich, Manny Farber, and Parker Tyler, and the teenager P.Adams Sitney -- this also being the editorial office of Film Culture magazine. And on some evenings you could even hear Salvador Dali clanking with his cane, up to the third floor of 414 Park Avenue South. It was my apartment, but Coop overran it, and I was squashed into the very back corner, next to the entrance into the bathroom, where I had a sleeping bunk under my editing table.

I don't know how it came about, but David Brooks or someone else got involved in a hot discussion on the subject ofthe younger generation, and David, who, as I said, was eighteen ,said something that Barbara didn't like. I don't remember what he said, but it was enough to break Barbara's silence. She spoke up. No, she didn't speak up: she came out like a spitfire. Like a painful, stammering torrent of words. When she spoke, she always had these strange, painful hesitations, as if there were so many words in her mind that she didn't know which ones to choose. So she called David and everybody else "full of shit" and proceeded to inform us all on the subjects of teenagers, drugs, parents, etc., and made us all sit straight in our corners and listen to her because she knew what she was talking about, she knew it first hand. And from there on, it was Barbara who spoke and we were silent. Or we argued. Ginsberg, Burroughs, Vosnesenski, Dylan, she argued with them all. Dylan -- she turned him back to life, after the motorcycle accident; for Harry she was acting as a matchmaker; Allen -- I think she wanted him to marry her. She was always busy, always making peace between the various factions of the underground. We were all bad children to her, not really doing our duties fully, not serving humanity enough, or not serving our art enough, or God, or ourselves.

And, of course, there was her own film-making, her own very special, swinging, shaking, swishing, flashing Bolex style, with innumerable superimpositions -- no matter from which end, upside down, or right or left. All those unrealized, huge projects, hundred page scripts staring practically everybody, from Lenny Bruce to Brando. And there was -- IS -- Christmas on Earth, which some of us thought was a masterpiece -- at least Ledoux and P.Adams and myself thought so -- but which she forbid to show in her lifetime. And her film with Ginsberg -- Allen for Allen -- unfinished. And the film with Vosnesenski.

And then, one day, she left town and moved to Allen's farm.
Then came Hassidism.
And she never came back. She left us all.

Ah, Barbara, you left us, like Rimbaud. You disappeared in the sands of some spiritual Africa, never to come back. Ah, we'd give a lot to know what was going in your head, during these last ten years, how your mind turned, what you felt.
Some day some explorer will bring us some shreds of information.
Now, however, I am staring at a white sheet of paper in front of me and I can't fathom any of it.

Jonas

NEWSSTAND

In the 1960s, the American press was at its peak: newspapers and magazines punctuated the political, intellectual, and artistic life of the country. A reflection of a booming consumer society, the majority of these publications were steeped in the ideology of a self-made America. In the margins, however, a multitude of smaller innovative publications emerged as new printing processes allowed for self-publishing. These publications were able to break free from conventions, upset the status quo, and give voice to free speech: the free press.

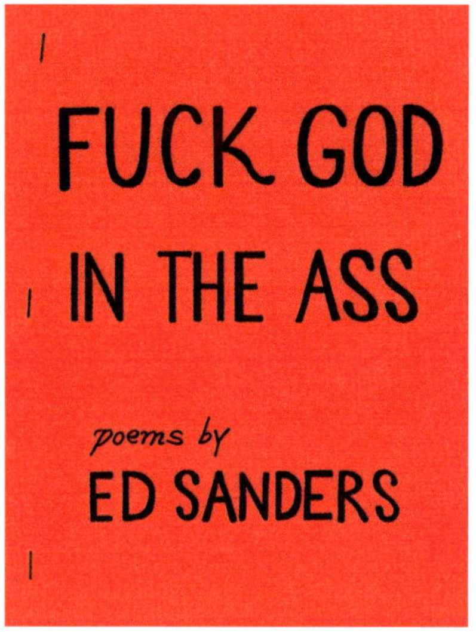

Above left: *Fuck God in the Ass* (1967), a book of poetry by Ed Sanders.

Above right: *Beat*, vol. 1, n°47, February 1966.

Below: "Cyn it Girl", *International Times*, vol. 1, n°16, June 1967.

Opposite page: *Love Street* magazine, The Haight Ashbury, San Francisco, 1968.

Pages 90-91: "Disneyland Memorial Orgy" by Wally Wood, in *Love Street*, The Haight Ashbury, San Francisco, 1968. Allan Rothschild Collection.

LOVE
STREET
25c
"LET
IT ALL
HANG
OUT"

PIERO HELICZER

(1937–1993)

Can't you see I am making a movie. Flyer by Piero Heliczer. Marisabina Russo Collection.

Piero Heliczer Screen Test from Gerard Malanga's book, *Screen Tests/A Diary*. © Gerard Malanga.

Poet, editor, filmmaker, celestial tramp, this tightrope artist, like many of his comrades from the underground, is impossible to classify. Scarred by the execution of his father, a Polish Jew, by the Gestapo, Heliczer also suffered from schizophrenia, which prevented him from realizing his full potential. Despite his incessant travels throughout Europe, Heliczer became the first to direct the Velvet Underground in his experimental film, *Venus in Furs*, in November 1965.

VENUS IN FURS

Piero Heliczer on the set of his film *Venus in Furs*, New York, November 1965.
Lou Reed on the left with Sterling Morrison and John Cale. Photograph: Adam Ritchie. © Adam Ritchie Photography.

November 1965. The eccentric Piero Heliczer wanted to include a band in his film *Venus in Furs*. He turned to his friend Angus MacLise who, at that time, was still collaborating with the Velvet Underground. As a result, Reed, Cale, and Morrison appeared nude, with paint-covered torsos, along with Moe Tucker as a masked bride, and Barbara Rubin as a nonchalant nun. The film did not survive Heliczer's nomadic lifestyle, however. Some images were captured by the young British photographer Adam Ritchie, who was working in New York with a crew from CBS and covering a story on the essence of underground cinema, intended for the general public. Barely formed, the Velvet Underground was shown on national television for the first and last time. During the five years of their existence, the group only allowed rare appearances on small local television stations of which there remains no trace.

Moe Tucker on set of *Venus in Furs*, November 1965. Photograph: Adam Ritchie. © Adam Ritchie Photography.

Above: CBS News filming the Velvet Underground on the set of *Venus in Furs*, November 1965. Photograph: Adam Ritchie. © Adam Ritchie Photography.
Below: Piero Heliczer on the saxophone on set of his film, November 1965. Photograph: Adam Ritchie. © Adam Ritchie Photography.

BIRTH OF THE VELVET UNDERGROUND

At the end of 1964, John Cale was hired to promote one of Lou Reed's songs for Pickwick Records. Cale and Reed took several months to rehearse together in order to develop the Velvet's sound. Sterling Morrison and Angus MacLise joined them for endless rehearsal sessions on the Lower East Side, and the group's sound slowly emerged. The original Velvet sound was found, characterized by a unique blend of acuity and insolence that the group went on to perfect at the Factory before unveiling it in their live performances and cementing it in their two first albums.

Angus MacLise, Lou Reed, Sterling Morrison, and John Cale on the stoop of 52 Ludlow Street, New York, 1965. Photograph: Donald Greenhaus.

Poster from the Caterpillar Changes festival organized by Barbara Rubin, February-March 1967. Jonas Mekas Collection.

STERLING MORRISON

(1942–1995)

Above left and right: Sterling Morrison as a child. Martha Morrison Collection.

Below left: Sterling Morrison and Jim Tucker (the elder brother of Maureen) as graduates. Martha Morrison Collection.

Opposite: Sterling Morrison circa 1963. Martha Morrison Collection.

In April 1965, Sterling Morrison and Lou Reed crossed paths in a subway station, having met initially three years earlier at Syracuse University. Morrison, an avid guitarist, bassist, and singer, immediately joined the group that Reed had formed with John Cale and Angus MacLise. Although they didn't yet have a name, the Velvet Underground already had songs coupled with Morrison's impeccable rhythmic timing. Morrison developed a technique that complemented the sound of Cale's keyboard and violin. With the addition of Morrison, who also specialized in medieval literature, the Velvet Underground went on to create some of its most soaring and groundbreaking work.

GOING BACK IN TIME TO PIERO HELICZER

Sterling Morrison

April 11, 1979, Austin, Texas.
Excerpt from *Little Caesar*, No. 9.

Poster for the Paris Film-Makers' Cooperative fundraiser, organized by Piero Heliczer, undated. Marisabina Russo Collection.

Whenever I hear the word "underground" mentioned, I am reminded of when the word first acquired a specific meaning for me and for many others in NYC in the early 60s. It referred to underground cinema, and to the people and lifestyle that created and supported this art form. And there were a lot of people involved, showing their work and otherwise performing at the old Film-makers' Cinematheque on Lafayette St., at the Bridge Theater on St. Marks Place, at the new Cinematheque on W. 41st St., and elsewhere. I'll leave it to others who are better informed to chronicle the movement, articulate its goals, and evaluate its achievements. But I was really excited by all that went on, and did as much as I could to take part in it; at the very least it was great fun. And the person who first introduced me to this scene was Piero Heliczer, a bona fide "underground filmmaker", the first one I had ever met.

Through Lou Reed I had met John Cale. John's neighbor, in another unheated flat on Ludlow St., was the redoubtable Angus MacLise, recently returned from eight years spent in Greece and India with his head filled with dervish dancing and exotic percussion. At the time, I was mostly interested in music (of one sort or another). Lou, however, had made a couple of student films at Syracuse University, and John was already a member of La Monte Young's cosmic ensemble that produced drone music with myriad harmonics and used slide-projection visuals. Angus was the most rabidly artistic of us all, with interests in literature, dance, music, film, lights, slides, incense, diaphanes, and religion—all at once. He mused day and night on a stage that might combine them all, and on what the dizzying effects of such a cataclysm might be. Angus, however, was not a filmmaker. But his friend Piero Heliczer, both inspired and shared his visions. And Piero was a filmmaker, an *underground* filmmaker. It wasn't long before I met him, and began learning what the underground film scene was about (and more besides).

On an early Spring day in 1965, John and I were strolling through the East Side slums and ran into Angus on the corner of Essex and Delancey. Angus said, "Let's go over to Piero's," and we agreed (John already knew him). Now that I think about it, dropping in on people was a lot more fun in those days since there was no telling what degree of far-outness you might encounter. There was also an excellent chance that your host would get you high. So it was certainly worth a walk of a few blocks to apt. 5E at 450 Grand Street (for the good that was in it, as the Irish say). Getting to the fifth floor, however, meant climbing 90 stairs; frequent visits would thus be proof of true friendship. But up we went, and entered the realm of Aquarium Productions, the name under which Piero and Angus published their literary journal, and mounted their theatrical productions.

The apartment was a bright place with a long hall ending in one of two living rooms, with two bedrooms opening off it along the way, and there was also a kitchen. Opening off the kitchen was a hallway that passed the bathroom to another bedroom, and another living room with an attached double-doored drawing room that served as yet another bedroom. The place was huge, and the rent was only $50 a month, for the landlord was a marvelous fellow named Arthur Brown who only rented to artists of all sorts (and to a few students). You could be months behind in the rent, and when he came around to see what was happening, he only needed to be reassured

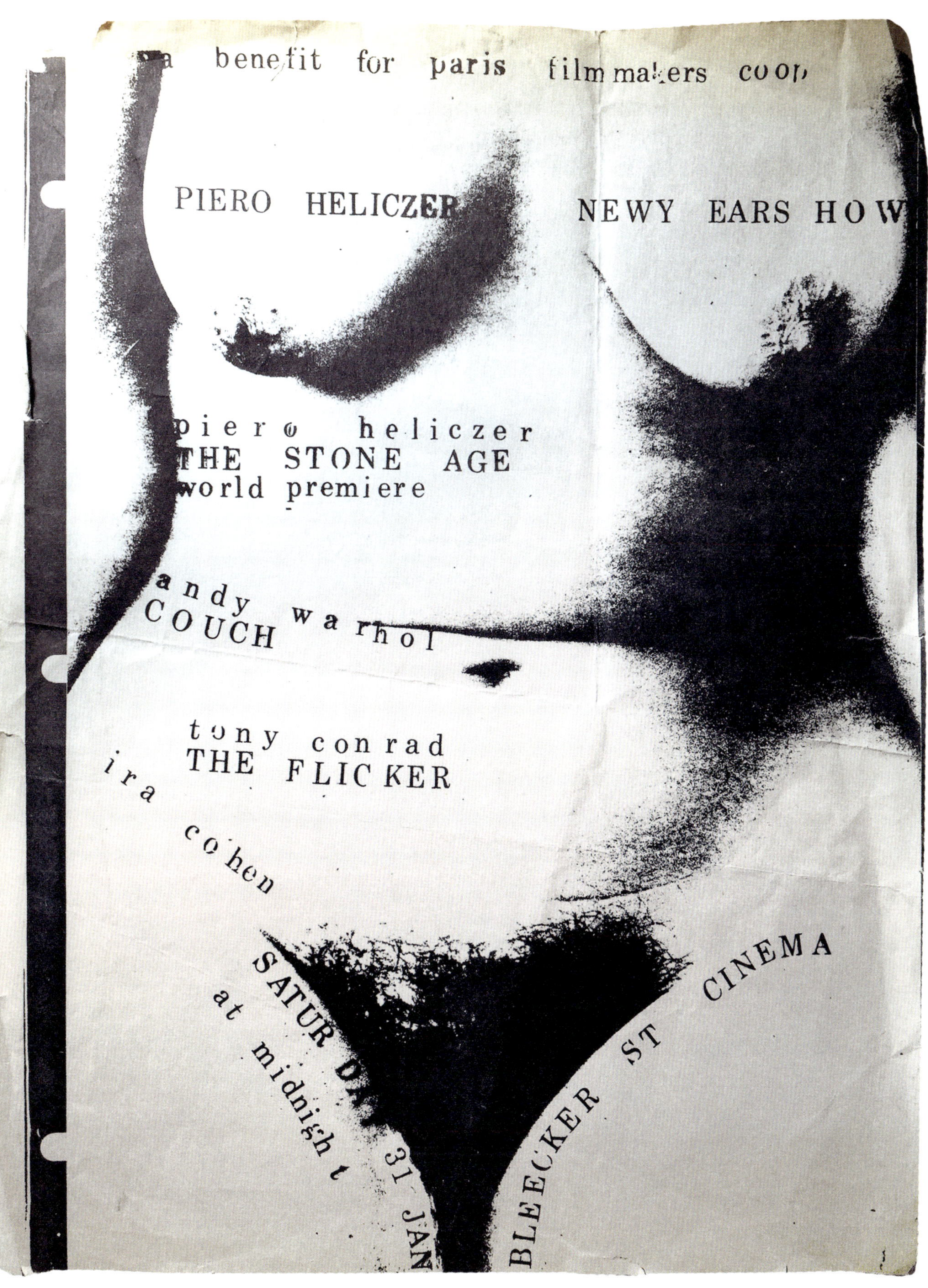
a benefit for paris filmmakers coop
PIERO HELICZER NEWY EARS HOW
piero heliczer
THE STONE AGE
world premiere
andy warhol
COUCH
tony conrad
THE FLICKER
ira cohen
SATURDAY 31 JAN
at midnight
BLEECKER ST CINEMA

that you were coming into some money eventually. He was delighted by any evidence that you could present of your artistic accomplishments—newspaper clippings and posters especially pleased him. He even gave you a card that said you were one of his tenants, and the card got you a discount from a list of merchants who were his friends. On top of that, once a year he took all his tenants to a free dinner at a local health food restaurant. I soon came to covet Piero's apartment and landlord, and eventually acquired both, although a misunderstanding sprang up between Piero and me on that account, and I had to give them back.

The place had some other unusual features, too. The first was that the wall separating the bathroom and the bedroom had been knocked down (by Piero in an attempt, he said, to create a "Hollywood Bedroom"); the debris was heaped up in the hall and blocked access to the living room (and harbored mice as well) until I hauled it up to the roof and got in trouble with the building super, who wanted it removed. I convinced him that the only way I was going to remove it was to throw it over the side to the alley below, where *he* could pick it up. He agreed then that perhaps it was best to leave it where it was. (I later vowed that I would hurl Piero off this same roof). The second feature was that every room, including the bathroom, had at least one telephone. It seems that they were always being installed, then turned off for non-payment of the bill, and hidden away when yet another phone was installed under a different name. When they were shut off no effort was made by the company to retrieve the phones—too many stairs to climb, I guess. But one glorious day my friend and roommate Joe Gallagher (who had knowledge of such things) hooked them all up! You can imagine the envy of all who beheld them, or chanced to hear their simultaneous ringing. We also never had to pay an electric bill because someone had meddled with the meters deep down in the cellar; we were thus tapping our electricity from who knows where (we never bothered to think about it).

Such, then, was the home of Aquarium Productions, and of Piero Heliczer. As for Piero himself, I have always found him to be genial, resolute, optimistic, and dedicated to filmmaking and to pleasure in general. There is a bit of the picaro about him, too. Of course, he had to get by on very little money because the expense of filmmaking was a definite burden. Nevertheless, he got his films made, and managed to travel about France, England, and Italy often enough. He should share the secret of how he did it; perhaps it was because so many people liked him and wanted to help him, or to work with him. I was eager to work with him, and the things we did changed the direction of my life. Why we did these things is too much to get into here.

It seems that Piero and Angus were organizing a "ritual happening" at the time—mixed media stage presentation to appear in the old Cinematheque. Naturally, this was well before such events became all the rage. It was to be a kinetic display of lights, film, dancers, music, and poetry; it was entitled "Launching the Dream Weapon." And needless to say, it got launched tumultuously. In the center of the stage there was a movie screen, and between the screen and the audience a number of veils were spread out in different places. These veils were lit by lights and slide projections, as Piero's films shone through them onto the screen. Dancers swirled around, and poetry and song occasionally rose up while from behind the screen a strange music was being generated by Lou, John, Angus, and me; I think that Piero was back there sometimes, too, playing his saxophone. The whole event took place in an atmosphere of dense smoke from all the incense that was burning. I thought that it was impressive and pretty; Archer Winsten said some nice things about it in the *Post* the next day, so I guess the launch was a definite success.

A while later there was another such celebration called "Rites of the Dream Weapon" with a similar format and equally free structure, and it, too, went over well. I hesitate to list the names of the other people involved in these two spectacles, because I am certain I don't remember them all (especially since I was mostly concerned with the music). The list should include Barbara Rubin, Marian Zazeela, Tony Conrad, Walter De Maria, and John Vaccaro.

For me the path ahead suddenly became clear—I could work on music that was different from ordinary rock 'n' roll since Piero had given Lou, John, Angus, and me a context to perform it in. In the summer of 1965 the four of us were the anonymous musicians who played at some screenings of "underground films," and at other theatrical events, the first of which for Piero's films (I think that Barbara Rubin and Kenneth Anger each showed a film also). Piero taped the music, and later played it at the screenings of his films—especially for "The New Jerusalem".

Something else happened in the fall of 1965. Angus was in Times Square subway station when he took a glance at a book rack. There leaping at him was the title "The Velvet Underground," and he joyfully rushed back to Ludlow St. to report his discovery to us. We had a name at last! And it was adopted by us and deemed appropriate not because of the S&M theme of the book, but because the word "underground" was suggestive of our involvement with the underground film and art scene. So there. Now you know.

From then on, Piero was able to identify his tape as "Velvet Underground's" music. We had some notoriety but no records (or offers to make any). A lot of people in England heard us for

Promo flyer by Piero Heliczer. Marisabina Russo Collection.

the first time when Piero played the tape at his film showings; I know a number of them came up to me afterwards and said so. We were very grateful.

Of course, with the underground scene flourishing in late 1965, the TV types eventually got around to checking it out. This set them up for what must have been one of Piero's greatest capers.

Somehow, CBS News decided that Walter Cronkite should have a feature on an "underground" film being made—you know, a film of a filming. By whatever selection process, Piero was able to be the "underground filmmaker"; since he had already decided to film us playing anyway, we got into the act (and besides, we had "underground" in our name, didn't we? Maybe someone at CBS reads Pirandello). Piero also wanted to film us where we lived, and so that is where the CBS film crew had to report. Where we were living, I should point out, was at no. 5E, 450 Grand Street: 90 stairs, hot-wired electric meter, telephones and all. Only a professional news team would have braved the hardships of this assignment.

The news crew showed up as it was getting dark, and we were already in the process of getting our faces completely painted by Margaret Boyce. They seemed a bit ill at ease, for some reason or other. First, the lighting man had to put stronger fuses in so that they could use their floodlights. We directed him toward the basement. Since Piero had left a lot of costumes in the closets when he moved, we decided to make use of a few of them. Maureen Tucker wore a bridal dress; Bobby Ritchkin had on bishop's regalia (and played bass). The rest of us had on more conventional clothing, but I suppose it looked weird enough to outsiders. Something should be said of Piero's outfit, though, since he looked the most splendid. He wore all black—boots, pants, turtleneck, and jacket—and topped it all off with a round-crowned, wide-brimmed black hat, the kind Italian peasants wear. What an image for the straight folks in videoland! Eventually, the lighting man returned, although he looked somewhat shaken by his experiences. He proceeded to reveal to us the secret of the free electricity (since none of us had ever dared enter the basement of our slum building and look), and mentioned his difficulties in installing the fuses. But by then the party the beautiful book

xviii stills by jack smith with a drawing by marian zazeela new york 1962

4 dollars or 16 nouveaux francs or 24 shillings

“we studied these photographs with keen eye discovering new & more beautiful images hidden in every dissolve & curve of the draperies & silks which ran through these masterpieces like some long lost mysterious fume from byzantium,, ron rice

the first battle of the marne

six poems by piero heliczer new york 1962

2 dollars 8 nouveaux francs or 12 shillings

“i see him through his poems & i see danger,, fielding dawson

loverman

a very free translation of the lemminkainen cantos of the kalevala by anselm hollo new york 1963

1 dollar or 4 nouveaux francs or 6 shillings

make checks payable to piero heliczer

The Beautiful Book promo flyer by Piero Heliczer. Marisabina Russo Collection.

was well in progress, with intoxicants of all sorts going down on all sides, so everybody just laughed. At that point, the crew decided to loosen up and have fun too, and soon everything was ready for the main action, whatever that might turn out to be.

We gathered our face-painted selves in the living room at the end of the hall, turned on the amps, and started to play. The TV guys turned on their lights and tape recorder, and got their camera ready. With that, Piero bounded into the middle of the room clutching *his* camera. He proceeded to whirl and writhe about, zooming and panning by body movement alone, in dazzling contrast to the stationary CBS cameramen gazing into a stationary camera. For Piero the action of the director is part of the action of the film, and he is not one for holding back. The band played on (without the vocals) while Barbara Rubin filmed the TV crew filming Piero filming us. Next, something happened that astonished everyone. Piero was shooting furiously, and then suddenly put down his camera (apparently out of film). Everyone expected some sort of break while he reloaded, but not Piero! Instead, he snatched up his saxophone and started playing with a passion, tooting and gyrating for all he was worth, dressed all in black, black hat pulled low over his forehead. What a show for the folks! There really was something different about underground filmmaker types! On the periphery of all of this and in all other rooms the party was in full swing. Soon, though, the official news gathering ended (with the crew very pleased with what they got), and everyone was amicable as they were leaving. The party lasted much longer.

All that remained was to see ourselves on the tube (and we all wondered whether it would actually be aired). But Walter, bless him, did indeed show it on New Year's Eve, 1965. You know how his last news segment each evening is a "human interest" sort of thing, or something offbeat, at least. Well, on that particular night, we were it, right at the mid-decade juncture. There it was on the screen for all to behold (Lou and I watched it at Danny Fields' place, because we didn't have a TV). Then, after a few minutes, there was a cut back to Walter, who said, "And that's the way it is, December, 31, 1965 … Goodnight." Then they rolled the credits over some more of the footage, as the eerie strains of "Heroin" played in the background. Good night to you, too, Walter, I thought, and thanks. You, too, Piero.

I should say something about that apartment hassle. In the fall of 1965, Piero moved in with his wife, Kate, (and with Margaret) at a different place, so I gave him his security back and took over 450 Grand Street (along with Lou, Joe, and Richard Cianci). There we all lived for over a year, with Piero a frequent visitor and occasional inhabitant; lots of other people were in and out too. But in late 1966 Piero came back with no place to stay and reinstalled himself at Grand Street, which was fine for a while. I wasn't around much anyway, so there was plenty of room. However, then Piero attempted to displace Joe and Richard, who complained to me about it and demanded that I say something.

Me: What's wrong with you guys? Just throw him out if he refuses to shape up.

Them: We can't do that! We really like him. Maybe you can talk to him because you have been his friend longer. No, you have to talk to him. We can't do it.

Like I said, Piero is really likable. Finally, though, I made a very loud phone call to him from the Warhol factory on East 47th St:

Me: Piero, you have to leave Grand Street.

Him: I can't. I have no place else to live.

Me: OK, live there. But what's this about taking the place over and kicking out Joe and Richard?

Him: I need the whole place for my work, and besides, it's mine anyway.

There then followed a long and heated discussion of whose place it really was, with a review of the transaction from the previous year. All this was to no avail. He was resolute. And so I began again on a new tack.

Me: Piero, do you believe that I am mad enough to come down there and throw you off the roof if you don't give up this business?

Him: Yes.

Me: Will you stop, then?

Him: No.

Me: Piero, I swear to Christ I'm coming down there and throwing you off the roof. Don't you believe me?

Him: Yes, I do.

Me: Well, what do you say?

Him: I have to have this place. So if you really want to throw me off the roof, I guess you'll just do it. I'm not able to stop you.

So I had to give up eventually, too; Richard and Joe moved to a different apartment in the same building. Then the city finally took the building over and gave everyone relocation money (which I suspect was Piero's motive in wanting the old place back). In the end, though, everyone was happy, and all my friendships have endured.

Nevertheless, the word was out that I hated Piero and was planning to kill him. I must confess to spreading those rumors myself, since I was trying to get his oldest and best friends to reason with him where I had failed, to convince him that I was serious about throwing him off the roof. They believed me, it seems, but Piero didn't. And he was right, of course.

How could I find fault with a picaro?

Pages 108-109: MacDougal Street at night, Greenwich Village, New York, May 1966. Cafe Wha? is in the center. Photograph: Fred W. McDarrah.

CAFFE

CIGARS SHERAMA
HAMMER
CANDY
7up

MOE TUCKER

In December 1965, on the eve of the Velvet's first concert, percussionist Angus MacLise refused to play at a specified hour. Thinking of a replacement, Sterling Morrison remembered that the sister of his childhood friend Jim Tucker played the drums and owned a car—a perfect combination. Maureen "Moe" Tucker, born in New York in 1944, possessed a rhythmic Bo Diddley beat, a boyish face, and a phlegmatic candor that rendered her impervious to the depravity of the Factory and the volatility of her new bandmates. A stabilizing force in the band and a motor for the music, Moe was also a singer with an airy, child-like voice that brought a lightness and joy to "After Hours" and "I'm Sticking With You". In the eyes of some purists, the absence of Moe prevented *Loaded* from being a true Velvet Underground album.

Spotlighting the Single Girl

She Gave Up Computers To Play Drums in Band

MAUREEN TUCKER

By LAURA WHITE

Maureen Tucker gave up a $100 a week job as an IBM key-punch operator so that she could play drums in a rock band for only $5 a night.

"A regular 9-to-5 job was too confining. I felt mentally as well as physically captured by machines," said 23-year-old Maureen, a petite redhead.

Maureen was a liberal arts student at Ithaca College in New York earning her tuition by working parttime and summers punching out computer cards. But music was her main interest. In high school she played the clarinet. She taught herself to play the guitar. And she even bought a small drum to accompany her favorite records.

Maureen's music career began by accident when she loaned a couple of amplifiers to a childhood friend, Sterling Morrison, a base guitarist with a brain-rock group known as The Velvet Underground. When the group needed a percussionist, Sterling asked Maureen to sit in.

"I loved it. At first, I tried to keep both jobs, but pretty soon it became impossible. One had to go, and it was the computer cards," she said.

The Velvet Underground was discovered by pop-artist Andy Warhol, who incorporated them into his mixed-media show, the first of its kind, "The Exploding Plastic Inevitable" which appeared at the Institute of Contemporary Art and toured the United States.

Warhol designed the group's first album jacket . . . a big yellow banana. The tour and the album started the Velvet Underground on the road to success.

Maureen is the only girl in the group and The only girl drummer with a rock-band.

"Except for girls in the all-girl bands," she said.

According to Maureen, being the only girl has plenty of advantages. The fellows in the group make sure nobody bothers her, and she always shows up at parties with three escorts.

But there are disadvantages, too.

"It gets a little lonely sometimes when we've traveling around the country. The guys don't really like to shop or go sightseeing, and I don't like to go around strange cities alone, so I end up reading," she said.

Boston Herald Traveler, 1967. Martha and Sterling Morrison scrapbook.

Moe Tucker at the Factory, photograph: Nat Finkelstein.

vibrations

year

VIBRATIONS, The Rock and Blues Magazine of the Zeitgeist, is published monthly by Insight Publications, 951 Massachusetts Ave., Cambridge, Mass.

THE JONATHANRICHMAN SUPPLEMENT

LATE WINTER 1969

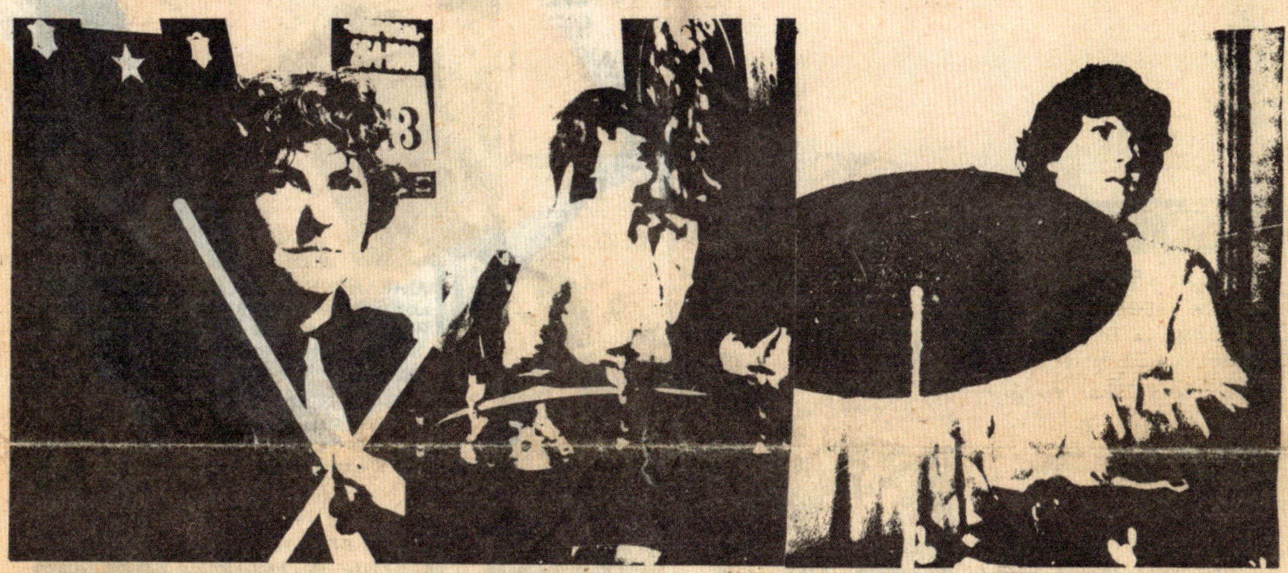

the QUEEN OF THE ROCK N'ROLL DRUMMERS

MAUREEN

We here at vibrations
have been th ng outloud
to oursel What
on arou ?"
I s ll al ys
her mbri e become
dua and $50 on
those fu ots because
they wr imitate New York."
B na, a new guy with us,
say p, everyone around here
has a New York complex."

second anniversary

J ATHAN RICHMAN

SUPPLEMENT

Vibrations, a fanzine with a special issue dedicated to the Velvet Underground, written by Jonathan Richman. Winter 1969. Alfredo Garcia Collection.

THE VELVET UNDERGROUND DEBUTED AT MY HIGH SCHOOL

Tony Jannelli

Tony Jannelli is the producer of the animated film *The Velvet Underground Played at My High School* (2016).

Tony Jannelli Collection.

I heard the Velvet Underground for the first time at a concert at my high school, in Summit, New Jersey, a small town situated 20 miles from the Big Apple, and yet so far away in terms of mentality. It was 1965. As a 10th grader sitting in the third row, this was one of the first concerts I had ever been to. It was also the first time I witnessed booing, shock, horror, and bewilderment in a public setting. On stage for merely 20 minutes, the Velvets performed three songs: "There She Goes", which appeared to be an inoffensive love song, "Venus in Furs", which referred to a sex slave, and finally "Heroin".

For suburban teenagers, completely foreign to the idea of the avant-garde and unable to decipher what we were seeing, it was a total shock. Almost everyone hated the concert and found the band to be amateurs, out of tune and strange. Half the audience walked out! A small, yet noisy minority of the audience loved it! For my part, I was disconcerted as it was so different from everything that I had ever heard. I naively thought that we were going to watch a professional and refined concert from New York … but it was far from that! It was not neat; it was not well produced.

Later, in university, I rediscovered my first Velvet album. Without trying to remember this particular concert, I started listening to their lyrics, to appreciate the distress in their music, and the way that they identify with the themes in their songs. Suddenly, it all spoke to me. Furthermore, I realized what their songs embodied; they evoked the real people that existed in their worlds, and they spoke about them with a lot of love and consideration.

Photo by John E. Lynch

the myddle class

IN CONCERT

Summit High School Auditorium
125 Kent Place Blvd. Summit, N. J.

8 p.m. December 11, 1965 Admission: $2.50

Tickets may be purchased in advance at:

Scotti's Record Shop
346 Springfield Ave.
Summit

Adams Haberdashers
1271 Springfield Ave.
New Providence

Henriksen's Pharmacy
415 Springfield Ave.
Berkeley Heights

Tickets may also be purchased in advance by sending a check or money order to
the myddle class, Box 221, Berkeley Heights, N. J.

Also appearing on the program:

The Forty Fingers

The Velvet Underground

Flyer for the first concert as the Velvet Underground.
The group opened for The Myddle Class in Summit, New Jersey,
December 1965. Allan Rothschild Collection.

AT CAFE BIZARRE

In December 1965, a few days after playing for the first time with Moe Tucker on drums, Velvet's manager, Al Aronowitz, secured them a residency as a house band in a tourist trap bar in Greenwich Village. They played there every night, to the bewilderment or general indifference of the patrons, and they took advantage of this opportunity to test new songs and sounds. They did this until Warhol and his crew, led by Barbara Rubin and Gerard Malanga, came to see them and immediately offered artistic asylum at the Factory.

Pages 114-117: The Velvet Underground at Cafe Bizarre, December 1965. Photography: Adam Ritchie. © Adam Ritchie Photography.

Jonas Mekas and Barbara Rubin at Cafe Bizarre for a Velvet Underground concert.
Photograph: Adam Ritchie. © Adam Ritchie Photography.

HOW I WAS THE FIRST TO PHOTOGRAPH THE VELVET UNDERGROUND

Adam Ritchie

I was born in London in 1949. At 29 years of age, with my green card in hand, I flew to New York and found work. I was an international economy researcher. After 18 months, I bought a camera and I started taking pictures. My boss convinced me to become a photographer and offered me three months salary to launch my new career. I started sharing a friend's darkroom. I quickly found work at *Mademoiselle*, *Glamour*, *Look*, *Esquire*, and the *Sunday Times*. At night, I managed the team at Bleecker Street Cinema that screened independent films. I met filmmakers and a lot of people from the underground. Among them was Barbara Rubin.

One day in 1965, she called me and said "I'm playing a nun in a film by Piero Heliczer called *Venus in Furs*. There's this incredible unknown band that plays in it. You have to hear them. Come with your camera!" I had met Piero in London. Twenty minutes later, I was walking up the steps to the building where they were filming. It was there that I heard the Velvet Underground play *Heroin* for the first time. In a dilapidated apartment, I found the members of the band, their bodies covered in paint, with Barbara dressed as a nun, and Margaret Boyce Cam playing a nurse. Piero was walking amongst them, filming everything with an 8mm camera. From time to time, he traded that for his alto saxophone which he played with the group. The cherry on top was the cameraman from CBS News who was filming Piero while he filmed.

Lou was inaccessible (I was told he was on heroin). Sterling Morrison and Moe Tucker remained quiet, but it was easy to talk with John Cale. He was from Wales and I was English, so we felt like two strangers amongst them. Angus MacLise played the drums before Maureen. I didn't know who that was until someone recognized him on my photos.

The music was incredible. I knew that the group was going to play at Cafe Bizarre two weeks later. I went along with the underground filmmakers Jonas Mekas and Barbara Rubin.

I then photographed them at Delmonico's Hotel during the annual psychiatrist's convention in New York. They probably had to understand what this new underground cultural revolution that their patients (children of the rich) where telling them about. Andy came with the Velvet Underground and Nico, along with a group from the Factory. Barbara Rubin disrupted the evening, aggressively filming the psychiatrists and asking them about their sex lives.

The last photographs I took of the Velvets were at the Open Stage, above Dom's in April 1966. They called the performance Andy Warhol's Exploding Plastic Inevitable. The Velvets played while Mary Woronov and Gerard Malanga danced with their whip and black leather pants. A Velvet film was playing on the giant screen behind the musicians.

To be honest, I didn't have much of a desire to approach Andy Warhol. He was too famous, too "plastic." His Factory and the somewhat deranged individuals who frequented it didn't interest me. But the Velvet Underground was a serious and hardworking group. Later on, I photographed Pink Floyd at the UFO Club when I returned to London in the summer of 1966. They were middle-class but were posing as an underground group.

In the 1960s, we couldn't take instant photographs with film. We had to play with exposure times because automatic didn't exist. To photograph Pink Floyd at the UFO Club in London, I opened the shutter speed by a second because the light from the projectors wasn't strong enough. With a flash, all the beauty of the lights would have been lost.

I concentrated on the image and I'm aware that I wasn't attentive to the music. There was always more light when I was photographing the Velvet Underground and their music pleased me. Today, these photos represent a historic interest and that makes me happy. It's too bad that the best ones were destroyed after my lab went bankrupt.

At Cafe Bizarre, 1965. Photograph: Adam Ritchie. © Adam Ritchie Photography.

FALL 35c

VIP THE PLAYBOY CLUB MAGAZINE

A recent fashion show–happening at the Windy City warren, sponsored by Mod shop Man At Ease, featured the nouvelle vague entertainment troupe, "The Velvet Underground," touting the most modern in way-out wearables.

CHICAGO: **Sam Lesner** of the *Chicago Daily News* reports: Man at Ease, the Wells Street Mod emporium, highlighted London Week at the Chicago Playboy Club with a lunchtime fashion show featuring rock-'n'-roll music and dancing by the cast of the *Exploding Plastic Inevitable*—a pop-art happening-show starring **Gerard Malanga** and **Ingrid Superstar.** In the fascinated audience was **Eric Nesterenko,** left wing for the Chicago Blackhawks . . . A VIP luncheon was held recently at the Windy City hutch with **Johnny** (Tarzan) **Weissmuller** as guest of honor. Johnny was in Chicago promoting the British comedy *Morgan!,* a record box-

Press clipping from *VIP: The Playboy Club Magazine*, Summer 1966. From Martha and Sterling Morrison's scrapbook.

FACTORY YEARS

Gerard Malanga, Nico, Lou Reed, Edie Sedgwick: movie stills from *Walden*, by Jonas Mekas.

the village VOICE, December 14, 1967 Page Forty-nine

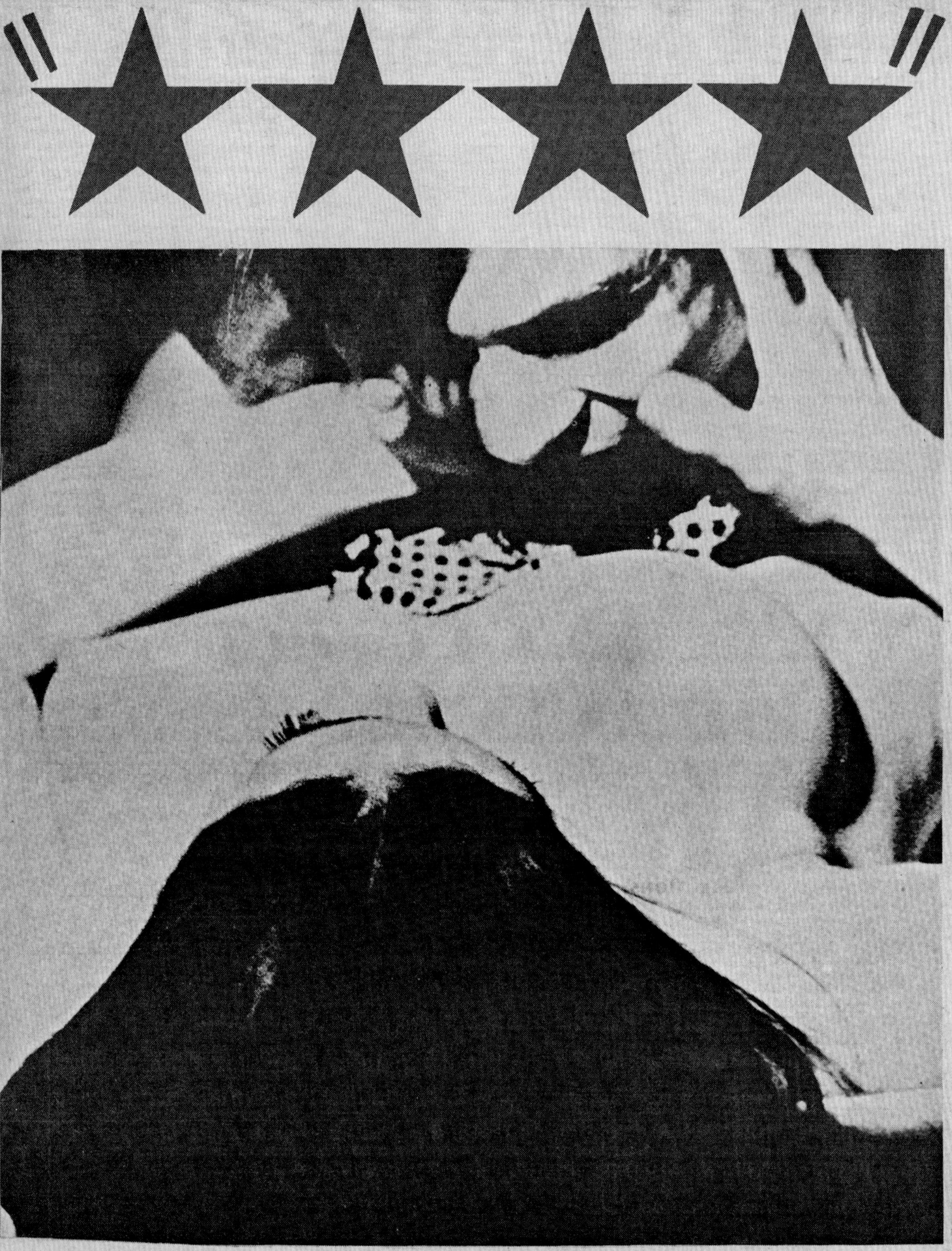

FRIDAY, DECEMBER 15 8:30 P.M. ONE SHOWING AT THE **NEW CINEMA Playhouse**

120 WEST 42ND (Inside The Wurlitzer Bldg.) 564-3818 THE 25-HOUR COLOR FILM FROM ANDY WARHOL FILMS INC.

SATURDAY, DECEMBER 16 9:30 P.M. THE 2-HOUR OVERTURE BEGINS A CONTINUOUS RUN

"★★★★" STARS NICO, INTERNATIONAL VELVET, IVY NICHOLSON, VIVA, ULTRA VIOLET,

EDIE SEDGEWICK, INGRID SUPERSTAR, BRIGIT POLK, KATRINA, ALAN MIDGETTE, ONDINE.

MUSIC BY THE VELVET UNDERGROUND AND INTRODUCING TIGER MORSE

Advertisement for a screening of Andy Warhol's "****" (four stars), a 25 hour movie, in *The Village Voice*, December 1967. Alfredo Garcia Collection.

The Velvet Underground forged a sound, universe, and identity that was a radically different form of rock'n'roll. It was innovative poetry that tackled sex and drugs, abuse and transgressions, and existential questions. The music was at once discordant and fluid, dark and luminous, and did not respect any codes. Their paradoxes and extravagances forced the listener to become involved and/or take a side. Fascinated, the Pop Art Prince, Andy Warhol, welcomed the group into the Factory. This venue—a talent incubator and particle accelerator—propelled the Velvet Underground into the spotlight.

ANDY WARHOL

(1928–1987)

Film still from *Andy Warhol: portrait of the Artist as a Young Man* (1964-1965) by Gerard Malanga. Gerard Malanga Collection.

Film still by Jonas Mekas. Jonas Mekas Collection.

At the end of 1965, Andy Warhol was far from the character and artist he would become over the next two decades. At 37, he had caused a sensation with his silkscreen prints of flowers and celebrities, Brillo boxes, and Death and Disaster series, and had become known for his system of seriality. However, he foresaw the future and sought to blur the distinction between the artist and works of art. He declared that he wanted to give up visual arts to explore new mediums: film and music were at the forefront. The Factory, Warhol's loft/studio, was the ideal venue for creation, where films and rehearsals were intertwined with parties and improvised exhibitions that attracted New York's artists and celebrities. Through what seemed to be a perpetual fair, an army of talent began to grow into what Warhol intended as a component of his “total art”.

POPISM

Andy Warhol

In his memoirs, Warhol described his personal vision of the Pop phenomenon in the 1960s in New York. He dedicates one chapter to his encounter with the band and how they worked and created together.

John Cale, Gerard Malanga, Nico, and Andy Warhol at the Factory, 1966. Photograph: Hervé Gloaguen.

As 1965 turned to 1966, the big new interest at the Factory was a group of musicians that called themselves the Velvet Underground. For New Year's Eve, the Velvets, Edie, Paul, Gerard, and I all went to the Apollo Theater up in Harlem, then raced back downtown to watch ourselves on the evening news. Eventually we passed out in front of the TV. Then later, when I went out on the street to go home, it was impossible to get a cab because the Great Transit Strike had started that midnight, just as John Lindsay, the city's Hollywood-handsome, love-comic beautiful new mayor, was stepping into office. That was another "happening," sort of like the black-out-people walking hundreds of blocks to work or riding bikes or hitching rides. In January, Jonas moved the Film-Makers' Cinematheque from Lafayette to West 41st Street. He was in the middle of a series called Expanded Cinema where artists like Jack Smith and La Monte Young and Robert Whitman would combine cinema images and projections with live action and music. I remember Oldenburg's piece where he dragged a bicycle down the aisle from the last row of the theater while a movie was being projected, and I remember Rauschenberg where he was a walking light metaphor, so beautiful to look at, electrified and standing on glass bricks holding a live wire and fluorescent tubes (the artist Arman had made glass shoes for him so that the electricity wouldn't be conducted).

We'd met the Velvets through a filmmaker friend of Jonas' named Barbara Rubin, who was one of the first people to get multimedia interest going around New York. She knew a lot of rock and folk performers, and she'd sometimes bring people like Donovan and the Byrds by the Factory.

The Velvets had done tapes for filmmakers to use while they projected their movies and they'd played live behind the screen during some screenings at the Lafayette Street Cinematheque.
But where we first really became aware of how fabulous and demented they were, was their act at the Cafe Bizarre on West 3rd Street–"On Go-Go Street for nine bucks a night," as Lou Reed, the sort of lead Velvet, put it.

When Barbara Rubin asked Gerard to help her make a movie of the Velvets playing at the Bizarre, Gerard asked Paul Morrissey to help, and Paul said why didn't I come along, and so we all went down there to see them. The Bizarre management wasn't too thrilled with them. Their music was beyond the pale–way too loud and insane for any tourist coffeehouse clientele. People would leave looking dazed and damaged. Anyway, the Velvets were about to get fired. We talked to them a little bit that same night while Barbara and her crew went through the audience pushing the blinding sun gun lights and the cameras in people's faces and asking, "Are you uptight? Are you uptight?" until they reacted, and then she would hold the cameras and lights on them while they got madder or cringed more or ran away or whatever.

We liked the Velvets and invited them to come by the Factory.

Paul wanted to do some shows with them. Coincidentally, we'd just been approached by a producer who'd taken over a film studio out on Long Island that he wanted to turn into a discotheque. He claimed that this studio was originally the airplane hangar that Lindbergh took off from. It was around 17,000 square feet and had a 3,000 capacity and he was going to call it Murray the K's World. He said he wanted the Factory crew to be disco mascots and hang out there every night making movies so he could get publicity for the place …

… If any band then could fill up 17,000 square feet with blasting sound, it was the Velvets. We liked the idea that their drummer was a girl, that was unusual. Sterling Morrison and Lou Reed—and even Maureen Tucker—wore jeans and T-shirts, but John Cale, the Welsh electric viola player, had a more parochial look—white shirts and black pants and rhinestone jewelry (a dog collar-type necklace and bracelet) and long black spiky hair and some kind of English accent. And Lou looked good and pubescent then—Paul thought the kids out on the Island would identify with that.

Poster for Exploding Plastic Inevitable at Trip, Los Angeles, May 1966. Martha Morrison Collection.

Another idea we had in mind when we went to check out the Velvets was that they might be a good band to play behind Nico, an incredible German beauty who'd just arrived in New York from London. She looked like she could have made the trip over right at the front of a Viking ship—she had that kind of face and body. Although Nico got more and more into the swirling capes and medieval monastery look as the 60s went on, when she first came on the scene, she dressed very mod and spiffy in white wool pants, double-breasted blazers, beige cashmere turtlenecks, and those pilgrim-looking shoes with the big buckles on them. She had straight shoulder-length blonde hair with bangs, blue eyes, full lips, wide cheekbones—the works. And she had this very strange way of speaking. People described her voice as everything from eerie, to bland and smooth, to slow and hollow, to a "wind in a drainpipe," to an "IBM computer with a Garbo accent." She sounded the same strange way when she sang, too …

… Nico was a new type of female superstar. Baby Jane and Edie were both outgoing, American, social, bright, excited, chatty—whereas Nico was weird and untalkative. You'd ask her something and she'd maybe answer you five minutes later. When people described her, they used words like memento mori and macabre. She wasn't the type to get up on a table and dance, the way Edie or Jane might; in fact, she'd rather hide under the table than dance on top of it. She was mysterious and European, a real moon goddess type.

I was invited to speak at the annual banquet of the New York Society for Clinical Psychiatry by the doctor who was chairman of the event. I told him I'd be glad to "speak," if I could do it through movies, that I'd show *Harlot* and *Henry Geldzahler*, and he said fine. Then when I met the Velvets I decided that I wanted to "speak" with them instead, and he said fine to that, too.

So one evening in the middle of January everybody at the Factory went over to the Delmonico Hotel where the banquet was taking place. We got there just as it was starting. There were about 300 psychiatrists and their mates and dates and all they'd been told was that they were going to see movies after dinner. The second the main course was served, the Velvets started to blast and Nico started to wail. Gerard and Edie jumped up on the stage and started dancing, and the doors flew open and Jonas Mekas and Barbara Rubin with her crew of people with cameras and bright lights came storming into the room and rushing over to all the psychiatrists, asking them things like:

"What does her vagina feel like?"

"Is his penis big enough?"

"Do you eat her out? Why are you getting embarrassed? You're a psychiatrist; you're not supposed to get embarrassed!"

Edie had come with Bobby Neuwirth.

Andy Warhol behind the projectors at Dom. Photograph: Fred W. McDarrah. © Estate of Fred W. McDarrah.

While the crews filmed and Nico sang her Dylan song, Gerard noticed (he told me this later) that Edie was trying to sing, too, but that even in the incredible din, it was obvious she didn't have a voice. He always looked back on that night as the last time she ever went out with us in public, except for a party here and there. He thought that she'd felt upstaged that night, that she'd realized Nico was the new girl in town.

Nico and Edie were so different, there was no good reason to compare them, really. Nico was so cool, and Edie was so bubbly. But the sad thing was, Edie was taking a lot of heavy drugs, and she was getting vaguer and vaguer. Her society lady attitude toward pills had changed to an addict attitude. Some of her good friends tried to help her, but she wouldn't listen to them. She said she wanted a "career" and that she'd get one since Grossman was managing her. But how can you have a career when you don't have the discipline to work at anything?

Gerard had noticed how lost Edie looked at that psychiatrists' banquet, but I can't really say that I noticed; I was too fascinated watching the psychiatrists. They really were upset, and some of them started to leave, the ladies in their long dresses and the men in their black ties. As if the music—the feedback, actually—that the Velvets were playing wasn't enough to drive them out, the movie lights were blinding them and the questions were making them turn red and stutter because the kids wouldn't let up, they just kept on asking more. And Gerard did his notorious Whip Dance. I loved it all.

The next day there were long write-ups about the banquet in both the *Tribune* and the *Times*: "SHOCK TREATMENT FOR PSYCHIATRISTS" and "SYNDROMES POP AT DELMONICO's." It couldn't have happened to a better group of people.

In January, when the Cinematheque moved to 41st Street, the Velvets and Nico played together again and we screened *Vinyl* and *Empire* and *Eat* in the background and Barbara Rubin and her crew ran around the audience as usual with movie cameras and bright lights. Gerard was up on the stage whipping a long strip of phosphorescent tape in the air. The whole event was called "Andy Warhol Up-Tight."

GERARD MALANGA

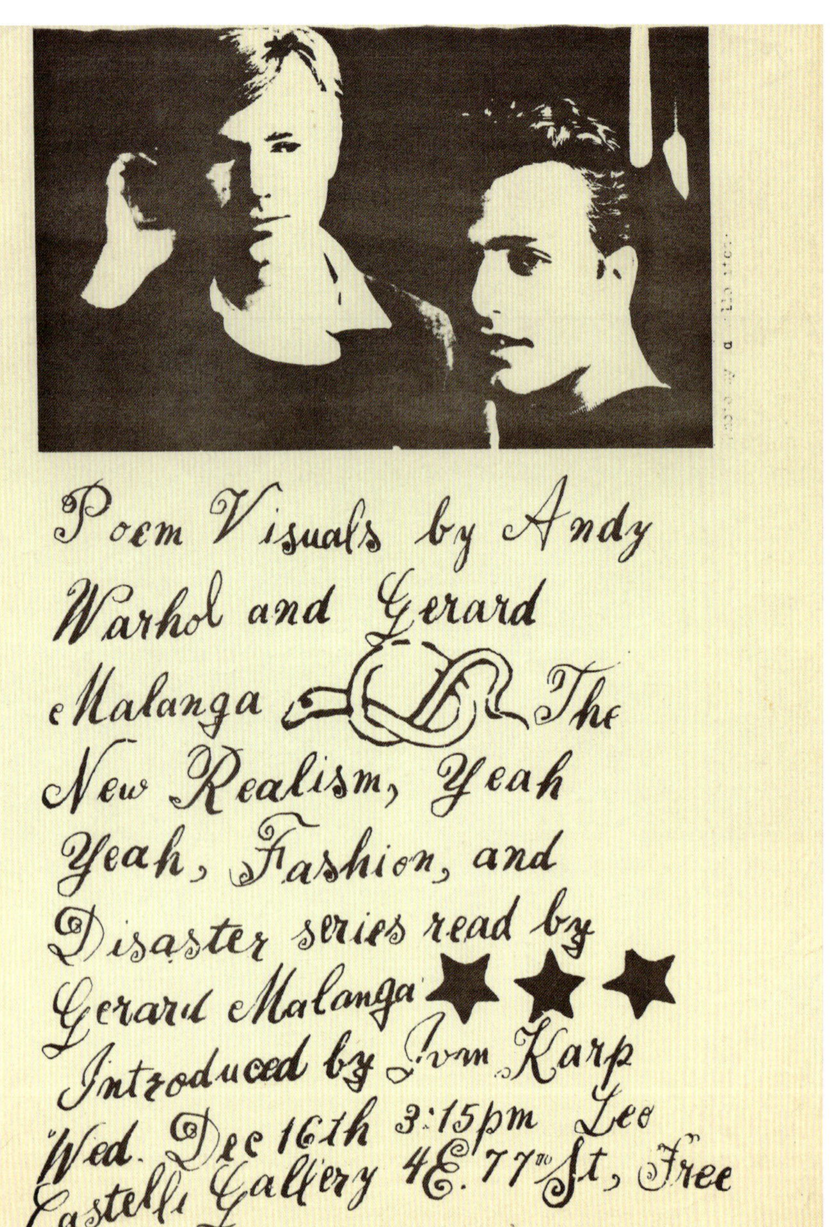

Left: Invitation to an evening of poetry, December 1964. Gerard Malanga Collection.

Right: Photobooth portraits of Andy Warhol and Gerard Malanga, 1963. Gerard Malanga Collection.

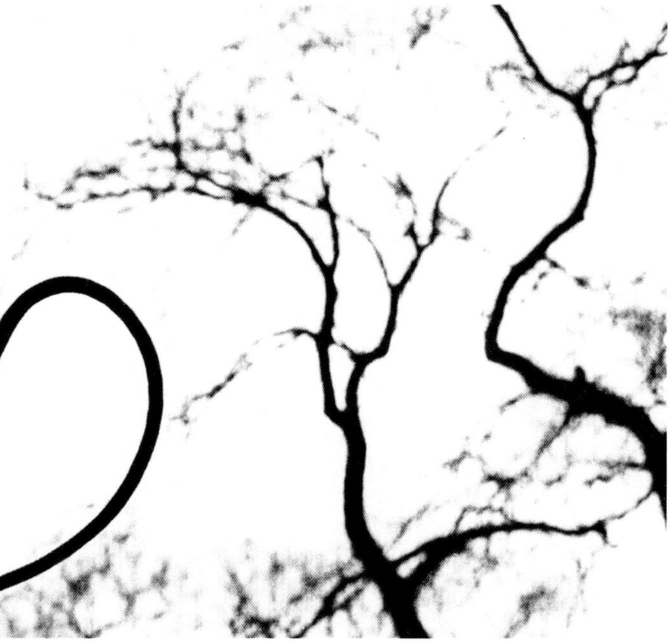

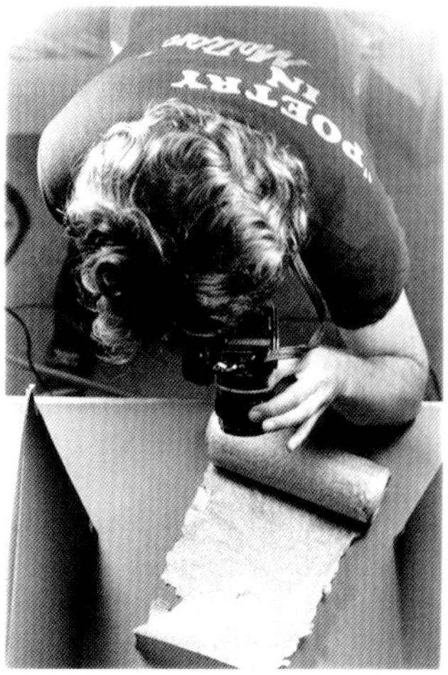

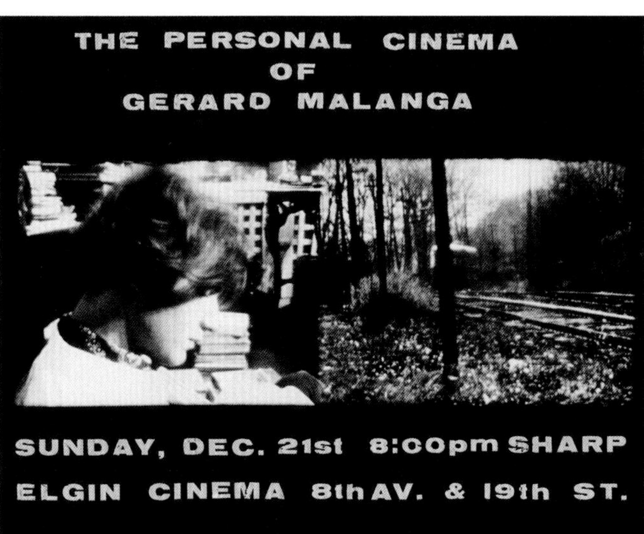

Gerard Malanga, born in 1943 to working class immigrants in the Bronx, became Warhol's main collaborator during his prosperous period. Initially recruited in 1963 for his mastery of silk-screen printing, he took part in Warhol's key works of the 1960s, from paintings to screen-tests, films, the Exploding Plastic Inevitable, and *Interview* magazine. His relentlessness at work and his curiosity made him a central figure of the Factory, as a collaborator, right hand, handyman, and even as Andy Warhol's body double. Paradoxically, he was also one of the most discrete figures, to the point that he hid his many talents which included poetry, his first and greatest passion, but also film, publishing, and photography. He stealthily shot the most famous photographic session of the Velvets in the spring of 1966 in Los Angeles. Shortly before, he had spontaneously joined the group to dance to their music. This gesture was at the same time both modest and flamboyant, much like this artist and first-hand witness.

Portrait of Gerard Malanga, 1966
Photograph: Diane Dorr Dorynek. Gerard Malanga Collection.

Middle: Malanga photographing the original manuscript of *On the Road* by Jack Kerouac, 1982. Photograph: Ira Cohen.

Below: Flyer for an evening of film projections by Gerard Malanga, Elgin Cinema, New York, 1970. Gerard Malanga Collection.

Andy Warhol with members of the Velvet Underground after the film premiere of *Our Man Flint* by Daniel Mann in January 1966. Photograph: Nat Finkelstein.

EDIE SEDGWICK

center on page

(1943–1971)

6 3/8 to 8 1/4

E-12

Edie Sedgwick in the film *Ciao! Manhattan* by John Palmer and David Weisman. David Weisman Collection.

Elf and depraved angel, heroine of a tragedy scripted by F. Scott Fitzgerald and staged by Vincente Minnelli: of all the Factory superstars, Edie Sedgwick was the most fascinating. While some were content to bask in the light, it seemed that she was its source. Born in Santa Barbara in 1943, from Massachusetts aristocracy, she was 22 years old when she met Andy Warhol. Inseparable from the artist, she starred in several of his films, danced on stage with Gerard Malanga while the Velvet Underground played, had an adventure with John Cale, inspired several songs by Bob Dylan, and Lou Reed's "Femme Fatale". Then suddenly, the star flickered out of Warhol's orbit. Worn out by addictions and mental health issues, Edie faded away in 1971. Her legend remains—fueled by the film *Ciao! Manhattan.*

Layout for the preparation of the *Film Culture* edited by Gerard Malanga, 1966. Jonas Mekas Collection.

Unplanned and unpublished photograph of Edie dancing to The Rascals while they are rehearsing, November 1965. Photograph Fred Eberstadt. The Life Picture Collection.

STEPHEN SHORE

Born in New York in 1947, Stephen Shore, the creator of the most intimate Velvet photographs, would later become a master of color photography. At just 17 years old, his black and white photography captured the Factory's atmosphere—during its calm hours—while the newly created Velvet Underground rehearsed in a corner.

Andy Warhol and Lou Reed. Photograph: Stephen Shore. © Stephen Shore, courtesy 303 Gallery, New York.

Top: John Cale and Nico. Bottom: Sterling Morrison, John Cale, and Lou Reed. Photographs: Stephen Shore. © Stephen Shore, courtesy 303 Gallery, New York.

Maureen Tucker at the Factory in 1966. Photograph: Stephen Shore. © Stephen Shore, courtesy 303 Gallery, New York.

John Cale. Photograph: Stephen Shore. © Stephen Shore, courtesy 303 Gallery, New York.

Sterling Morrison. Photograph: Stephen Shore. © Stephen Shore, courtesy 303 Gallery, New York.

Nico. Photograph: Stephen Shore. © Stephen Shore, courtesy 303 Gallery, New York.

Sterling Morrison, John Cale, and Lou Reed. Photographer: Stephen Shore. © Stephen Shore, courtesy 303 Gallery, New York.

Sterling Morrison, Lou Reed, and John Cale during the filming of *Symphony of Sound*, 1966. Too much noise for the police. Photograph: Stephen Shore. © Stephen Shore, courtesy 303 Gallery, New York.

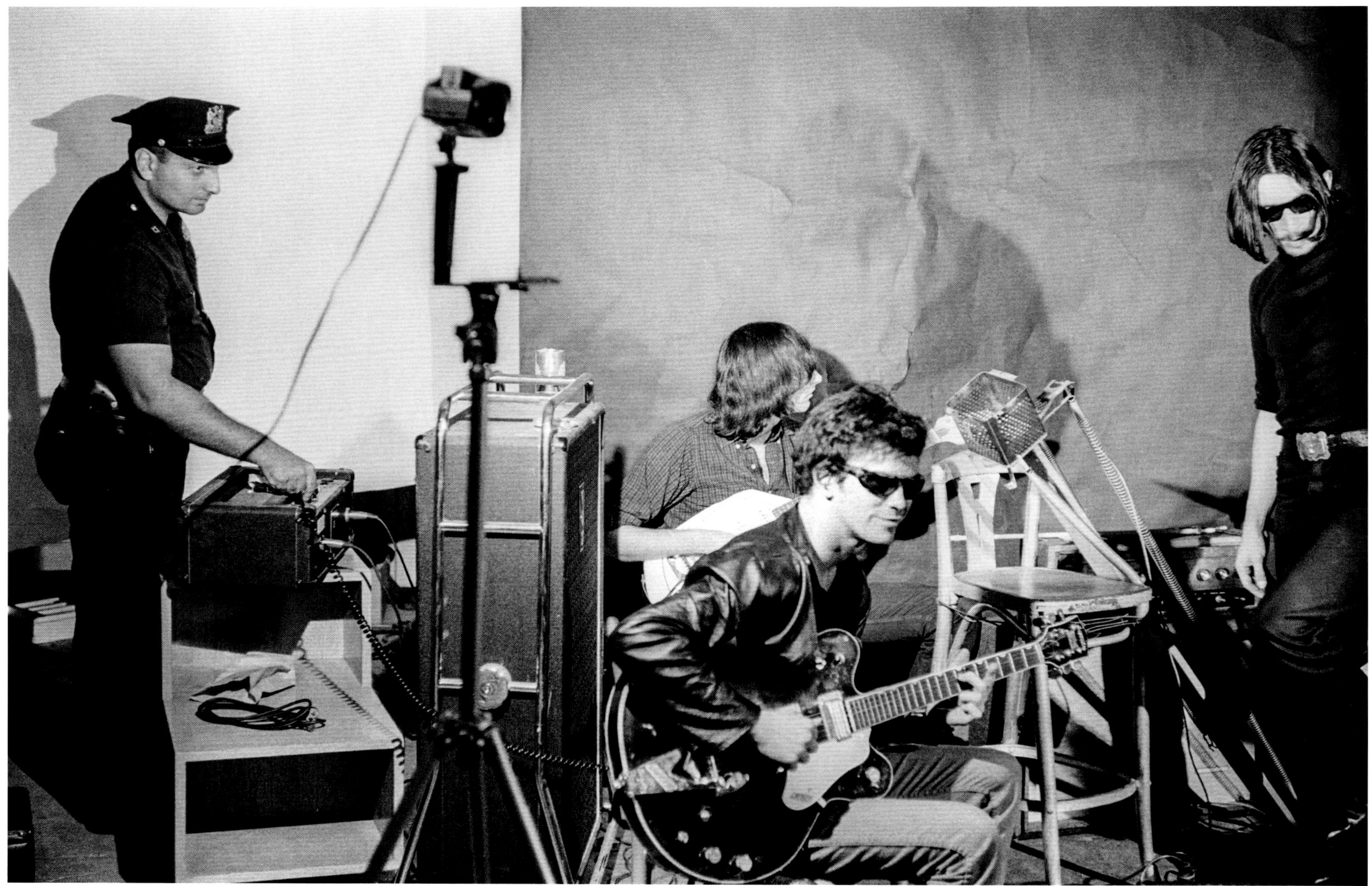

NICO

(1938–1988)

center ~~of~~ on page.

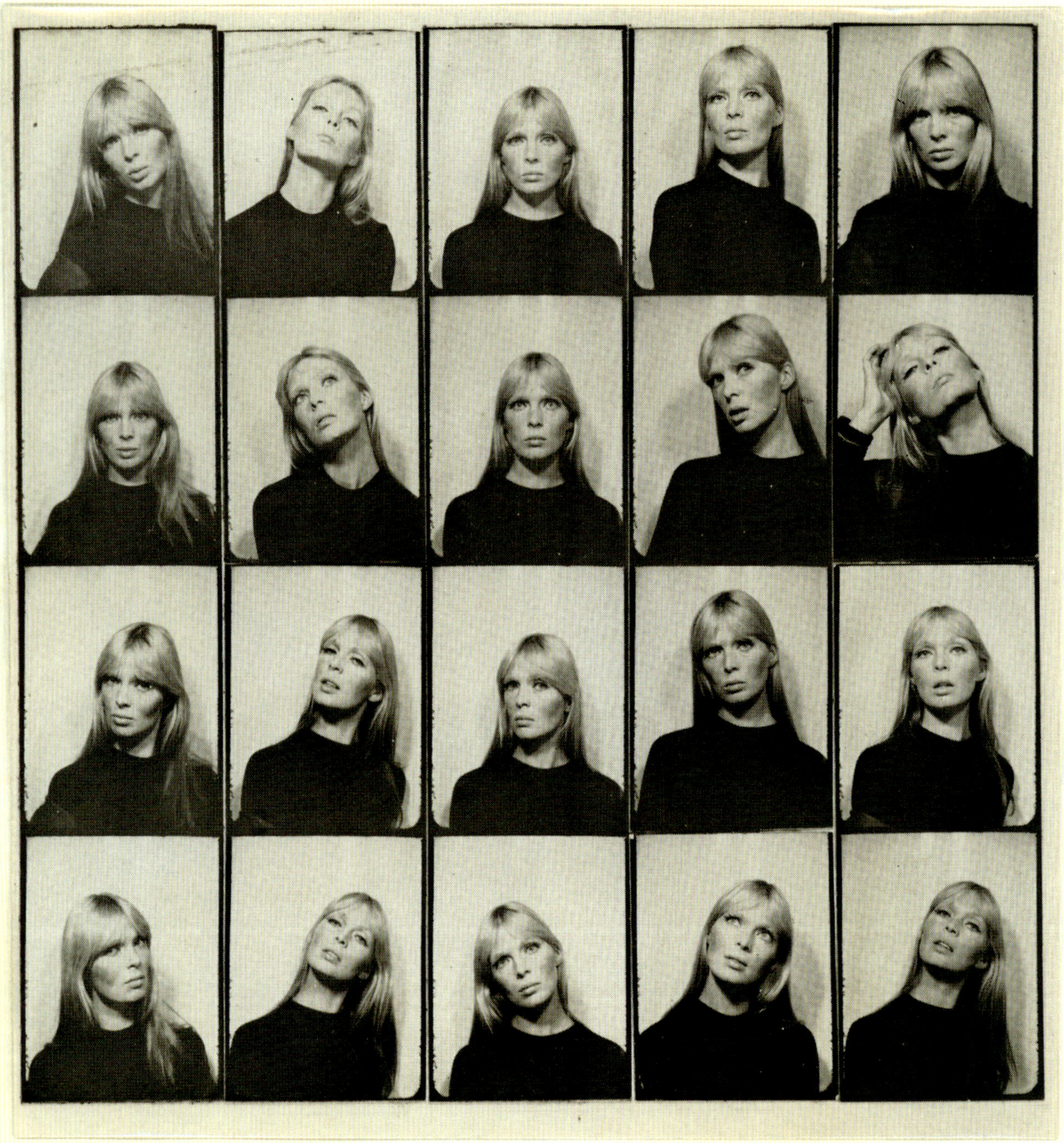

6 3/8 to 8 1/4

(7)

E-12

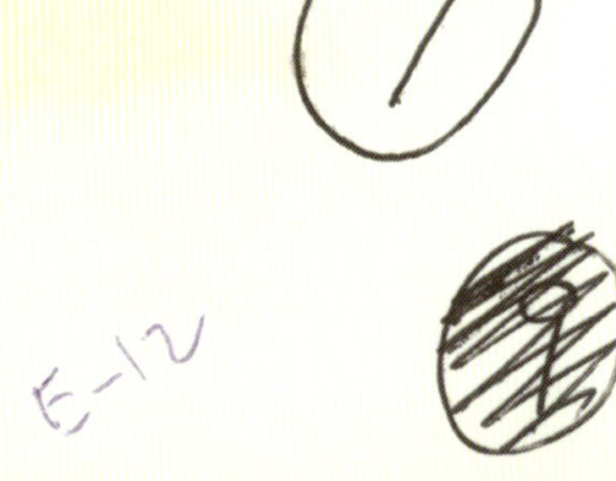

Assistant cameraman Ennio Guarnieri, Nico, and Federico Fellini on the set of *La Dolce Vita*, 1960. © Arturo Zavattini / Solares Fondazione delle Arti.

When Nico began to sing with the Velvet Underground in January 1966, her life was already a novel. Born Christa Päffgen in Cologne in 1938, she began her modeling career as a teenager. What followed was a nomadic life, from Berlin to Rome to Paris, then from London to New York, from the catwalk to the covers of the most prestigious magazines, on to cinema and recording studios. Her blonde locks are featured in Fellini's *La Dolce Vita*, she has a son with Alain Delon, Bob Dylan wrote her a song, and Brian Jones gave her the opportunity to release her first single, "I'm Not Sayin'". As soon as she arrived at the Factory, her sweet, distant vocals and nonchalant looks seduced Andy Warhol and his acolyte Paul Morrissey. They saw her as the "figurehead of a Viking ship", carried by a wave of success.

Layout for *Film Culture*, edited by Gerard Malanga, 1966. Jonas Mekas Collection.

Advertisement in the *Village Voice*, February 1967. Alfredo Garcia Collection.

THE VELVET UNDERGROUND AT THE PSYCHIATRIST'S CONVENTION

Jonas Mekas, Edie Sedgwick, Gerard Malanga, and Nico at the Delmonico, New York, January 1966. Photograph: Adam Ritchie. © Adam Ritchie Photography.

Edie Sedgwick and Jonas Mekas present the Velvet Underground at the Psychiatrist's Convention at the Delmonico, New York, January 1966. Photograph: Adam Ritchie. © Adam Ritchie Photography.

Grace Glueck, "Andy Warhol and his gang face the psychiatrists", *The New York Times*, January 14, 1966.

The New York Society for Clinical Psychiatry survived an invasion last night by Andy Warhol, Edie Sedgwick, and a new rock 'n' roll group called "The Velvet Underground."

"The Chic Mystique of Andy Warhol," described by an associate of the painter as "a kind of community action-underground-look-at-your-self-film project," was billed as the evening's entertainment for the psychiatry society's 43rd annual dinner at Delmonico's Hotel. And until the very last minute, neither group quite believed the other would show up.

But sure enough, as the black-tied psychiatrists and their formally gowned wives began to trickle into Delmonico's lobby at 6:30, there was Andy, and in evening get-up, too—sunglasses, black tie, dinner jacket, and corduroy work pants. And right there with him were some of his "factory" hands—Gerard Malanga, poet; Danny Williams, cameraman, and the "factory" foreman, Billy Linich.

The "factory," as any Warhol buff knows, is the big, silver-lined loft where he and his coterie make their underground films and help mass-produce Andy's art.

What "The Chic Mystique" was nobody explained. The Warhol part of the program included the showing of his underground films as background for cocktail conversation and at dinner, and a concert by the rock 'n' roll group. And Warhol, and his cameramen, moved among the gathering with hand-held cameras, using the psychiatrists as the cast of a forthcoming Warhol movie.

The psychiatrists who turned out in droves for the dinner, were there to be entertained—but also, in a way, to study Andy. "Creativity and the artist have always held a fascination

for the serious student of human behavior," said Dr. Robert Campbell, the program chairman. "And we're fascinated by the mass communications activities of Warhol and his group."

Delmonico's elegant white-and-gold Colonnade and Grand Ballroom had probably never seen such a swinging scene. Edie Sedgwick, the "superstar" of Warhol's movies, was on full blast—chewing gum and sipping a martini.

There was John Cale, leader of "The Velvet Underground," in a black suit with rhinestones on the collar. There was Nico, identified by Warhol as "a famous fashion model and now a singer," in a white slack suit with long blonde hair. And there were all those psychiatrists, away from their couches but not really mingling, not letting their hair down at all.

"I suppose you could call this gathering a spontaneous eruption of the id," said Dr. Alfred Lilienthal. "Warhol's message is one of super-reality," said another, "a repetition of the concrete quite akin to the L.S.D. experience." "Why are they exposing us to these nuts?" a third asked. "But don't quote me."

Dr. Arthur Zitrin, director of psychiatry at Bellevue Hospital, was slightly worried. "We've had everyone appear at these annual dinners, from Paul Tillich to Warhol," he said. "I'm program Chairman for next year. How the hell are we going to follow this act?"

The act really came into its own about midway through the dinner (roast beef with string beans and small potatoes), when "The Velvet Underground," swung into action. The high-decibel sound, aptly described by Dr. Campbell as "a short-lived torture of cacophony," was a combination of rock 'n' roll and Egyptian belly-dance music.

The evening ended with a short talk by Jonas Mekas, film director and critic. But long before that, guests had begun to stream out. The reaction of the early departees was fairly unanimous. "Put it down as decadent Dada," said one. "It was ridiculous, outrageous, painful," said Dr. Harry Weinstock. "Everything that's new doesn't necessarily have meaning. It seemed like a whole prison ward had escaped."

"You want to do something for mental health?" asked another psychiatrist. "Kill the story."

At the Delmonico, New York, January 1966. Photograph: Adam Ritchie.

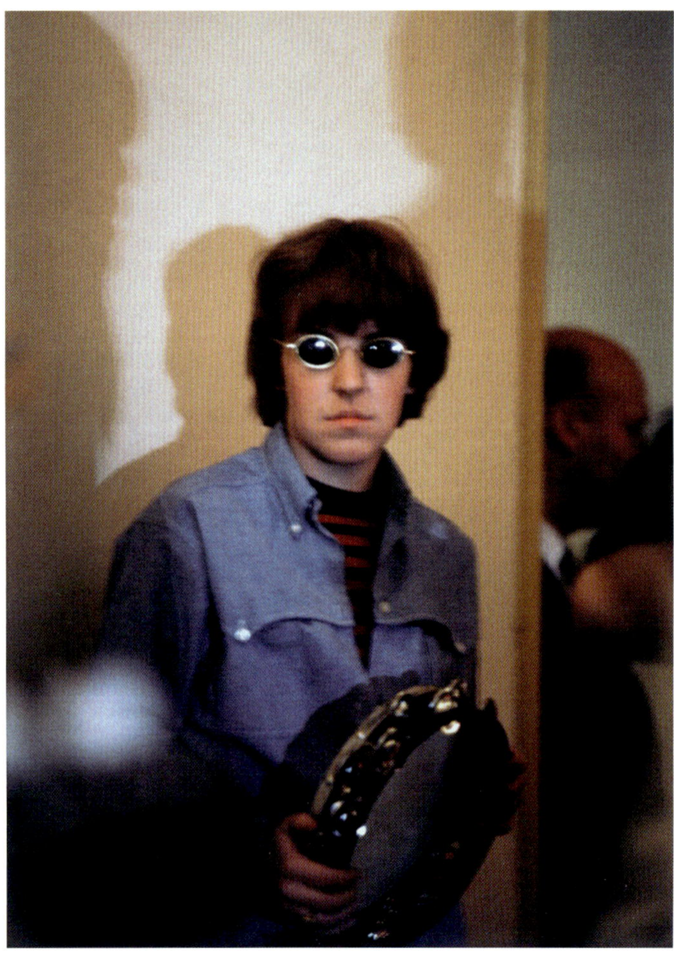

At the Delmonico, New York, January 1966. Photograph: Adam Ritchie. © Adam Ritchie Photography.

ON THE ROAD TO ANN ARBOR

For their first outing from New York in March 1966, the Warholian caravan headed for Ann Arbor, Michigan. The performance series initiated by Warhol in collaboration with the Velvets was still called Up-Tight, but all the ingredients of the Exploding Plastic Inevitable were already together. The “happening” began well before the show: during preparations and on the road in a van driven by Nico. On board was photographer Nat Finkelstein.

Warhol’s trip with the Velvets in Ann Arbor, March 1966. Photograph: Nat Finkelstein.

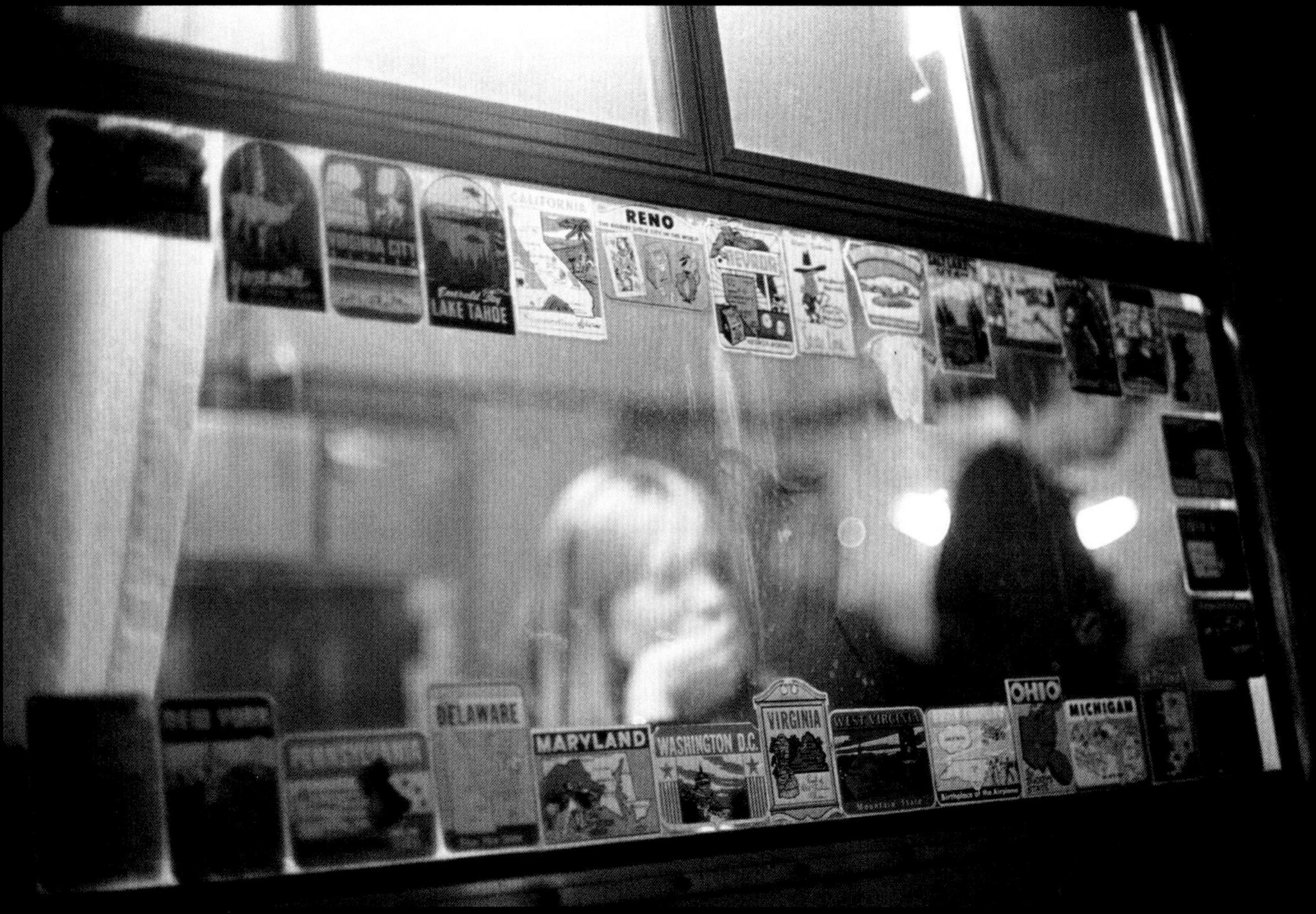
CALIFORNIA
RENO
LAKE TAHOE
DELAWARE
MARYLAND
WASHINGTON D.C.
VIRGINIA
WEST VIRGINIA
OHIO
MICHIGAN

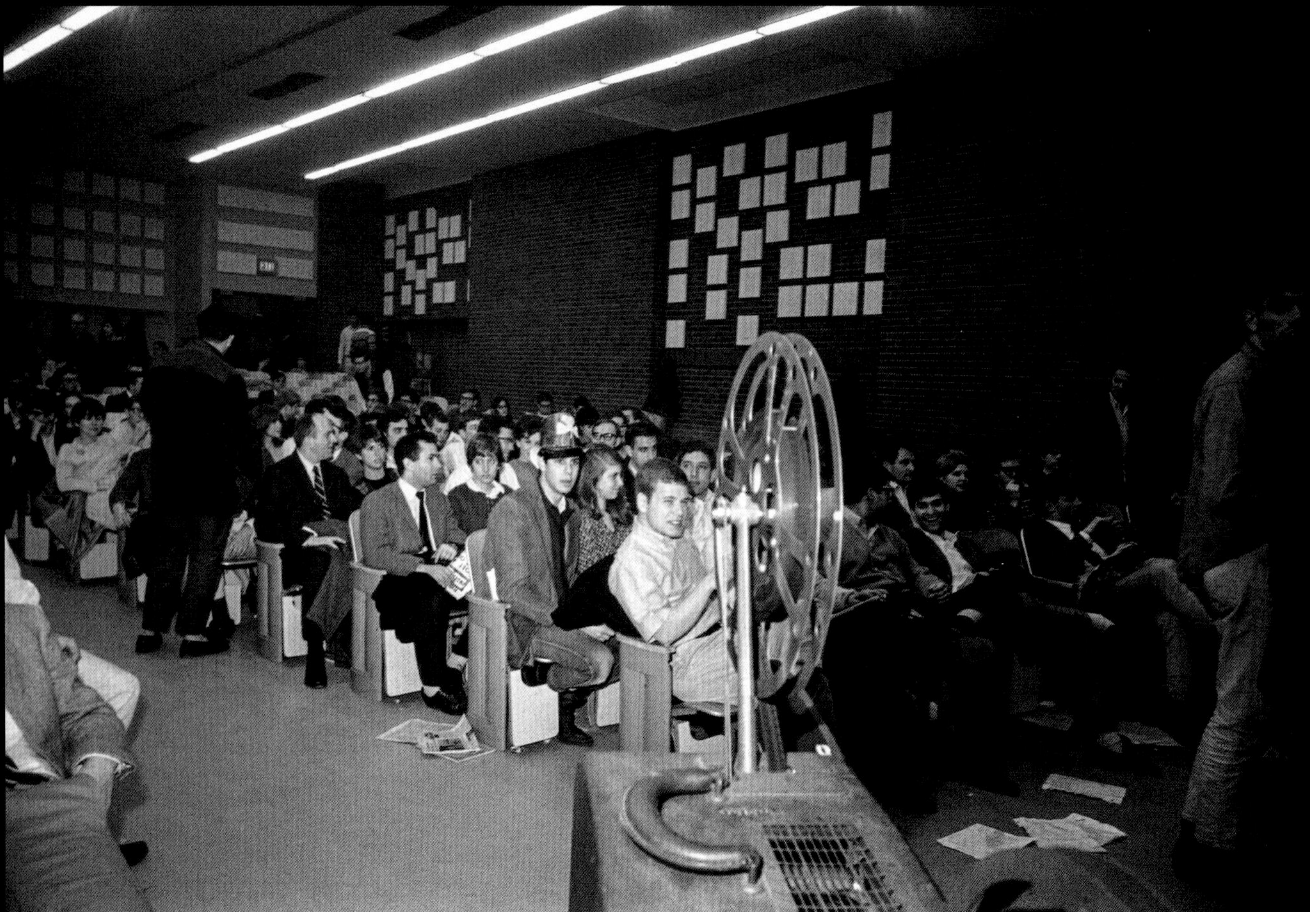

DANNY WILLIAMS

In the group photos of members of the Factory, we never noticed him. However, in Warhol's entourage, nobody remained anonymous because no one was innocuous. There was nothing extravagant about Danny Williams, with the exception of the fact that he mysteriously disappeared at 26 years old. His niece Esther Robinson directed the investigative documentary, *A Walk Into the Sea: Danny Williams and the Warhol Factory* (2007), which revealed his talents as the mastermind behind the light show of the Exploding Plastic Inevitable. Williams was also the only person who Warhol entrusted with his Bolex camera. As a result, in January 1966, Danny Williams was the first to film the young Velvet Underground, in his own style, when they arrived at the Factory.

At the Factory, 1966. Bottom left to right: Nico, Gerard Malanga, Moe Tucker, Danny Williams (eyes closed); at center: Stephen Shore, Andy Warhol, Lou Reed, Sterling Morrison; above: John Cale, Paul Morrissey. Photograph: Nat Finkelstein.

EXPLODING PLASTIC INEVITABLE

In the spring of 1966, a new "happening" designed by Warhol combined music, dance, projection, film, and light shows. Baptised Exploding Plastic Inevitable, the show first took place in a ballroom located on the East Village's most Bohemian street, St. Marks Place. For the first time, the Velvets played on a real stage, facing a dance floor below a mirror ball and strobe lights. They performed Lou Reed's songs in front of an audience that included Salvador Dalí, Robert Rauschenberg, and Allen Ginsberg. That same month, the Velvet Underground would begin recording their first album.

Andy Warhol's touri
ploding Plastic Inevi
cophony for dancers
Angeles, while films
Warhol, are shown

pe. The Ex-
reates a ca-
Trip in Los
e, made by
ns at rear.

Exploding Plastic Inevitable at Trip, Los Angeles, May 1966.
From Martha and Sterling Morrison's scrapbook.

May 28, 1966 THE BEAT Page 13

"Out of sight" . . . Sonny Bono, actor.

"It's like eating a banana nut Brillo Pad" . . . David Crosby, Byrd.

"It doesn't leave anything for the imagination" . . . Tony Hicks, Holly.

A Happening!

What is it? It's Andy Warhol, it's The Plastic Inevitable, it's The Velvet Underground, it's Nico, it's a pair of dancers, a candle, two whips, a candy bar, a violin, a pop bottle and movies.

It's from New York and it's on the West Coast for the first time at The Trip in Hollywood. It's going to other parts of the nation soon.

It's drawing crowds of curious celebrities and it's confusing crowds of curious.

It's happening.

See it for yourself, no questions allowed.

BEAT Photos: Howard L. Bingham

"I'm glad I've got short hair" . . . Ryan O'Neal, Rodney

"The Velvet Underground should go back underground and practice" . . . Barry McGuire, chicken rancher.

"It's where entertaining's going" . . . John Phillips, Papa.

From *The Beat* magazine, May 1966.

CINEMA GUILD PRESENTS

2 SHOWS - ONE NIGHT ONLY - HILL AUDITORIUM

AN EVENING WITH

ANN ARBOR

ANDY WARHOL

FEATURING

"Exploding Plastic Inevitable"

films

music

THE

VELVET UNDERGROUND

NICO : GIRL OF THE YEAR GERARD : SUPERSTAR

added attraction

the

New Generation

THE WORLD OF THE FLOWER PEOPLE

WATCH FOR THE

BANANA --TRUCK

TOTAL INVOLVEMENT

STRANGELY SEDUCTIVE...... TRIP OUT.... TURN ON....

"BE IN"

SUNDAY

APRIL 9 -- -- HILL AUD

6:30 - 9:00

TICKETS AVAILABLE AT HILL AUD. BOX OFFICE

Flyer for the Exploding Plastic Inevitable, April 1967. From Martha and Sterling Morrison's scrapbook.

the Rolling Stones but by refusing to position themselves on this axis, the Velvet Underground took listeners backwards. Fatalistic, cold, and feverish, Velvet songs held up an unflattering mirror to the reality of New York. Disregarding the comfort of the ears as much as the comfort of the soul, their music and arrangements favored steep rhythm, squeaky violin, guitars, barbed wire, and icy singing. Under the intransigence of the sounds were hidden celestial melodies, of which its heady singularity would trigger a revolutionary aesthetic.

Andy Warhol at the Factory, working on his "Peelable Banana" that adorns the cover of *The Velvet Underground and Nico*, 1967, *Peel Slowly and See*. Photograph: Hervé Gloaguen.

SCEPTER/WAND RECORDS
FIRST GOLD ALBUM
WAND 657 "LOUIE LOUIE"

April 1966. The Velvets & Nico at Scepter Studios for the initial recording of their first album. In a corner, Warhol is watching, listening, producing. Photographs: Nat Finkelstein.

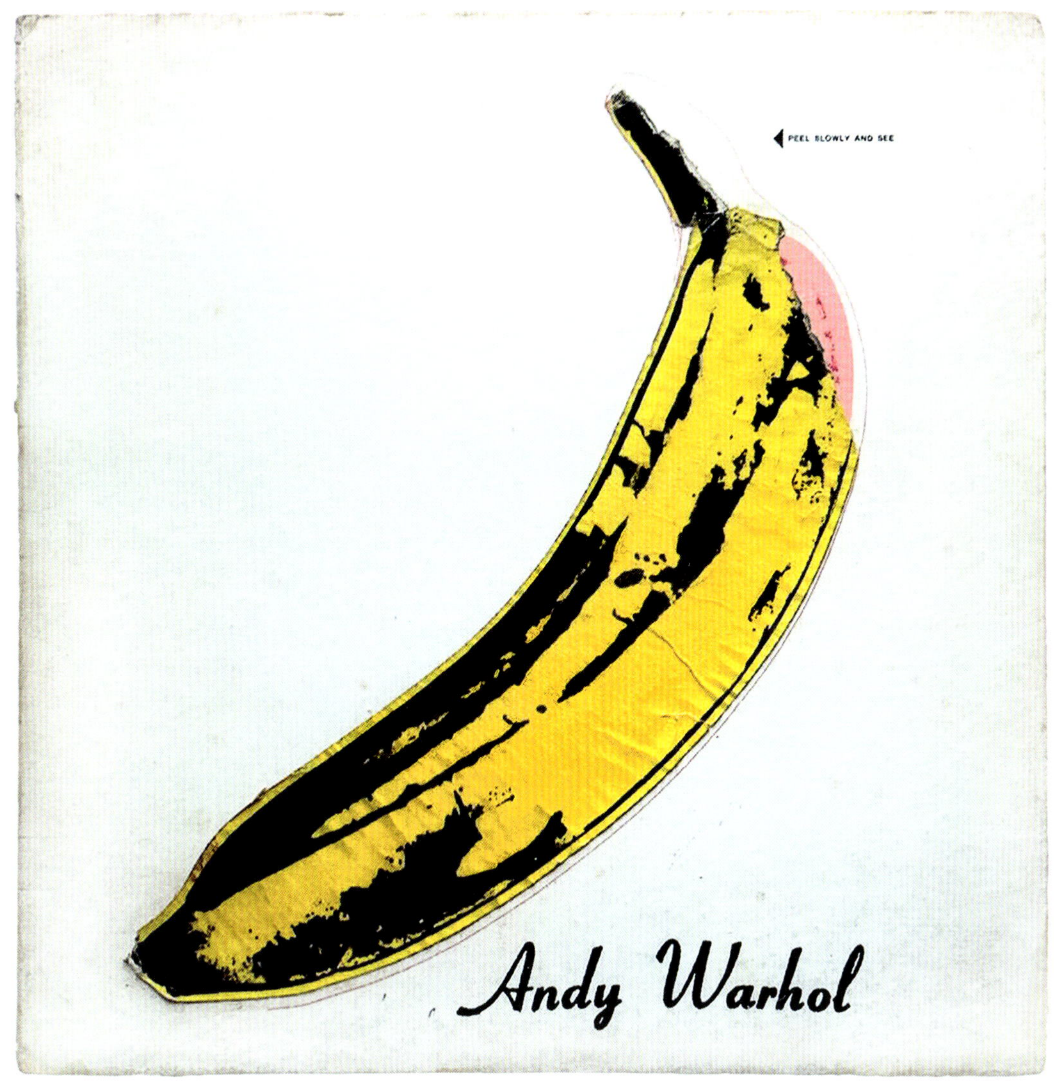

Original album cover for *The Velvet Underground & Nico* (1967).

"An extremely pretty sexy banana, and the album cover peels, which is nice, to reveal the inside of a very sexy, groovy banana."
—Lou Reed

Nico on Times Square, New York City, 1966. Photograph: Steve Schapiro. © Steve Schapiro.

NICO BY ARI

Nico had an affair with the French actor Alain Delon and had a son on August 11, 1962, Christian Aaron Boulogne, whom Nico called "Ari." Delon denied paternity and Nico had difficulty raising him, so Ari was raised by Delon's parents. Ari wrote this introduction for a book of his mother's poems, lyrics, and writings.

Years after the death of my mother Nico, I remember the words of a friend in common who had just come out of prison: "Your mother, you know, she was a great lady."

There's no need for interpretations or commentaries, I simply wanted to pass on her dreams. With that, I reunited her texts and songs for her fans/readers. They are brought together for the first time in a trilingual volume. Nico wrote equally well in French, German, and English.

It is a heavy heritage to carry, and the task wasn't easy—especially since I needed to do the work of an archivist to bring together pieces of her art since she had the annoying habit of misplacing it. In Delhi, for example, where she spent a month working, all her writings were lost forever. They were in a piece of luggage that, rather than returning to England, got lost in India, where her father had lived during the Second World War on a houseboat in Srinagar. It was also in this bag that she had the only photograph of her father. She wanted to return and retrace her/his steps. Unfortunately, the war raged on and continues to do so in Kashmir.

These texts, as you will discover, are beautiful in my eyes. The poetry of a *great lady*, like our friend had said.

I am proud to add that she gained immortality and died at the age of 49 years old, like the great Jacques [Brel].

Does this mean she had a sharp conscience, an appreciation of life?

I will be quiet/shut up and leave you with her words:

"I don't read biographies. They are filled with lies since it says that life has a beginning, middle, and end. I don't believe in the middle. And the end drives you to another end: it's the subject of Jim's song "The End"…. One day I would like there to be a novel about me that would come from the imagination and would explain my spirit, not my life. My spirit and my life are two different things. My spirit is named Christa. My life is Nico. Christa made Nico, and now she will leave Nico because Nico has left herself. Nico went to the summit and depths of life. What she discovered is that both these spaces are empty. But Nico also doesn't want to find herself in the middle, where people turn their backs on her. To avoid these unhappy areas, it is better to be nowhere. This is the conclusion that I have come to."

Cible mouvante by Nico

Ad for Nico's solo show in the *Village Voice*. Alfredo Garcia Collection.

THE ABOVE-GROUND SOUND OF THE VELVET UNDERGROUND

The Velvet Underground's velvet, leather, satin, and brass stuff was designed by Betsey Johnson of Paraphernalia.

Photos by Ralph Garcia

We always get a thrill when a great underground rock group finally breaks through the surface to full-fledged popularity. And we get an even bigger thrill when the group in question happens to be the Velvet Underground.

Spurred to semi-fame, underground style, by Andy Warhol in his Dom days, the Velvet Underground have been laboring in the murky depths for far too long. Now, with the advent of their sensational new album, "White Light/White Heat" (Verve), that problem has been solved, once and for all.

Welcome to the hot glare of fame, fortune, and publicity, group! HULLABALOO gives its first happening party in honor of the four valiant Velvets: Lou Reed (vocals, lead guitar, piano), John Cale (vocals, electric viola, bass guitar), Sterling Morrison (vocals, guitar, bass guitar), and Maureen Tucker (drums).

Happy sunshine!

56 HULLABALOO

Promotional article for the album *White Light/White Heat*, in *Hullabaloo*, June 1968. Alfredo Garcia Collection.

THE VELVET UNDERGROUND

by COPPER

Have you ever been on a trip? If you have I can assure you, you've never taken one the likes of The VELVET UNDERGROUND AND RON BRITAIN EXPERIENCE.

Verve's midwest regional promotion manager, JACK KATZ, has done it again! He and his lovely wife hosted a "Press Trip" in honor of the Velvet Underground's new album "WHITE LIGHT, WHITE HEAT" on the Verve label.

After the get-together of stars and press, the entire entourage tripped over to the Aardvark Cinemateque in Old Town. There, 200 lucky teens awaited The Velvet Underground, Andy Warhol movies, and the me of the evening, WCFL's Ron Britain. (We mus'nt forget to add the history-making appearance of the one and only TAB MATHIS. How sweet it is)

The Velvet Underground, Lou — lead singer & electric guitar, John — electric organ, Sterling — electric guitar and Maureen (Mo) — on drums took everyone ten miles high on their unique hard-rock sound.

Velvet Underground w/Eva Dolin & Jack Katz of Verve

l-r Allen Shaw, Velvet Underground's manager, Jack Katz, George Yeheares

Ron Britain

From Martha and Sterling Morrison's scrapbook.

The Velvet Underground:

Taking the Country By Storm!

By Margo Rose

Because Andy Warhol discovered them, everyone thought the Velvets were just a put-on. They're kooky and wild, all right—but their music proves they're for real!

It was a hot August Saturday night, and the very hip resort in Sag Harbor, Long Island was packed. Artists, writers, all the beautiful people in the New York show business scene, were on hand. Young people, teenyboppers, marrieds, the crowd was thickening, braving the heat, forgetting about it even, as they sat rapt. The Velvet Underground was beginning to play. The sound was hard rock, electronic, with a lot of fuzz, and a primitive, pulsating rhythm that dared you not to become part of it. Soon the dance floor was full. It was difficult to just hear the music without getting up and m-o-v-i-n-g! Hot, intricate blues, worked in with sophisticated harmonies and rhythms, and piercing strains of sometimes beautiful, yet more often cynical and pointedly sardonic lyrics, floated in the air. Four figures at the guitars, organ, and drums, were silhouetted in the darkened, smoke-filled *(Continued p. 61)*

From Martha and Sterling Morrison's scrapbook.

CANDY DARLING

(1944–1974)

Candy Darling. *Last Hurrah to Hollywood*. 1971. Photograph: Gerard Malanga.

Born James Lawrence Slattery in 1944 in the New York suburb of Queens, the future Candy Darling was still a child when he began to mimic Hollywood actresses in front of his television. Faced with misunderstanding and/or rejection from those around him, it became clear that he would become a glamorous blonde. As a transwoman in the Factory, she was first referenced in 1969 by Lou Reed who opened his first post-John Cale album with “Candy Says”. Candy went on to ephemeral glory in films by Warhol, Paul Morrissey, and Werner Schroeter.

Above left: Drawing from *Candy Darling's Journal*, 1969-1972, New York, Outlaw Art Museum.

Above right: Album sleeve from Lou Reed's *Walk on the Wild Side*, November 24, 1972. Allan Rothschild Collection.

Below: Candy Darling in *Women in Revolt* (1971), directed by Paul Morrissey. © Everett Collection.

NEW YORK

ART

AND

THE VELVET UNDERGROUND

by JONATHAN RICHMAN

From Martha and Sterling Morrison's scrapbook.

REINVENTION OF THE VELVET UNDERGROUND

After Nico, Warhol, and John Cale left the Velvet Underground, the group that appeared left for dead reinvented itself. Lou Reed, at the helm of the ship, found an inexhaustible source of inspiration in introspection. He layered luminous harmonies with his tormented verses and recruited Doug Yule, a multi-instrumentalist who was able to reproduce his voice. The “new” Velvet Underground traveled the United States but skipped New York, where they didn’t perform between the spring of 1967 and the summer of 1970. Instead, they performed in clubs in Boston, Chicago, Philadelphia, and in cities along the West Coast. As is evidenced with the posthumous album, *1969: Velvet Underground Live*, which was released in 1974, underground music was gaining ground and taking off in notoriety.

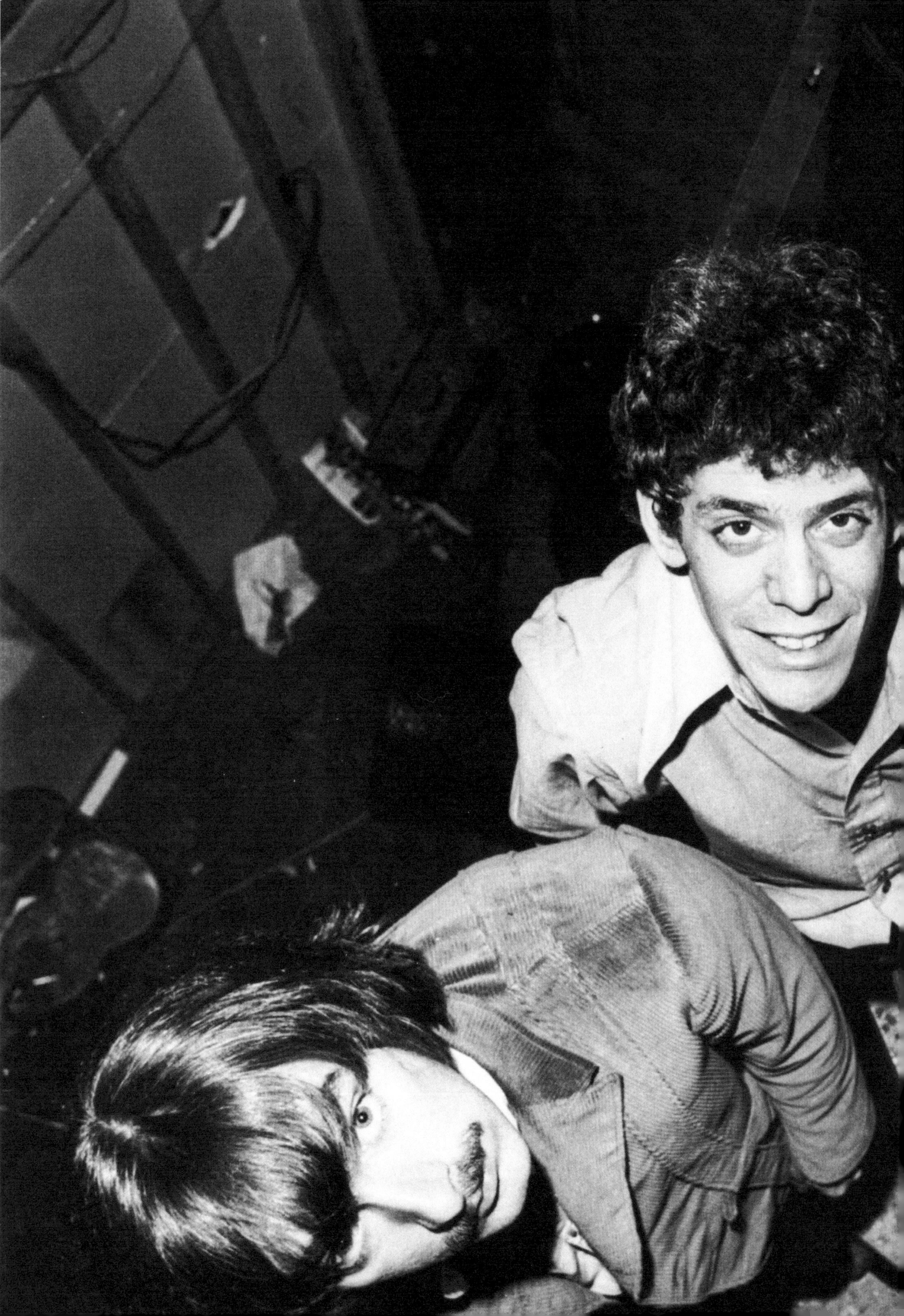

The Velvet Underground with the arrival of Doug Yule, end of 1968. Photograph: Lynn Goldsmith.

DOUG YULE

At their concerts in Boston, Lou Reed and Sterling Morrison sometimes stayed at the home of a young local musician, Doug Yule (born in 1947). He was recruited to replace John Cale on short notice in October 1968. A bassist with a melodious and multi-instrumental touch, he was able to sing in Lou's style, although with less ruggedness.
With Yule, the Velvet Underground made a third album that was fluid and nuanced. Taking advantage of his resemblance to his elder, Yule was promoted by their manager, Steve Sesnick, to the rank of substitution leader. This was most evident during the sessions for *Loaded*, their last album, where he sang four tracks. From the autumn of 1970 to 1973, Doug Yule remained at the helm of a ghost group that had been orphaned by its founders.
In 1973, he wrote and recorded *Squeeze* almost entirely by himself, which would be a Velvet Underground record by name only.

The Velvet Underground, 1969; *Loaded*, Cover illustration: Stanislaw Zagorski, 1970; *Squeeze*, 1973.

Lou Reed and Doug Yule during the recording of *Loaded*, New York, 1970. Photograph: Henri ter Hall.

RETURN TO ROCK

Lou Reed

Interview done in 1969 for *Third Ear* magazine.

Is your new album already released at Atlantic?
No, it won't come out for a while. [*Speaking to Doug Yule*] You should come over here, because it's not going to be much of an interview with only me. I'm warning you. I messed up my voice the other day in the studio, which is why I have a weird voice.

It's really great, because we'd never done a real album before. All the albums that we recorded, we made in one or two days. We left the tape running, and we more or less did the editing live, so all our albums seem to have been recorded in a basement. Each album corresponds to a specific period but what I prefer is what we do now. This is the first time that the final result is so close to the original idea: what we had in mind will finally be released on an album. This has never happened before, because we did not know how to make an album and we never had a producer that understood what we were talking about. This album, for the first time, sounds exactly as we wanted it to sound.

Is the music that you are doing now different?
No, you can hear that it's us. People will have no trouble recognizing us.

And the texts?
It's really rock songs, much more than before.

In some songs, there are some chord changes that you wouldn't expect to find in an ordinary rock song. Doug and I have always dreamed of making symphonic rock songs that are not vulgar. The idea was to lead an orchestra … of guitars.

Do you think that your audience will be the same as previous albums?
I think that there is a whole new audience to seduce, an audience that does not even know about the existence of the other three albums. Fans of the first albums hated the third one, and those who liked the third didn't buy it because of the first two. As far as we are concerned, it didn't really affect us. The new album is exactly what it is supposed to be, and it's so cool to listen to.

Has the media misunderstood you?
They didn't have enough information. People say that our first albums are scary, and I understand what they mean and why they say that. We portray things so realistically that it's scary. We hang out in a very strange milieu because it's New York. We just had to exorcise certain things and that's what we did. There were certain things going on and we really felt that someone had to talk about it, so we did it and really paid for it. I don't like this esoteric stuff. We never really wanted to be avant-garde, even if people thought we were. You know … if I ever hear another rock band say that Stockhausen … Honestly, have they ever even listened to Stockhausen? It's the most annoying thing in the world, who are they trying to fool? That's why rock is so great, because it puts the listener in the middle, it's an incredible thing.
You take a room full of people and you put on a record, and everyone will do the same thing, at least almost everyone. It is magic.

Do you identify yourself less with what is happening in New York today?
I do not identify with anything at all. I identify with myself.

At the beginning your music identified with all that, right?
No, it's all that identified with us. It was us

Lou Reed and Doug Yule during the recording of *Loaded*, New York, 1970. Photograph: Henri ter Hall.

who went through all this stuff in New York.

It's simply that you relate your impressions and experiences in your music?
We do not lie, that's the thing.

Do you feel closer to your audience today than before?
Much more. It took a lot of time to understand what it was like to be on stage. You know, we were nervous because we were in demand on all sides. There was a moment when we wanted to concentrate on our concerts, and there was all this stuff that was happening to us and we didn't understand what was going on. The most important thing was that we sat down and realized that we really wanted to be a rock band. If God showed up tomorrow and asked me what I want to do, I would tell him I want to be in a rock band. Yeah, if he showed up tomorrow and he asked me what I wanted to do, I'd tell him I'm doing it already. Do you want to be the President? No. Do you want to be in politics? No. Do you want to be a lawyer? No. What do you want then? I want to be a rhythm guitarist.

SOMETHING DIFFERENT

Put your mind to it and discover
What Goes On

K-14057

in a high-flying single that digs deep. And digs big.

THE VELVET UNDERGROUND

Written, Arranged and Conducted by The Velvet Underground

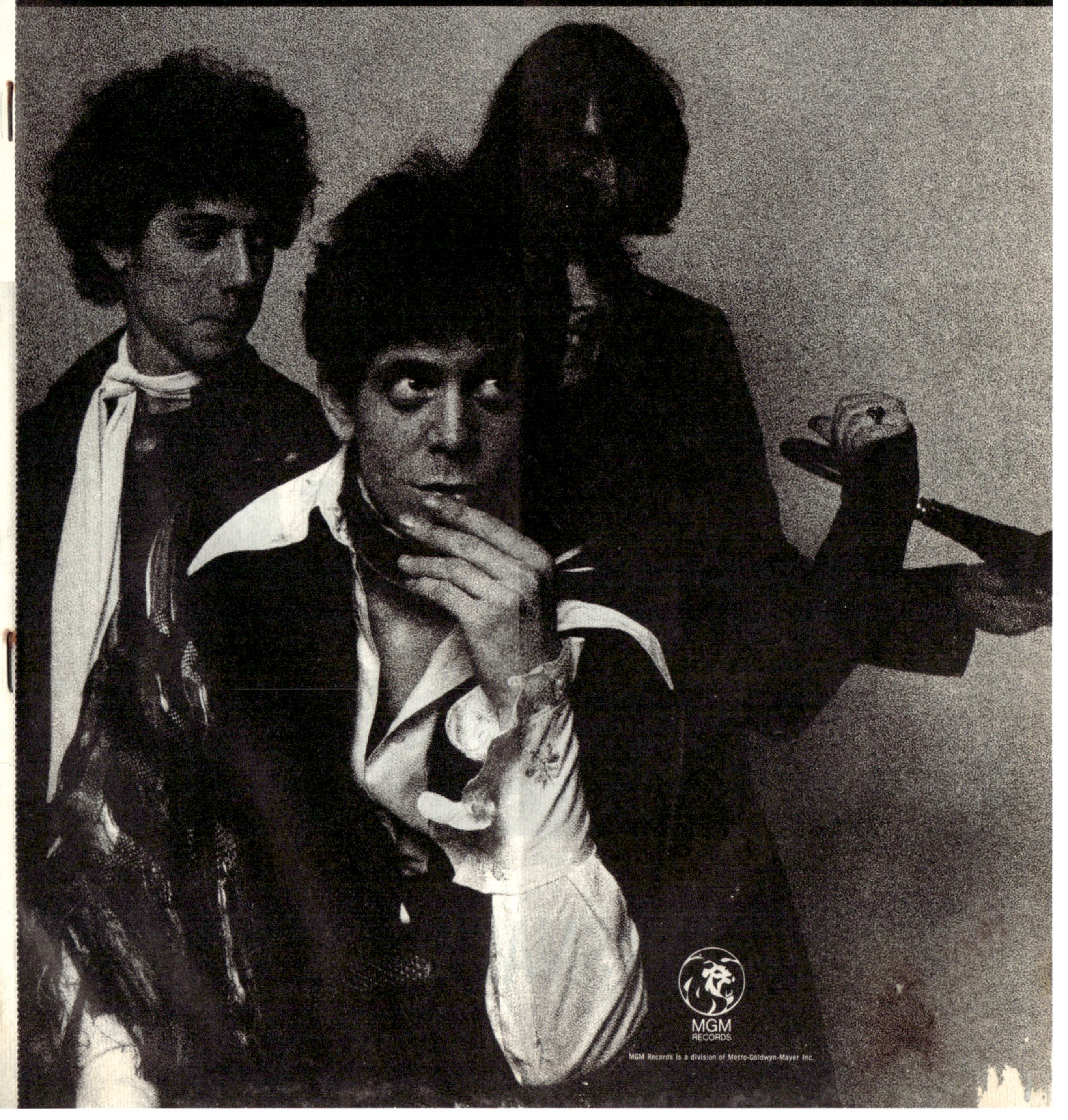

Advertisement for the single "What Goes On" in *Cash Box* magazine, May 1969. Alfredo Garcia Collection.

ANOTHER STORY OF THE VELVET UNDERGROUND

Doug Yule

Interview by Christian Fevret for *Les Inrockuptibles*, 1996.

Did you have any influence on the sound of the third album that was recorded just two months after you joined the band?
I believe that my main influence on the third album was my voice. It was more melodic, more harmonious. I sang in a veiled manner. Lou realized that we could do vocal harmonies together that made his voice sound better. On this album, melodies are more present. A track like "Jesus" would probably not have been on the album if John had been there because he would not have wanted it. "Jesus" works for two reasons: the vocal harmony and bass line, two elements that come from me. As for the bass lines, I always played what I wanted. My style is not traditional but rather symphonic: the guitar does its thing and the bass moves around it, with very sweet vocal harmonies.

You had barely arrived and you were already singing the very first song on the album, "Candy Says".
Lou wanted something particularly melodious. His voice is husky, he has to push it. When he sings softly, it derails and cracks, it is hard to control. Making me sing enabled him to get a softer rendering, but also to relieve himself of the pressure he felt in the spotlight. If you sing all the songs, you never have a moment to breathe. On the first album, he let Nico sing when he wanted a sweet sound, like "I'll Be Your Mirror".

In what kind of places did you play?
It went from places like The Cave in Cleveland, where there were 250 people to the Boston Tea Party, which had a capacity of 1,500 people, and then small clubs like the Avalon in San Francisco and Whisky a Go Go in Los Angeles. The spectators followed the group and knew the songs. There were always some to reclaim this or that piece. One of Lou's favorite jokes was to look at someone who asked us to play a song and he would tell them, "No, we will not play it."

A few months later, in 1969, you recorded what is considered the fourth lost album.
In 1969, we went to the Record Plant every night for one or two weeks. We were not thinking that much. Sesnick said that we should record in the studio. We answered, "Great, let's go." It was as simple as that. I believe that the Velvet Underground of 1970 was a logical extension of the original Velvet. Lou has matured a lot during these few years. His writing and his interpretation had changed. His desire for success led him to adopt a more public approach, a sine qua non condition to play on the radio.

I remember a discussion that we both had in a limousine about songs that would sell and we opened ourselves to this path. You can not play in basements forever for peanuts, you aspire for more recognition, to make records that sell, to a certain material comfort. When we entered the studio to record *Loaded*, in the spring of 1970, we wanted to make a popular record. The banana album sells better now than when it was released. At the time, it was a curiosity, just like *White Light/White Heat*, a rather strange album that did not sell very well. *Loaded* was the logical conclusion for a group that needed commercial success to continue to exist.

Were you able to react to Lou Reed's departure?
It was not really him who decided, it was Sesnick. Lou was going through a personal crisis that Sesnick was refusing to manage. He sent him for a walk. I don't really know if drugs had anything to do with it, he never spoke to me about it. It was a shock to me. Sesnick arrived an hour before the show and said, "Lou will not come tonight." And that was it.

Were you, the other members of the group, and Sesnick seriously able to consider that the Velvet Underground could go on without Lou?
The question never came up. It was not necessary to think, but to act. It also came from Sesnick, who with his strong personality lifted everyone's spirits up by saying that it was not going to be a problem. VU on stage, without Lou, was not that bad. I think that there are good pirated recordings of the group in Europe. What was missing was Lou's writing. And I was not mature enough to write at the time.

After Lou left, Sterling stayed in the band for a year?
Sterling went off like that … pouf! I think we were flying out of Houston, and he was standing there in the middle of the airport. He just said, "I'm not going. I'm going to Austin, I'm going back to school." He continued to Austin, to the University of Texas. It was a shock, maybe bigger than Lou's departure. Lou is fickle, but Sterling was usually more solid, always true to himself.

Do you now feel that continuing under the same name afterwards was a mistake or a betrayal?
Sesnick was still involved, his influence was very strong. Then he left and there was no momentum. We were singing new songs that I had written, which I then turned into the album *Squeeze* in England. Sesnick had organized everything, sold the project under the name Velvet Underground and pocketed the money.

I went into the studio alone, accompanied by Ian Paice from Deep Purple on the drums. If Maureen did not play on the album, it's because Sesnick had convinced me that she would not do it under a bogus pretense, and he probably told her something completely different about me. *Squeeze* was not a good album, it lacked sensibility, it was done entirely in the studio, without interaction with members of the group. Even for this record, I did not touch a penny. Sesnick received his bonanza and he gave them an album. He was a junkie: he lived in the present without worrying about the future.

What happened after the release of *Squeeze*?
I returned to New York shortly after since nothing was happening. I went to New Hampshire and worked at a gas station. Six to eight months later, as I was about to settle down in Denver, I went back to New York and talked to Sesnick. He said that people in Europe wanted the group to come back. He asked me if I was interested and we put together a group with three other people. We arrived in England, where Sesnick was supposed to have advanced the deposit for the amps, but there were no amps and no hotel. We ended up in London without a penny. We slept on the floor. Finally, the developer arrived with money and we did the tour, which ended up working. The audience was happy. But it left me with a bitter taste in my mouth. This was the last time I saw Sesnick.

Was this the last time you played under the name the Velvet Underground?
Yes, but only intentionally. While I was shooting with a band from New Hampshire, the promoter sold us under the Velvet Underground name, without my consent. I had to stop. I no longer wanted to be the Velvet Underground at that time … This was around 1973-1974.

Do you not find the end of the story mediocre, in light of what the group had been?
We just kept playing; it was easier than starting something new. It did not really matter to the public that some of us were no longer there. They were enjoying it, and so were we.

Do you think that your role in the Velvet Underground has been underestimated by history?
The story is told by the winners.
Half of what was recorded by the Velvet Underground was with John and the other half with me. My contribution and my influence were not insignificant, there was a real change in the group because of my presence. *Loaded* was mainly made by Lou and me, because Sterling and Maureen were not really available for this album. I sometimes thought of writing my version of the story, in the form of a long letter [*laughs*]… But anger would not change anything. Velvet, on the banana album, was a dark and mysterious group. Very underground, very cult, musically in the margin. *Loaded* is aimed more at the general public. From this point of view, it is probably more romantic for people who write on this subject to take the first album and say, "Here's the real band." It makes a better story when you accentuate the drama …

Lou Reed and Doug Yule during the recording of *Loaded*, New York, 1970. Photography: Henri ter Hall

Poster for the Boston Tea Party concert, January 1969. Martha Morrison Collection.

Poster for the Boston Tea Party concert, March 1969. Martha Morrison Collection.

LAST CONCERTS

Richard Nusser

Riffs column, *The Village Voice*, July 2, 1970

Lou Reed left the Velvet Underground in August 1970, but before he did, the band played two shows a night for nine weeks at Max's Kansas City on Park Avenue. Their stint there was memorialized with an album, *Live at Max's Kansas City*, which was put out by Cotillion Records two years later. Richard Nusser was there, chronicling the scene in his Riffs column in the *Voice*.

The Velvet Underground at Max's Kansas City? At first I thought it was some kind of joke. As if someone was trying to rig a re-run of the Terrible 60s by conjuring up old ghosts in old haunts. The Velvets, after all, had been the darlings of the Pop/amphetamine culture, whose spiritual center was often to be found at the round table in Max's back room, and it was not inconceivable to imagine some entrepreneur attempting to cash in on what would certainly be a premature revival of those jaded, faded years.

But no. The Velvets have changed considerably since they left Warhol's gang. No more demonic assaults on the audience. No more ear-wrenching shrieks of art. No more esoterica. "We once did an album with a pop painter," Lou Reed told the audience last Wednesday as the group began a two-week engagement upstairs at Max's, "because we wanted to help him out." "You're doing better without him," a fan yelled back.

And so they are. It seems the Velvets are now back to where they once belonged, functioning as a genuine rock 'n' roll dance band, dedicated to laying down strong rhythms and a steady beat that gets the vital juices flowing. No fuzz tones, no academic exercises. They were always good musicians, sometimes precocious and lacking discipline, but admired by their peers, nevertheless, for originality and innovation. Now they are all bloody virtuosos, with a mature sense of knowing when they are good and enjoying it. The result can be positively exhilarating.

The audience told me that opening night, of course, was something of an event, a kind of Old Home Week that brought together various elements of the rock/pop hierarchy, plus nostalgia seekers and true believers, most of whom had not seen the Velvets since they exercised at the Gymnasium three years ago. I don't know what they expected to hear, but they certainly weren't disappointed.

The Velvets served up scads of crisp, new material, along with what Lou calls "rock 'n' roll versions" of the group's old standards, like "I'll Be Your Mirror" and "I'm Waiting for the Man." The first set was done "in concert," with the audience seated behind tables, but in no time at all everyone was fighting the urge to dance. People started smiling, sometimes in amazement, as the boys began pulling these incredible notes from their instruments, and then they started beating time on their knees and bobbing their heads.

By the time they were halfway through the first set, people were yelling "Right on!" and you know what that can do to a performer, especially if he's white and the guy yelling is

Poster design by Steve Nelson, copyright 1970, all rights reserved.

black. The room is small, and very conducive to that kind of rapport. After two nights of this, the group was firmly convinced that they had done the right thing by coming into Max's to make their return appearance on a New York stage.

By Friday night, they were at the peak of their power. The word must have gotten out that the Velvets were back and in rare form, because the audience was right there from the beginning. They applauded the first notes of each old number and when Doug Yule, playing lead guitar, went into the bluesy, heart-tugging solo on "Sweet Nothing," which is the Velvets' "Hey Jude," they went wild, interrupting it twice with applause.

I don't know what effect this will have on their careers, but judging from past audience reactions to the Velvets (and other groups), I would say things are at an all-time high. I, for one, have always believed that the Velvets have never received the attention they deserve, but I attributed this to the fact that they have never tried to be commercial. They seemed to enjoy being artsy and esoteric. I also think that they were so indigenous to New York City that they were probably too sophisticated for the rest of the country. Oh, they always had a loyal following, even in the most obscure burgs, but it was all purists. No mass market. They're more eclectic now, so things may change.

They have made significant contributions to rock music, that's for sure. They have influenced many groups, including the Beatles, the Stones, and the Airplane (who lifted one of Maureen Tucker's drum riffs line for line and used it on one of their biggest singles). The Velvets are also the foremost exponents of something I call white/urban East Coast rhythm and blues, a form that doesn't rely on a white singer doing black face. All rock has black roots but the Velvets are one of the few groups around (along with the Stones) who have succeeded in developing their own style without coming off like a pale imitation. They have managed to evoke a culture born of the Long Island Expressway, and what's wrong with that?

They'll be at Max's another week, at least. Two shows a night, Wednesday through Sunday, starting at 11:30. There's a $3 admission fee, but once inside you can relax and enjoy. There's no hustle.

[FA]LLEN KNIGHTS [A]ND FALLEN LADIES

[L]ou Reed

One year after quitting the Velvets, Lou Reed published this text in *No One Waved Good-bye: A Casualty Report on Rock and Roll.* Edited by Robert Somma

At the age when identity is a problem, some people join rock and roll bands and perform for other people who share the same difficulties. The age difference between performer and beholder in rock is not large. But, unfortunately, those in the fourth tier assume those on stage know something they don't. Which is not true. It simply requires a very secure ego to allow yourself to be loved for what you do rather than what you are, and an even larger one to realize you are what you do. The singer has a soul but feels he isn't loved off stage. Or, perhaps worse, feels he shines only on stage and off is wilted, a shell as common as the garden gardenia. But we are all common as snowflakes, aren't we?

Brian Epstein built an empire but lived long enough to have a lot of time on his hands. Those who hate the nine-to-five regimen do not know the blessings that it holds. It masters the mind and protects it from itself. It soothes the ego. *This* is what I do. I have a family and I provide. When one has free time one tries to enjoy it, if only for its rarity. We are a race that needs to work. Brian Jones died for the lack of it and Janis Joplin and Jimi Hendrix from too much of the wrong kind.

I remember the early days of The Beatles as well. I had recently been asked by the Tactical Police Force of the city, which housed my large eastern university, to leave town well before graduation because of various clandestine operations I was alleged to have been involved in. In those days few people had long hair and those who did recognized each other as, at the very least, a good guy and one who smoked marijuana. And so I was lining up medical proof in order to evade the draft when along came the moptops, with their pictures in every window and their records on the jukebox where the local poets furrowed their brows and read to each other, where sophisticated elderly townies came to prey on callow youth and where I often went to drink alone to that week's lost anything. It was the world of Kant and Kierkegaard and metaphysical polemics that lasted well into the night and it was into this world that the Beatle music came, first as novelty and later as the style, the Spanish heeled boots, the banged haircuts, the accents (so delightful, cooed the girls to their Wellington-footed American counterparts), a style which was to proliferate and finally dominate the 60s.

I had recently been introduced to drugs at this time by a mashed-in-faced Negro whose features were in two sections (like a split-level house) named Jaw. Jaw gave me hepatitis immediately, which is pathetic and laughable all at once, considering I wrote a famous amplified version of the experience as a song. Anyway, his bad blood certainly put an end to my abortive excursions and consequently tempered whatever enthusiasm I might have had for pop music at this time. The Beatles were innocent of the world and its wicked ways, I felt, while I no longer possessed this pristine view. I, after all, had had jaundice.

This other-worldly approach vanished, however, and after my mind and my liver kept me from the Army, I, too, danced to Beatle music. Had Epstein realized what he had unleashed on the world? Did he tie his kite to their comet or was it vice versa? Had it been a sure thing any fool could have bumbled through or was the whole enterprise a masterful scheme of plotting (10 records in the Top 10 at once!)? We will never know and if John or Paul do, it does not seem they are talking.

If Brian Epstein had nothing to do, really, with The Beatles' success, one can understand his death more easily. We see him worthless, feeling, perhaps, the pawn of circumstance, to which he had not added his true bit of fuel. Feeling that he had nothing to give. After all he did, in his autobiography, describe himself as bland, as having only come to life through them. Had he not failed at becoming an actor? I remember him on the old *Hullaballoo* TV show looking so pale and wan and out of place. So quiet! Was this the mastermind tycoon, the successor to Col. Parker, the new Barnum?

But perhaps he was the genius some say, filling up his day with devious and splendid machinations, plotting and coursing the trail of our idols so that they did eventually blaze above each and every one of our heads. If he was a great businessman, expressing his will through four musicians, bringing honesty and integrity to an otherwise murky business, how he then must have suffered when The Beatles decided to tour no longer. What left after two movies and no tours? No more organizational meetings, plots, plans, and devices. Does one pore endlessly over monstrous manuscripts praying to find the sacred words, to resurrect once again the excitement, the glory, and the power?

Or do you spend your time flitting from one party to another, continent to continent, experimenting with this or that, savoring the fruits of one's endeavors but endeavoring no more? Do you find new groups, Gerry and the Pacemakers, The Cyrcle, Cilla Black? There is only one group. And they do not want to perform.

I remember him best for a story that may or may not have been true. In his mansion Brian Epstein kept Spanish servants, none of whom could speak English. Let that be a lesson to us all in discretion.

After The Beatles came The Stones and of The Stones one could never have ignored Brian Jones with his puffed up Pisces, all-knowing, suffering fish eyes, his incredible clothes, those magnificent scarves, Brian always ahead of style, perfect Brian. How could Brian have asthma, a psychological disease (we're told) and certainly something strange for a member of a rock and roll group. We read in interviews that Brian saw himself as the original lead Stone, a position he held until their American tour singled out Mick for the honor in the hearts of the American female.

Can you remember 1964 when The Stones were called homosexual for long hair? (Were you?) Brian, with two 14-year-old girls draped on each arm, must have laughed. And yet, the center of attention was drifting. In a group the attention may be evenly distributed (we all knew and loved John, Paul, George, and Ringo) but in The Stones it was to be Mick. Now normally in a group an instrumentalist can never overshadow a lead singer. (Exception: The Yardbirds where Eric Clapton, Jeff Beck, and Jimmy Page did just that to poor Keith Relf.) In The Stones there was Mick, the pivotal center. Charlie and Bill were for gourmets. That left Keith and Brian.

Lead guitar always, always beats rhythm guitar for popularity, so that left Brian, who one assumes therefore turned to more and more exotic instruments to establish his presence both to himself and others. This is what I'm worth. Let me see *you* play the damn thing.

It would be a mistake I think for someone to compete with Jagger on his own terms. Jagger has literally rewritten the book on strut scowl and scruffy and the role of street urchin versus society he played perfectly and mercilessly. Had Brian thought of competing it would have been a mistake. No one can overtake the lead vocalist.

New drugs, new countries, new sounds, back to the blues, my own music (everyman's conceit and dream), I must redefine myself because the self I wanted to *become* is occupied by another body. And still he was identified as a Stone which was contrarily identified as Mick's group, a backup band, a sideman. Now connoisseurs of course know that the band is a Band, but the great mass looked to Mick not Brian to be their leader through this fall from grace. And how can you take that? "But I started the thing," you might say. "It was my records in the first place, I turned them on, must I be a damn singer to turn on the world?" Yes. Or the champion of guitar.

Then, of course, there are more problems, the drug arrests, the constant mental turmoil. What if they tour without me? Financial. Could I starve? (He died well in debt.) If they play without me I shall be disgraced and have nothing whereas if I leave and strike out on my own I'm out before they get me (how sad! how inevitable!), and I create my own myth, style, voice, the eyes will be on me, I have a future, there's so much I know, music, music, music, who would know it from THAT, I can do it, I have to do it, I will do it, I must do it.

And of course the disorientation, am I backwards, forwards, the asthma attack (I am going to choke), the fall (where is the pool?!) and everything settles like a quiet bubble coming in spurts and then thin streams until finally the last one has popped itself right out of earthly existence.

Do people realize that at the age some of our entertainers are, most people have settled into a lifestyle from which they will reap rewards the rest of their lives? That is security of job and family. Most have found their soul-mate and are busy with one child, if not two, and life seems ordered and with purpose. No strange meanderings for them. That is for lesser or greater or at the very least different mortals from you or I. And yet there is no son more delinquent, no family more in chaos than the audience which comes to sit at the table of rock. Who else withdraws emotions so arbitrarily? And yet if the audience is just one big person, it should not be thought any more or less dependable than anyone else. Therefore performer beware. If you come looking for love, come prepared with a thick skin or a thick heart. Or, as my analyst put it, don't depend on anyone, not your lover, your friend, or your doctor.

Hendrix, that most supple of guitarists, the true electronic extension, depended on his audience to take him anywhere but where he was. But, as he insisted on taking their trip rather than taking them on his, he was ultimately forced to face a vision of himself which screamed clown. One cannot get to the top and switch masks. The lover demands consistency, and unless you've established variance as your norm *a priori* you will be called an adulterer. You can accept illogic as logic if it's presented all the time but not when sprung as a ripe pomegranate in a grove of erstwhile peaches.

Hendrix was at the mercy of so many people one wonders how he stood it as long as he did. He was the other side of Joplin's coin. If she traded off the black, he was trading off the white. When his management brought him here from England with two white sidemen, the die was cast. For Jimi Hendrix could never have been accepted in white America as a first-rate phenomenon had he had an all-black band.

When Jimi Hendrix came over the most striking thing besides his truly incredible guitar virtuosity was his savage, if playful, rape of his instrument. It would squeal and whine going off into a crescendo of leaps and yells that only chance could program. (See, we *are* extensions of Mr. Cage, it's all so modern and primitive at the same time, how simultaneous.) Anyone who does that night after night must go mad. It was the frenzy of self, for frustration can only so long be acted out in violent ways, never mime. If any part of it becomes sham, then vital energies are used to mimic the worst aspects of self and both mind and body are soon exhausted.

Jimi Hendrix's shows became sex shows, the idol erotically gliding, so … diffident, through a performance with two playmates clearly not in his league. Bitterness developed over attention to the star. But he was the star, wasn't he (lead guitarist and vocalist)? So the group dissolves. Comes the amorphous dawn and he realizes, I am not a strip-teaser, an Ann Corio con artist of the pelvis, I am a guitar player, now that I have, uh, arrived *why don't they take me seriously*? The zenith of burlesque wants to play rock Macbeth and so, they say, do all comedians, ha, ha, want to be tragedians. But I! Am! An! Artist! I! Can! Play! And he could (running counter to the Cassandra-like predictions of management) have played a sinewy Lear or a sweet and loving Hamlet, for Jimi played music, beautiful music every waking minute moment, noon and sun-music permeated his every thought and action and it had to be, I repeat, *had* to be, that he would have to say I must play real music or shrivel up and die one wind-swept morning.

And so, as Joplin is to do also, he forms a new band, to play what he attempts. And yet, there is no money for that, it is not so successful (where are the fans?) and so the old band is sporadically reformed for jobs in Oregon and the need to perform for an audience goes on, only this time to be forced to, this time, knowingly violate the self and soul (the body is the temple that houses the soul activated by the spirit which is energy) it was all right before, when we didn't understand what we were doing (the Shadow of Men witnesses all we do), when we had to get there … but to break the principles (so newly discovered) now! the spirit breaking, now! And so one runs back to the room to clarify the goals, get one's head straight, get it together, sort it all out, and dimly, dimly, may or may not perceive that management was lying.

Who can you talk to on the road? Long-haired dirty drug people wherever you look. The boy passes over a bag of green powder (for Christ's sakes as Holden would put it, Samwise come protect the master) and passes out. Don't take that, it has horse tranquilizer in it. Oh, I shot up to your song. I got busted to your song. Oh please bless me and touch me and make it all go away, I loved to you.

Who did Janis Joplin talk to on the road? She brought excesses of feeling into moribund white music. On the road when one sees only nights, never the pretty days of a flat Midwestern sun. And all your companions are drugged and hip and so sophisticated (we talk on such a high level only dogs can hear us) about the scene and who did what to whom and three puns on why, far out … She's so … twisted. Who can you talk to when you're famous and alone and all the people idolize you and want … to … get high with you and show you that they too are HIP, that they KNOW what is happening and watch let's get her drunk she's so funny when she's drunk you'll love her do you remember …

I remember people who do encore after

Lou Reed. Photograph: Henri ter Hall.

encore and after being pressed into a role they may have wanted, either consciously or unconsciously, emulate a pattern, gradually become the persona and, then alone, have to live up to it because the wretched THEY want it and what if they are right? Perhaps I should die, after all, they all (the great blues singers) *did* die, didn't they? But life is getting better now, I don't want to die, do I?

And if it's true all so true that you can't live up to everyone's expectations, and if it's true you cannot be all things to all people, and if it's true you cannot be other than what you are (passage of time to the contrary), then you must be strong of heart if you wish to work the problem out in public, on stage, through work before "them" who fully expect and predict in print their idol's fall. And if it was true it was inevitable and oh yes we know sad, and oh nothing could be done about it after all that's how she started out she just realized too late the habits of years are not undone in days, then if it's true that princesses are besmirched, then all of us are fallen knights.

DEAD LIE THE VELVETS UNDERGROUND! R.I.P. LONG LIVE LOU REED!

This is a facsimile of Lester Bangs' typescript
for the May 1971 feature in Creem Magazine.
Used by permission of CREEM Media, Inc. ©2007
200 copies printed by Jerry Kelly LLC for Ectoplasm Press
Dedicated to Bill A. and Connie R.

Quis nos operor est specialis.

Lester Bangs

DEAD LIE THE VELVETS UNDERGROUND!

R.I.P.

LONG LIVE LOU REED!

by Lester Bangs

The Velvet Underground have been one of the most consistently advanced musical organizations of our time, paid the price, and endured on the strength of their commitment. The mass audience which they've deserved for so long may finally be coming around to them after exhausting all that "safer," flashier music which eventually proved so stereotyped. Not that there is anything intrinsically difficult about the Velvets' music, then or now. But a combination of bad press, guilt-by-association and public defensiveness have dogged them, absurdly, ever since they agreed to donate their manifold talents to dramatize the milieu of a Pop artist/filmmaker who had reached the stage where he needed a rock 'n' roll band to deliver both his vision and his image to every still-safe living room in Middle America.

So the Velvets hit the pop music scene with a grinding fanfare, and brought countless quivers to the flesh of harried parents gaping at their children huddled in quietly intense circles around speakers oozing the ultimate nightmare as a resinnous hymn building into a roar of agonized hostility as inescapable as one honed fingernail shrieking across a blackboard: "Heroin/Be the death of me....And thank your god that I'm not aware!"

If the kids embraced it with all the grim receptivity of a new age of ruthlessly self-consuming hedonism, the more responsible listenners set on high as arbiters of the kid culture --rock critics, writers of teen mag album surveys, industry voices--flinched back with dual reflexes of shocked disapproval and glum silence: maybe this cancer (and isn't it aimed at our very vitals?) will just go away if we ignore it long enough.

Some of the more adventurous approached it with gimmicks: well, it has something to do with Warhol, so it must be a put-on, right? Call it camp. Call it New York sickness and write it off musically--doesn't the chick drummer (and whoever heard of that, either?) lose the beat in "Heroin," isn't much of it grinding feedback noise? Who can take an album like this in the spring of '67, when the prospects for a Love utopia shine so and Sgt. Pepper is just around the corner? (And B. Kramer threw it out the window, first playing 2d.)

The early Velvet Underground certainly had a capacity to threaten people, whether they intended to or not, but what both their detractors and many of their most ~~fanatical~~ fanatical fans failed to grasp was the distance between the Velvets and their subject matter, a distance as implicit in "Venus in Furs" as in an American slice-of-life portrait like "Lonesome Cowboy Bill." The band has evolved through several fruitful stages of musical experimentation and thematic comment in the last five years, some of the best of it unrecorded, but to many they are still a needle-driven instrument of Andy Warhol's supposed S&M conspiracy against the mass libido, and their first album remains their best seller while typing them yet as evil incarnate, spokesmen for the self-destructive fringe and parent of more precisely-aimed assaults like Alice Cooper and the Stooges.

Perhaps it's just that the Woodstock Nation has been brainwashed by the narcissistic, vibe-ey albums of groups content to serve as PR squads for the youth culture's "beautiful gentle people" ~~[struck]~~ hype, and fails to see that art doesn't necessarily support darkness by treating it. In any case, the first Velvet Underground album is as solid a documentation of the last decade's malaise as we're going to see. "Heroin" is a classic testament that stares death in the face and comes back poetic if unresolved. But all the Velvets' songs mark the progress toward that resolution, toward life and joy achieved honestly, outside all the ~~counterfeit~~ counterfeit wisdom and popular shortcuts to salvation which have failed so miserably. The drug song that corrupts most is the one that advertises <u>any</u> chemical as the mechanism ~~of~~ ultimate self-realization. If heroin is the absolute alternative to enlightenment, it at least makes no false claims, and those who would use this music to score their own self-destructive programs will find no support from the Velvets. ¶ I talked to Lou Reed last month, and he spoke long and eloquently on this. He was especially surprised when I mentioned the ~~Rolling~~ anecdote of the <u>Rolling Stone</u> writer who had asked me if the Velvets were still doing "fag stuff": "We were never doing 'fag stuff,' although some people associated us with that. Just like some people that don't know her think that Maureen has some sort of really hard, dyke-ish image, and when they meet her they're surprised to find out what a beautiful, sensitive girl she really is. So I know that those first two albums and that image hurt us a lot. Those songs that everybody typed us with were reflections of certain scenes around us, and some of it manifested where we were at at the time. But later we changed and our music changed but nobody else could seem to shake their preconcieved notions. Like at the time I wrote 'Heroin' and 'Sister Ray' I felt like a very rather negative, strung-out, violent, agressive person. I meant those songs to sort of exorcise the darkness, or the self-destructive element in me, and hoped that other people would take them the same way. But when I began to see how people were responding to them it was disturbing. Because like people would come up and say, 'I shot up to "Heroin,"' things like that. For awhile I was even thinking that some of my songs might have contributed formatively to the consciousness of all these addictions and things going down with the kids today. But I don't think that anymore; it's really too awful a thing to consider.

"But I do know that that was only one aspect of our music, and we've gone through lots of changes since then, and I wish more people would recognize that fact. All of a sudden we started looking out when we went onstage and seeing audiences full of stoned-out, violent people asking for those songs. We didn't want to appear to be supporting that, which is why we won't play most of those songs anymore."

If the Velvets' first album was thematically grim, it was musically as bold as any statement from any band of the last five years. It rendered the dark street life of New York City in a vision as fully realized as anything in Burroughs or Alexander Trocchi's Cain's Book; songs like "Heroin" and "Waiting For the Man" were obvious, but "Sunday Morning" was so lush and lyrical that you might not at first notice that the words described urban paranoia with a terse chill: "Look out/The world's behind you/There's always someone around you who will call/It's nothing at all...."

The humor in songs like "Femme Fatale" and "There She Goes Again" was missed by a lot of people, as was the authentically absorbed Oriental influence in the viola track of "The Black Angel's Death Song" (just compare its originality with the obvious "raga rock" scales indulged in by so many other groups at the time, and recall that the Velvets were doing it long before the rest, in 1965), and its lyrics with their strange smears of imagery ("So you fly/Through the cozy brown snow of the east....") Which was also where Lou Reed began to branch out vocally into the distended chants that eventually became a whole system of delivery in "Sister Ray." Here it just found the syllables shifting from the word "choose" to briefly take wing in nonsense syllables, a kind of expletive shorthand: "I chi chi/Chi chi I/Chi chi chi/Ta ta koooah/If you choose/Choose to choose/Choose to go."

White Light/White Heat was the album, though, that firmly proved the Velvets to be much more than a Warhol phase, and established them for anyone with ears to listen as one of the most dynamically experimental groups in or out of rock. This great album, which was all but ignored when it appeared except for a couple of reviews in Crawdaddy, will probably stand to future listeners looking back as one of the milestones on the road to tonal and rhythmic liberation which is giving rock all the range and freedom of the new jazz. "Sister Ray" represented the ultimate extension of the pioneer work of the Yardbirds, marked the first truly successful attempt at applying the lessons of free jazz to rock, and threw a fierce light towards the future and further definitions in the new vocabulary by people like Beefheart and the Tony Williams Lifetime (dig especially the similarity between "Ray"'s jam and "Right On" on the Lifetime's second album). It also led Velvet fans to expect a consistent pattern of fiendishly intricate experiments, even though the band didn't want to limit and type themselves as part of the avant-garde any more than they expected to fixate themselves lyrically in the worlds of darkness conjured by the first album and much of the second. Partly because they knew that they had many more stories to tell, and partly in response to an audience as unprepared for futuristic music as for nightworld lyrics, the Velvets left White Light/White Heat to stand for the time being as their ultimate statement in the new musical vocabulary of electronic abstraction.

Lou reminisces and shrugs: "Sister Ray's jam came about right there in the studio--we didn't use any splices or anything. I had been listening to a lot of Cecil Taylor and Ornette Coleman, and wanted to get something like that with a rock 'n' roll feeling. And I think we were successful, but I also think

we carried that about as far as we could, for our abilities as a band that was basically rock 'n' roll. Later we continued to play that kind of music, and I was really experimenting a lot with guitar, but most of the audiences in the clubs just weren't receptive to it at all."

But it wasn't only the outer-edge forays on Side Two which made White Light/White Heat a classic--each of the other songs was a solidly individualistic entity of its own, as distinct from the songs around it as from the dim gropings so many other groups were into at the time. The title track had a steaming piano riff and marvellous little rhymes that clicked through the funk with a perfect loose precision ("Watch that side, watch that side/Doncha know gon' be dead on arrival," or "Ohh, sputter butter, ev'body gone gon' see the mother"), and "Lady Godiva's Operation" injected a coarse urban humor into the grandeur of a Byrds-like guitar riff, "turning on the machines that--" (enter Lou's streetkid cackle to finish the line begun in rather effete tones by John Cale's cultured voice): "--sweetly pump air!"

Perhaps the most interesting piece was "The Gift." Lots of oppressively banal "stories" and spoken passages have clogged LP grooves in the last few years, but only "The Gift" remains to stand as a successful fusion of literature and programmed rhythm--despite the contrived black humor of the denouement, the total work is witty, well-written and just realistic enough to be right on target. As Lou says today: "I wrote 'The Gift' while I was in college. I used to write lots of short stories, especially humorous pieces like that. So one night Cale and I were sitting around and he said, 'Let's put one of those stories to music.' So we did and I still wasn't sure about it--I'm never sure about things I write for about two weeks--but I guess it turned out really good." If the rest of them are as good as he guessed this one to be, we CAN ONLY HOPE ~~he'll do well to try~~ we find some publishers.

Just how many leagues ahead of predictability the Velvets are was brought home stunningly in their third album, as the simplicity and eloquence of such little masterpieces as "Candy Says," "Some Kinda Love" and "I'm Set Free" permeated our consciousness as surely as the vast baroque architecture and deliberately placed sonic smog of "Sister Ray." But the sense of universality was new. Anybody should be able to see both themselves and others they've known in songs like "Candy Says," as Lou points out: "I've gotten to where I like 'pretty' stuff better (than drive and distortion), because you can be more subtle, really say something and sort of soothe, which is what a lot of people seem to need right now. Like I think if you came in after a really hard day at work and played that third album, it might really do you good. A calmative, some people might even call it muzak, but I think it can function on both that and the intellectual or artistic levels at the same time. Like when I wrote 'Jesus,' I said: 'My god, a hymn!,' and 'Candy Says,' which is probably the best song I've written, which describes a sort of person who's special except that I think all of us have been through that in a way--young, confused, with the feeling that other people, or older people, know something you don't. And those and things like 'Sunday Morning' have always been my favorite Velvet Underground songs; I wish somebody else somewhere would record them."

"That's the Story of My Life" is really the story of the paradoxical mood of our times boiled into a couple of short sentences. What other band would answer "the difference between wrong and right" with "both those words are dead," and finish without drawing a moral conclusion? The Velvets' music, far from the pretentious dogma so rampant since 1967, solicits both intellectual involvement and an independent judgment.

Patti Smith and Robert Mapplethorpe, 1971. Photograph: Gerard Malanga.

VELVET LEGACY

In August 1970, with the departure of Lou Reed, the end of the Velvet Underground was greeted with general indifference. Two years later, however, the name was nevertheless on everyone's lips. Reclaimed by David Bowie, the group's influence would not stop growing. Bootleg records, unpublished titles, and a generalized mea culpa of the press gradually elevate the Velvet Underground and its creators to the skies. The spirit and catalyst of New York rock quietly conquers the planet, as a posthumous revenge. Far from being limited to music, the Velvet waves pollinate the visual arts, photography, film, and fashion and continue to inspire pop culture and rock.

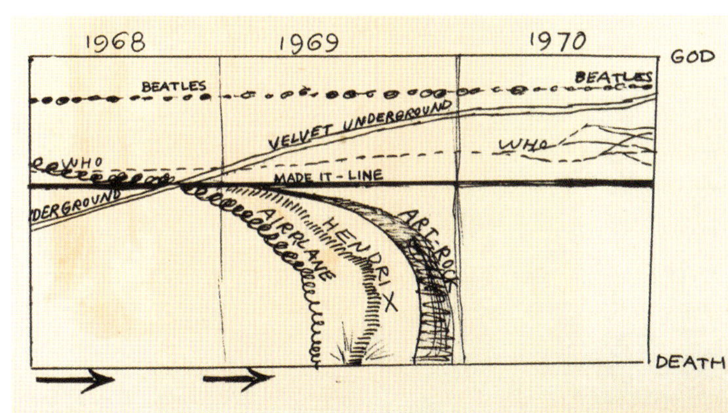

Hand-drawn graph by Jonathan Richman comparing the Velvet Underground to other bands. Martha & Sterling Morrison's scrapbook.

THE VELVET REVOLUTION ROCKS ON

Simmy Richman

The Independent, October 14th, 2012.

What is the most influential album of all time? Music lovers can (and do) argue about such things at length, but few would deny the first Velvet Underground album its right to be up there. It was number one when another British newspaper published its "50 albums that changed music" list back in 2006. The rock critic Lester Bangs stated that "Modern music starts with the Velvets," and Brian Eno told an interviewer in 1984: "I was talking to Lou Reed the other day and he said that the first Velvet Underground record sold 30,000 in the first five years. I think everyone who bought one of those 30,000 copies started a band." The record is now, unbelievably, 45 years old, but its influence shows no sign of waning. To celebrate this milestone, a six-CD boxset with all the trimmings is just about to be released–so now seems as good a time as any to ask what it is about the record that continues to fascinate and enthrall.

The simple answer is to listen to the album. For the long answer you have to go back to 1965. In the UK, The Beatles are just hitting their sweet spot with pop ditties such as "Yesterday" and "Ticket to Ride". In New York, meanwhile, a literature student turned songwriter named Lou Reed had recently met an avant-garde musician named John Cale and the pair started writing songs together. Two of these songs would go on to appear on their seminal debut: one, "Heroin", requiring no explanation (sample lyric: "It's my wife and it's my life"), and the other, "Venus in Furs", about sadomasochism. Talk about out of step with the times.

And then they met the artist Andy Warhol and things got really weird. In 1966 Warhol made the group, now including guitarist Sterling Morrison and drummer Mo Tucker, the house band for his multimedia events, the Exploding Plastic Inevitable. Providing drone-heavy jams to accompany Warhol's film, light, and dance shows, the Velvet Underground found the perfect backdrop to their unholy symphonies, as well as a sugar daddy to finance and indulge their experimentation.

And the first, ahem, fruit of that relationship was that 1967 debut LP. With three tracks sung by German Warhol muse turned chanteuse Nico, it has become known as "the banana album," thanks to Warhol's peelable cover artwork bearing only the instruction to "Peel slowly and see" and the artist's signature (because who needs anything as mainstream as, like, the band's name, man?). The album duly flopped: if Cale and Reed and co. had been out of step in 1965, by the time the album was released, it was the summer of peace, love, and flower power, a touchy-feely world far away from the Velvets' dirty, dirgy melange of hard drugs and decadent sex.

But over the following decades, word of that debut would pass from person to person, establishing it as the underground music scene's worst kept secret. It did no harm to the cause that Lou Reed's David Bowie-produced solo single "Walk on the Wild Side" became a bona fide hit in 1972. Or that any number of new wave bands found themselves turning to the band's back catalogue for cult cover versions. Suddenly, a band that had lasted only a couple of years in

PLEASE KiLL ME

the UNCENSORED ORAL HISTORY *of* PUNK

by Legs McNeil *and* Gillian McCain

Prologue

■ All Tomorrow's Parties 1965–1968

LOU REED: All by myself. No one to talk to. Come over here so I can talk to you . . .

We were playing together a long time ago, in a thirty-dollar-a-month apartment and we really didn't have any money, and we used to eat oatmeal all day and all night and give blood, among other things, or pose for these nickel or fifteen cent tabloids they had every week. And when I posed for them, my picture came out and it said I was a sex maniac killer that had killed fourteen children and tape-recorded it and played it in a barn in Kansas at midnight. And when John Cale's picture came out in the paper, it said he killed his lover because his lover was going to marry his sister, and he didn't want his sister to marry a fag.

STERLING MORRISON: Lou Reed's parents hated the fact that Lou was making music and hanging around with undesirables. I was always afraid of Lou's parents—the only dealings I'd had with them was that there was this constant threat of them seizing Lou and having him thrown in the nuthouse. That was always over our heads. Every time Lou got hepatitis his parents were waiting to seize him and lock him up.

JOHN CALE: That's where all Lou's best work came from. His mother was some sort of ex-beauty queen and I think his father was a wealthy accountant. Anyway, they put him in a hospital where he received shock treatment as a kid. Apparently he was at Syracuse University and was given this compulsory choice to either do gym or the Reserve Officers Training Corps. He claimed he couldn't do gym because he'd break his neck and when he did ROTC he threatened to kill the instructor. Then he put his fist through a window or something, and so he was put in a mental hospital. I don't know the full story. Every time Lou told me about it he'd change it slightly.

LOU REED: They put the thing down your throat so you don't swallow your tongue, and they put electrodes on your head. That's what was

... 3

LOU REED: Estoy solo. Sin nadie con quien hablar. Acércate, quiero hablar contigo...

Llevábamos mucho tiempo tocando juntos, en un piso de 30 dólares al mes, y no teníamos ni un pavo. Comíamos copos de avena de día y de noche, y donábamos sangre, entre otras cosas, o posábamos para aquellos tabloides semanales que costaban diez o quince centavos. Una vez publicaron mi foto, y el texto decía que yo era un maníaco sexual de Kansas que había asesinado a catorce niños, lo había grabado todo, y escuchaba la cinta a medianoche dentro de un granero. El texto que acompañaba a la foto de John Cale decía que había matado a su amante porque éste iba a casarse con su hermana, y él no quería que su hermana se casara con un maricón.

STERLING MORRISON: Los padres de Lou Reed detestaban que Lou hiciese música, que se relacionase con aquellos indeseables. Yo les tenía pánico. Sobre nuestras cabezas pendía siempre la amenaza de que los padres de Lou vinieran a buscarlo y lo metieran en el manicomio. Cada vez que Lou cogía una hepatitis, sus padres estaban al acecho para internarlo.

JOHN CALE: De ahí procede lo mejor de la obra de Lou. Su madre había ganado algún concurso de belleza en su juventud, y creo que su padre era un contable bastante rico. Parece ser que, de niño, internaron a Lou en un hospital, donde recibió tratamiento de shock. Después, en la universidad de Syracuse, le obligaron a escoger entre la gimnasia o entrar en los Cuerpos de Entrenamiento de Oficiales en Reserva. Se negó a hacer gimnasia porque no quería romperse el cuello, y al entrar en los CEOR amenazó con matar al instructor. Más adelante, rompió una ventana de un puñetazo, y lo internaron en un hospital psiquiátrico. No conozco la historia completa. Cada vez que Lou me la contaba, la cambiaba ligeramente.

LOU REED: Te meten esa cosa por la garganta para que no te muerdas la lengua, y te ponen electrodos en la cabeza. Es lo que recomendaban por aquel entonces en el condado de Rockland para reprimir los sentimientos homosexuales. En realidad, pierdes la memoria y te conviertes en un vegetal. No puedes leer un libro, porque cuando llegas a la página diecisiete tienes que volver a la página uno.

59

Легс Макнил

Джиллиан Маккейн

«ПРОШУ, УБЕЙ МЕНЯ!»

«Прошу, убей меня!» явно стоит в ряду величайших рок-н-ролльных книг всех времен и народов.

The New York Times

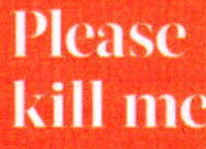

Пролог

■ Все будущие вечеринки[1] 1965–1968

Лу Рид: ...Все время один. Не с кем словом перекинуться. Давайте, приходите, поболтаем...

Играть вместе мы начали очень давно, еще когда снимали квартиру за тридцатник в месяц. С деньгами в то время была полная засада, мы питались исключительно овсянкой, а зарабатывали тем, что сдавали кровь или фотографировались для всяких дешевых газеток, для местной прессы. Как-то у них вышла статья с моей фотографией, они написали, что я сексуальный маньяк-убийца, убил четырнадцать детей, заснял это дело на пленку и показал ее в сарае в Канзасе в полночь. А под снимком Джона Кейла написали, что он убил своего любовника за то, что этот самый любовник хотел жениться на Джоновой сестре, а он не хотел, чтобы сестренка вышла замуж за педика.

Стерлинг Моррисон: Предки Лу Рида терпеть не могли то, что он занимается музыкой и шляется с какими-то придурками. Лично я боялся родителей Лу: они славились тем, что в любой момент могли его отловить и отправить в дурку. Над нами всегда висел этот дамоклов меч. Каждый раз, когда Лу заболевал гепатитом, его родители пытались поймать его и упечь в психушку.

Джон Кейл: Так и рождались лучшие работы Лу. Его мать была бывшей королевой красоты, а отец – кажется, преуспевающим бухгалтером. В любом случае, они уложили его в больницу, где ему, тогда еще ребенку, проводили шоковую терапию. Вроде бы он учился в университете в Сиракузах и ему надо было пройти один из курсов по выбору: гимнастику или военную подготовку. Он заявил, что не пойдет на гимнастику, потому что сломает там шею. Так что он пошел на военку и попы-

[1] «All Tomorrow's Parties» – название песни The Velvet Underground.

DEN OCENSURERADE HISTORIEN OM PUNKEN

PLEASE KILL ME

LEGS McNEIL OCH GILLIAN McCAIN

Prolog

All Tomorrow's Parties 1965–1968

LOU REED: Alldeles ensam. Ingen att prata med. Kom hit så får jag snacka med dig ...

När vi började spela ihop så hade vi inga pengar och bodde i en lägenhet som kostade trettio dollar i månaden. Vi åt gröt morgon, middag, kväll och livnärde oss på att ge blod och ställa upp på bilder i billiga veckotidningar av det snaskigare slaget. När bilden på mig publicerades stod det att jag var en galen våldtäktsman och mördare och att jag hade dödat 14 barn, bandat alltihop och sedan spelade upp det i en lada i Kansas om nätterna. När John Cale var med stod det att han hade dödat sin älskare för att han ville gifta sig med Cales syster och han ville inte att hon skulle gifta sig med en bög.

STERLING MORRISON: Lou Reeds föräldrar gillade inte att han höll på med musik och hängde med slödder som oss. Jag var skraj för dem trots att det enda jag såg eller hörde av dem var deras ständiga hot om att låta omhänderta Lou och spärra in honom på dårhus. Vi hade det hängande över våra huvuden. Varje gång Lou fick gulsot så ville de låsa in honom.

JOHN CALE: Det var därifrån Lou fick inspiration till sina bästa låtar. Hans mamma hade varit någon slags skönhetsdrottning och jag tror att hans far var förmögen revisor. De satte honom på sjukhus när han var bara barnet. Där gav de honom elchockbehandling. Tydligen var det så att när han läste på Syracuse University var man tvungen att

11

Please kill me

Punkowa historia punka

LEGS McNEIL

GILLIAN McCAIN

PROLOG

Wszystkie bale jutra 1965–1968

LOU REED Sam jak palec. Nie ma do kogo gęby otworzyć. Chodź, to sobie pogadamy… Graliśmy razem dawno temu, w mieszkaniu za trzydzieści dolarów miesięcznie, i naprawdę nie mieliśmy żadnej kasy, dniami i nocami żarliśmy tylko płatki owsiane, oddawaliśmy krew i takie tam albo pozowaliśmy do zdjęć, które później ukazywały się w brukowych tygodnikach po piętnaście centów. No i wychodził kolejny numer, a w nim moja fotka podpisana: „Maniak seksualny, który zamordował czternaścioro dzieci i nagrał to wszystko na taśmę, a potem puszczał ją sobie o północy w stodole w Kansas". Albo zdjęcie Johna Cale'a z podpisem: „Zabił swojego kochanka, który miał się ożenić z jego siostrą, bo nie chciał, żeby siostra wyszła za pedała".

STERLING MORRISON Rodzice Lou Reeda nie znosili tego, że Lou robił muzykę i zadawał się z nieciekawymi typami. Zawsze bałem się rodziców Lou – wszelkie kontakty, jakie z nimi miałem, wiązały się z ciągłą obawą, że go złapią i wpakują do wariatkowa. Ta groźba stale wisiała nad naszymi głowami. Za każdym razem, gdy Lou dostawał zapalenia wątroby, rodzice tylko czekali, żeby go dopaść i zamknąć.

JOHN CALE Z tego właśnie brały się najlepsze rzeczy, jakie zrobił Lou. Jego ojciec był, jak mi się wydaje, bogatym księgowym,

[11]

PROLOG

ALL TOMORROW'S PARTIES
1965–1968

Lou Reed: Ich bin ganz allein. Niemand da zum Reden. Komm rüber, damit ich mit euch reden kann.

Wir haben vor Urzeiten in einem total verdreckten Apartment, das nur dreißig Dollar Miete im Monat kostete, Musik gemacht und hatten wirklich überhaupt kein Geld. Es gab normalerweise mittags, morgens und abends Haferflocken, und wir haben Blut gespendet oder für diese wöchentlich erscheinenden Fünfzehn-Cent-Boulevardheftchen als Fotomodelle gearbeitet. Ich habe dann für sie posiert, und die Bildunterschrift unter meinem Foto besagte, dass ich ein Sexbesessener und Triebtäter sei, der vierzehn Kinder umgebracht und davon einen Film gedreht habe, der um Mitternacht in einer Scheune in Kansas City gezeigt wurde. Und als ein Bild von John Cale in der Zeitung erschien, hieß es, er hätte seinen Liebhaber gekillt, weil der seine Schwester heiraten wollte, so habe er verhindert, dass seine Schwester eine Schwuchtel ehelicht.

Sterling Morrison: Lou Reeds Eltern hassten es, dass Lou Musik machte und sich mit zwielichtigen Typen rumtrieb. Ich hatte ständig Angst vor Lous Eltern – aber eigentlich hatte ich immer nur dann mit ihnen zu tun, wenn sie wieder einmal damit drohten, dass sie sich Lou schnappen wollten, um ihn in die Irrenanstalt einzuweisen. Das schwebte ständig über unseren Köpfen. Jedes Mal, wenn Lou eine Hepatitis bekam, warteten seine Eltern schon darauf, ihn zu schnappen, damit sie ihn einsperren konnten.

John Cale: Aus dieser Zeit stammten die besten Arbeiten von Lou. Seine Mutter war so etwas wie eine Exschönheitskönigin, und sein Vater war, glaube ich, ein ziemlich reicher Wirtschaftsprüfer. Wie dem auch sei, jedenfalls steckten sie

16

LOU REED : Tout seul. Personne à qui parler. Viens un peu par là que je te cause…

On jouait ensemble il y a des années, dans un appartement à trente dollars par mois, on avait vraiment pas un rond, on bouffait des flocons d'avoine matin et soir et on faisait des dons du sang pour se faire offrir un petit déj', entre autres, ou encore on posait pour des tabloïds hebdomadaires bas de gamme. Quand ma photo est parue, la légende disait que j'étais un maniaque sexuel qui avait tué quatorze enfants et filmé les meurtres pour les projeter dans une grange du Kansas à minuit. Et quand ç'a été le tour de John Cale, la légende disait qu'il avait tué son amant parce que celui-ci était sur le point de se marier avec sa sœur, et qu'il ne voulait pas que sa sœur épouse un pédé.

STERLING MORRISON : Les parents de Lou Reed ne supportaient pas qu'il fasse de la musique et qu'il traîne avec des indésirables. J'avais tout le temps peur de ses parents – la seule relation que j'aie eue avec eux, c'était cette menace constante qu'ils chopent Lou pour l'envoyer chez les dingues. C'était une véritable épée de Damoclès. Chaque fois que Lou attrapait une hépatite, ils se précipitaient pour lui mettre la main dessus et l'enfermer.

JOHN CALE : C'est de là que Lou a tiré le meilleur de son œuvre. Sa mère était une espèce d'ancienne reine de beauté et il me semble que son père était un comptable fortuné. Ce qui est sûr, c'est qu'ils l'ont mis dans un hôpital où il a reçu des électrochocs quand il était gamin. Apparemment, il était à l'université de Syracuse, et on l'a forcé à choisir entre faire de la gym ou entrer dans le Corps d'entraînement des officiers de réserve. Il a refusé de faire de la gym sous prétexte qu'il risquerait de se casser le cou, et, quand il a intégré le bataillon d'entraînement, il a menacé de mort le sergent instructeur. Puis il a explosé une fenêtre ou une

LE VELVET UNDERGROUND, AVEC ANDY WARHOL, ARI, GERARD MALANGA ET MARY WORONOV DANS LA FACTORY EN 1966 (PHOTO : BILLY NAME, © BILLYNAME/OVOWORKS, NYC)

PROLOGUE | 15

Prologo: 1965-1968

All Tomorrow's Parties
(Velvet Underground & Nico – album omonimo)

Lou Reed: Sempre da solo. Nessuno a cui parlare. Vieni qui, così ti posso parlare…

Suonavamo insieme, molto tempo fa. Vivevamo in un appartamento da trenta dollari al mese e non avevamo un soldo. Mangiavamo focacce d'avena mattina e sera e facevamo di tutto, tipo vendere il sangue e roba simile, oppure posavamo per quei settimanali spazzatura da dieci centesimi. Una volta uscì un articolo con la mia foto. Dicevano che ero un maniaco sessuale omicida che aveva ucciso quattordici bambini. Dicevano che avevo registrato tutto e che riascoltavo il nastro in un fienile del Kansas a mezzanotte. Quando uscì la foto di John Cale, dissero che aveva ucciso il suo amante perché quello voleva sposare sua sorella e lui non voleva che sua sorella sposasse un finocchio.

Sterling Morrison: I genitori di Lou Reed odiavano il fatto che Lou facesse il musicista e che frequentasse gente indesiderabile. Ho sempre avuto paura dei genitori di Lou – ciò che mi spaventava era che minacciavano sempre di impacchettare Lou e farlo sbattere in manicomio. Era come una spada di Damocle sulla nostra testa. Ogni volta che Lou si beccava l'epatite i suoi genitori erano pronti a impacchettarlo e farlo rinchiudere.

John Cale: Le cose migliori di Lou vengono tutte da lì. Sua madre era una specie di ex reginetta di bellezza e credo che suo padre fosse un contabile piuttosto benestante. A ogni modo, da ragazzino lo misero in ospedale e gli fecero fare l'elettroshock. Pare che poi, ai tempi della Syracuse University, lo avessero costretto a scegliere tra l'andare in palestra o nei Corpi di Adde-

21

MATE-ME POR FAVOR
(PLEASE KILL ME)
A HISTÓRIA SEM CENSURA DO PUNK
POR LEGS MCNEIL & GILLIAN MCCAIN
L&PM

PRÓLOGO

Todas as festas de amanhã
1965-1968

Lou Reed: Estou completamente sozinho. Ninguém pra conversar. Dá uma chegada aqui, daí posso falar com você...

Há um tempão a gente tocava junto num apartamento de trinta dólares por mês e não tinha grana pra nada; comia mingau de aveia todo o dia e vendia sangue, entre outras coisas, ou posava praqueles tabloides semanais baratos. Quando posei pra eles, minha foto saiu dizendo que eu era um maníaco sexual assassino que tinha matado quatorze crianças e gravado tudo, e que rodava aquelas fitas num celeiro no Kansas à meia-noite. E quando a foto de John Cale saiu no tabloide, dizia que ele tinha matado o amante porque o cara ia casar com a irmã dele, e ele não queria ver a irmã casada com um veado.

Sterling Morrison: Os pais de Lou Reed odiavam o fato de ele estar fazendo música e andando por aí com indesejáveis. Eu vivia com medo dos pais de Lou – o único envolvimento que eu tinha com eles era a ameaça permanente de eles agarrarem Lou e jogarem-no num manicômio. Essa ameaça pairava sempre sobre nossas cabeças. Toda vez que Lou pegava hepatite os pais dele estavam à espreita pra agarrá-lo e trancafiá-lo.

John Cale: O melhor do trabalho de Lou veio todo daí. A mãe dele era aquele tipo de ex-rainha de concurso de beleza, e acho que o pai era um contador endinheirado. De qualquer modo, quando ele era garoto, os pais o puseram num hospital onde ele passou por um tratamento com choque elétrico. Parece que ele estava na Universidade de Siracuse e teve que fazer uma escolha compulsória entre ginástica ou as Corporações de Treinamento dos Oficiais de Reserva. Ele alegou que não podia fazer ginástica porque quebraria o pescoço e, quando foi pra corporação, ameaçou matar o instrutor. Então ele deu um soco numa janela ou coisa parecida e aí foi posto num hospital pra doentes mentais. Não sei a história toda. Toda vez que Lou me conta, ele muda alguma coisinha.

19

PRÓLOGO

Todas as festas de amanhã
1965-1968

Lou Reed: Estou completamente sozinho. Ninguém pra conversar. Dá uma chegada aqui, daí posso falar com você...

Há um tempão a gente tocava junto num apartamento de trinta dólares por mês e não tinha grana pra nada; comia mingau de aveia todo o dia e vendia sangue, entre outras coisas, ou posava praqueles tablóides semanais baratos. Quando posei pra eles, minha foto saiu dizendo que eu era um maníaco sexual assassino que tinha matado quatorze crianças e gravado tudo, e que rodava aquelas fitas num celeiro no Kansas à meia-noite. E quando a foto de John Cale saiu no tablóide, dizia que ele tinha matado o amante porque o cara ia casar com a irmã dele, e ele não queria ver a irmã casada com um veado.

Sterling Morrison: Os pais de Lou Reed odiavam o fato de ele estar fazendo música e andando por aí com indesejáveis. Eu vivia com medo dos pais de Lou – o único envolvimento que eu tinha com eles era a ameaça permanente de eles agarrarem Lou e jogarem-no num manicômio. Essa ameaça pairava sempre sobre nossas cabeças. Toda vez que Lou pegava hepatite os pais dele estavam à espreita pra agarrá-lo e trancafiá-lo.

John Cale: O melhor do trabalho de Lou veio todo daí. A mãe dele era aquele tipo de ex-rainha de concurso de beleza, e acho que o pai era um contador endinheirado. De qualquer modo, quando ele era garoto, os pais o puseram num hospital onde ele passou por um tratamento com choque elétrico. Parece que ele estava na Universidade de Siracuse e teve que fazer uma escolha compulsória entre ginástica ou as Corporações de Treinamento dos Oficiais de Reserva. Ele alegou que não podia fazer ginástica porque quebraria o pescoço e, quando

13

Prologi

ALL TOMORROW'S PARTIES
1965–1968

LOU REED: Yksikseni tässä istuskelen. Ei ketään, jolle jorista. Tulepas tänne, niin rupatellaan...

Kauan sitten me soiteltiin kimpassa kolmekymmentä dollaria kuussa maksavassa huoneistossa, eikä meillä koskaan ollut latin latia. Me elettiin kaurapuurolla ja tienattiin rahaa esimerkiksi luovuttamalla verta tai poseeraamalla kerran viikossa ilmestyviin, viisi tai kymmenen senttiä maksavien juorulehtien valokuviin. Kerran erään tuollaisen valokuvan kuvatekstissä ilmoitti meikäläisen olevan seksihullu murhaaja, joka oli tappanut neljätoista lasta, nauhoittanut koko hoidon kasettimankalla ja diggaillut nauhaa keskiyöllä jossain kansasilaisessa ladossa. Ja kun John Calen kuva painettiin lehteen, siinä kerrottiin sen tappaneen poikaystävänsä, koska poikaystävä oli menossa naimisiin sen siskon kanssa eikä se halunnut siskonsa naivan homoa.

STERLING MORRISON: Lou Reedin vanhemmat eivät ollenkaan pitäneet siitä, että Lou teki musaa ja pyöri epämääräisissä porukoissa. Henkilökohtaisesti pelkäsin koko ajan, että ne ottavat sen kiinni ja passittavat hourulaan. Se uhka leijui jatkuvasti ilmassa. Joka kerta kun Lou sai hepatiitin, sen mutsi ja faija väijyivät sitä, jotta olisivat voineet napata sen kiinni ja lyödä rautoihin.

JOHN CALE: Siitä Loun parhaat jutut syntyivätkin. Sen äiti oli joku entinen missi ja isä muistaakseni hyvin toimeentuleva kirjanpitäjä. Oli miten oli, ne lähettivät Loun lapsena johonkin sairaalaan, jossa sille annettiin sähköshokkeja. Loun opiskellessa Syracusen yliopistossa sille ilmeisesti annettiin ukaasi: joko alat urheilla tai lähdet upseerikouluun. Lou ilmoitti, ettei se voi urheilla, koska siinä menisi niskat nurin, ja upseerikoulussa se uhkasi tappaa kouluttajakersanttinsa. Sitten se tempaisi nyrkkinsä ik-

its original line-up became a name to drop and a force to be reckoned with.

The band hit these ears around the time of punk rock. I was about 13 and mainly listening to 10cc and The Beatles. Here was a dark glimpse into a beatnik, Bohemian counterculture then unavailable to a middle-class Jewish kid from northwest London. Songs could be sweet and short or stretch into feedback jams lasting seven minutes. On that first album alone, the Velvets invented—or at the very least inspired—art rock, punk, garage, grunge, shoegaze, goth, indie, and any other alternative music you care to mention. It didn't matter that the music was made before my time. The debut album was and still is ahead of everyone's time.

If it is name-checked less these days, that's only because its influence has become a given: in the same way that you don't need to ask a reggae musician if they've heard Bob Marley or a singer-songwriter if they've listened to Nick Drake.

But make no mistake, its power is undimmed. So, to mark 45 years of spreading its corrupting magic and mayhem, we recall the impact of "the banana album" on musicians from down the decades.

UNDER THE INFLUENCE

The 1970s

"If the Velvet Underground had a protégé," said the group's guitarist Sterling Morrison, "it would be Jonathan Richman." Latterly known for sweet acoustic ditties, the Boston-born musician began his career as frontman of garage band the Modern Lovers and was directly inspired by the ragged energy of the Velvet Underground. Indeed, the fan/fanatic saw the group play 80 times, slept on their manager's couch when he first moved to New York, and wrote an article titled "New York Art and the Velvet Underground" for a Boston magazine as early as 1967. By the late 1970s, his band's "Sister Ray"-inspired single "Roadrunner" had become an unlikely top-20 hit in the UK in the wake of the new wave phenomenon. Richman would later top that with a song called "Velvet Underground". The lyrics speak for themselves: "Both guitars got the fuzz tone on/ The drummer's standing upright pounding along/ A howl, a tone, a feedback whine/ Biker boys meet the college kind/ How in the world were they making that sound?/ Velvet Underground."

1980s

Before Chrissie Hynde was a rock star, she was a writer for the *NME* who had landed in London from Akron, Ohio, in 1973 with three records in her possession: the first two Velvet albums and Iggy Pop's *Raw Power*. She wrote of the band: "Takes me right back to the teenage years of my virginal innocence; the evening I spent in some dingy hall, eyes fixed on the cat in the striped T-shirt and wraparound shades, those songs made my eyes water like I was chewing on a wad of aluminum foil, me hoping I could score some dope after the show; me wishing I could be like them."

1990s

It goes without saying that the British "shoegaze" phenomenon of the early 1990s could not have existed without the Velvet Underground, indebted as it was to the Velvets' love of distortion and feedback. And at the heart of that scene were Slowdive, a band fronted by Neil Halstead, who went on to form Mojave 3 as well as being a solo artist. Halstead says: "I remember seeing the name a lot in *Melody Maker* when I was 15. I was a big Jesus and Mary Chain fan and I remember hearing "Sunday Morning" and thinking it didn't sound much like the Mary Chain. After that I was sucked into the record. It still sounds as exotic and dark and beautiful and cool to me now as it did then. The further I got into it, the more I realized that not only did the Mary Chain owe the Velvets a debt, but so did every other 'alternative' band I was listening to at that point."

2000s

While the band's influence was everywhere by now, The Strokes' first album, the 2001 release, *Is This It*, probably comes as close to any record since the banana album to directly capture that balance between passionate authority and cool detachment. In 2004, The Strokes' singer Julian Casablancas told *Rolling Stone*: "The Velvet Underground were way ahead of their time. And their music was weird. But it also made so much sense to me. I couldn't believe this wasn't the most popular music ever made. In the beginning, The Strokes definitely drew from the vibe of the Velvets."

Now

Freddie Cowan is the guitarist of The Vaccines. He says: "I remember hearing 'All Tomorrow's Parties' when I must have been about 13 and Tom [his older brother and the keyboardist for The Horrors] was about 15. It was a rite of passage to discuss the importance of it and beyond that, it was the best intro to a song I'd ever heard. One of that first album's biggest advantages is that Andy Warhol 'produced' it and he knew nothing technically about music. Not obeying the rules made for a sound that's still unique and those ideas are still being used. The whole thing is this aggressive, deadpan perfection. It is adult rock 'n' roll; brutal and not dumbed down. The influence remains because of the whole approach and attitude. If you write about what you know and do things as if you really fucking believe it, you can't go wrong."

FROM THE VELVET UNDERGROUND TO THE STROKES

Julian Casablancas

Julian Fernando Casablancas is the lead singer for The Strokes.
Excerpt from "The Velvet Underground" by Julian Casablancas, which appeared in the *Rolling Stone* 100 Greatest Artists in 2004.

When you listen to a classic-rock station today, why don't they play the Velvet Underground? Why is it always Boston and Led Zeppelin? And why are the Rolling Stones so much more popular than the Velvets? OK, I understand why the Stones are more popular. But there is also a part of me that has always felt that it should have been the other way around. The Velvet Underground were way ahead of their time. And their music was weird. But it also made so much sense to me. I couldn't believe this wasn't the most popular music ever made.

Listening to those four studio albums now is like reading a good book that takes place in a distant time. When I hear *The Velvet Underground and Nico* or *Loaded*, I feel like I'm in Andy Warhol's Factory in the 1960s or hanging out at Max's Kansas City. The way Lou Reed wrote and sang about drugs and sex, about the people around him—it was so matter-of-fact. I believed every word of "Heroin." Reed could be romantic in the way he portrayed these crazy situations, but he was also intensely real. It was poetry and journalism.

A lot of people associate the Velvets with feedback and noise. *White Light/White Heat* is the kind of record you have to be in the mood for. You have to be in a shitty bar, in a really shitty mood. But the Velvets created some very beautiful music, too: "Sunday Morning," with John Cale's viola; "Candy Says"; "All Tomorrow's Parties"—I can't imagine that song without Nico singing it, although I thought Maureen Tucker had a cool voice, as well as being a really cool drummer. She had a femininity. I thought she sounded hotter than Nico.

In the beginning, the Strokes definitely drew from the vibe of the Velvets. I listened to *Loaded* all the time when we started the band, while I was writing my first songs. For four solid months, it was just *Loaded* and this Beach Boys greatest-hits record, *Made in the U.S.A.* A lot of our guitar tones are based on what Reed and Sterling Morrison did. I honestly wish we could have copied them more. We didn't come close enough. But that was cool, because it became more of our own thing. Which is something else I got from the Velvets. They taught me just to be myself.

the stooges

FADE YO LA TENGO

DINOSAUR Jr
GREEN MIND

PSYCHIC TV
DREAMS LESS SWEET
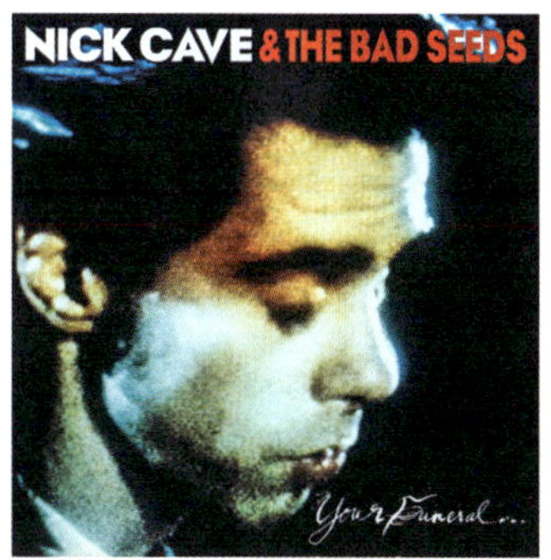
NICK CAVE & THE BAD SEEDS
Your Funeral...

ANIMAL COLLECTIVE
PAINTING WITH

Patti Smith Horses

CAN I KICK IT?
A TRIBE CALLED QUEST

mogwai
young team
富士銀行
富士銀行

Radio City Big Star

The MODERN LOVERS

lcd soundsystem

TELEVISION
MARQUEE MOON

Suicide

Brian Eno
Before and after Science

bad brains
attitude
THE ROIR SESSIONS

THE KILLS
NO WOW

CLOCK DVA
BREAKDOWN
REMIX
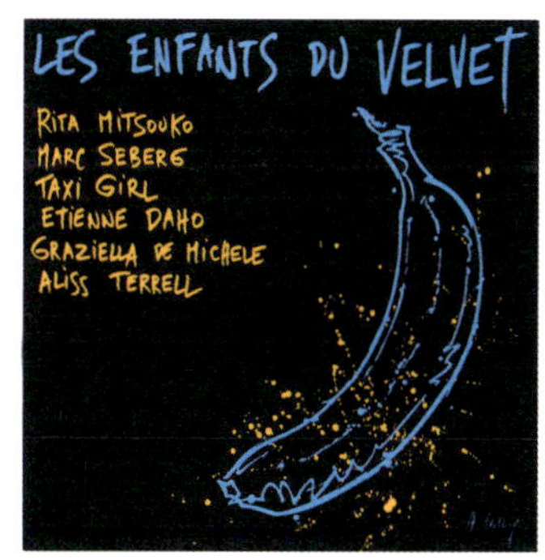
LES ENFANTS DU VELVET
RITA MITSOUKO
MARC SEBERG
TAXI GIRL
ETIENNE DAHO
GRAZIELLA DE MICHELE
ALISS TERRELL

BANNED IN CZECHOSLOVAKIA
UNDERGROUND PRAHA
musical activism under communism, 1975–90

luna
luna
lunapark

NEU!

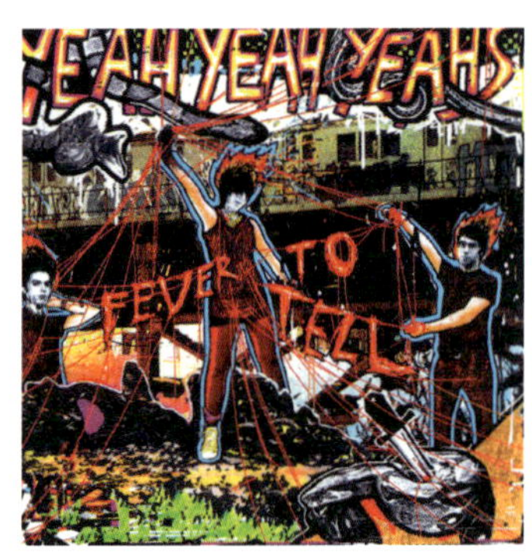
YEAH YEAH YEAHS
FEVER TO TELL

RICHARD HELL
&THE VOIDOIDS
BLANK
GENERATION

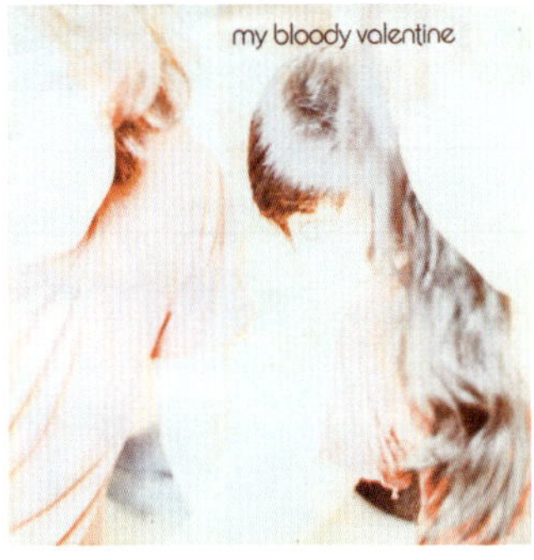
my bloody valentine

SPACEMEN 3
The Perfect Prescription

the feelies

HERE SHE COMES NOW
NIRVANA

RAMONES

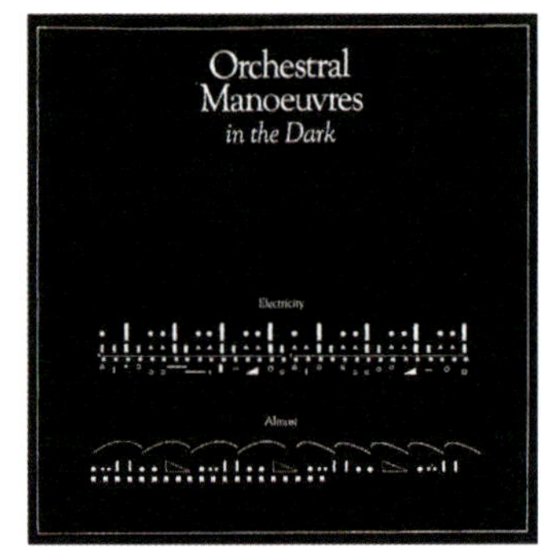
Orchestral
Manoeuvres
in the Dark

AUTOMATIC FOR THE PEOPLE
R.E.M.

New York Dolls

TALKING HEADS:77

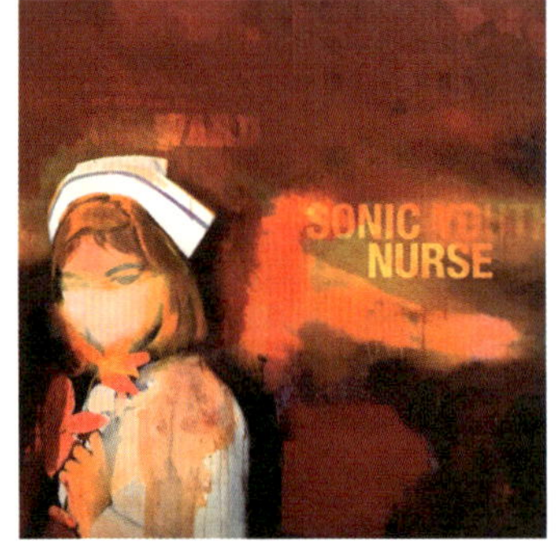
NURSE

Stereo
the dream
syndicate
the days
of wine
and roses

THE RAVEONETTES IN AND OUT OF CONTROL

Andy Warhol

ECHO
and the
BUNNYMEN

PSYCHO
CANDY
PSYCHO
CANDY
THE JESUS AND MARY CHAIN

Above: Arthur Kane and David Johansen of the New York Dolls on stage at Mercer Arts Center, NYC. December 31, 1972. Photograph: Bob Gruen.

Middle: Danny Fields, Arturo Vega, Joey Ramone, David Johansen, and friends outside of CBGB, NYC. August 1977. Photograph: Bob Gruen.

Below: The Ramones May 19, 1977 at Eric's Club on Mathew Street, Liverpool. Photograph: Ian Dickson.

NOTHING COMPARES TO VU

Christian Fevret witnessed the historic reunion of the Velvet Underground in Paris in 1990. This was the first time that the original four members had played together since 1968.

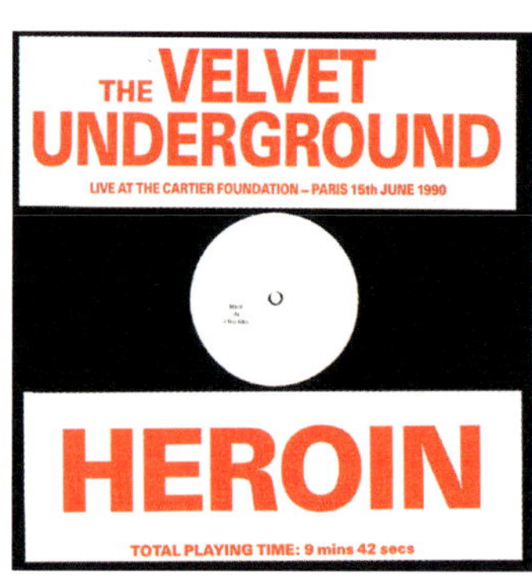

Weeks ahead of the concert, everyone was already talking about it. Lou Reed, John Cale, Sterling Morrison, and Moe Tucker, the original four members of Velvet Underground, would be at the *Andy Warhol System: Pub, Pop, Rock* exhibition at the Fondation Cartier, in Jouy-en-Josas (just outside of Paris) which opened on June 15th, 1990.

Although the four members were all going to be at the exhibition, each would have their own corner. Moe Tucker had remained friends with all her old colleagues, Sterling and John had met up from time to time, and John and Lou had buried the hatchet, after 20 years, for the Warhol tribute, *Songs for Drella*. Unfortunately, Lou and Sterling had been in a state of cold war and had not spoken in over 10 years, and there were spiteful claims in the press about royalty payments. The dream of seeing the four of them play together 22 years after their last show had been scornfully and emphatically denied by Cale and Reed.

Their interest grew, however, and they became more engaged in the event, with each of them helping to set up the exhibition, by rummaging through their personal effects to loan articles and documents that they had kept. A week before the opening, Reed and Cale agreed to play five songs from *Drella*.

The evening before the opening, I met Sterling Morrison in his Paris hotel. He was anxious, and became very agitated when he learned what Reed and Cale were playing the next day. "What am I supposed to do? What are people going to think? People will think that I can't play guitar anymore." It was another stab in the back, for somebody who thought that his role in the band had been underestimated.

At noon, the Fondation Cartier Park was welcoming the first of 500 guests. On the balcony of a private house, isolated at the back of the park, three figures were chatting. The vision of Cale, Morrison, and Tucker together was already a bit of an event for those who managed to see it. Three minutes later, a pair of dark glasses, curly hair and a leather jacket came forward timidly: Lou shook Sterling Morrison's hand nervously. The four of them sat down on a balcony table, and didn't leave until lunch was over.

Lou and his wife Sylvia then drove a few hundred metres to an open air stage: Cale and Reed were supposed to be playing in 10 minutes. "I think it would be nice to ask Sterling and Moe to join," said Lou. There was an astonished silence in the car. "And what about doing 'Pale Blue Eyes'?" he wondered, before somebody discreetly mentioned that Cale hadn't been around when they recorded that one.

One hour later, a commotion began at the back of the stage. They found Moe, but it was impossible to track down Sterling who was still unaware of what was going on. He was in a corner of the park when Reed and Cale played "Style It Takes" from *Songs for Drella*. No lights, a white stage, a background of pine trees, and pale sunlight. It was like being at a school fair. On the lawn, a few hundred attendees were stiff with excitement at the idea of witnessing the musical moment of their lives. The rumour went round in trembling voices: They had found Sterling.

"We have a surprise for you …" A shy grandmother took off her jacket and emerged as Moe Tucker: a purple silk shirt, necklace, buttoned-up collar, and dark glasses. There was another one, a beanpole of a man, dressed like a Texan going to church, and hidden behind a pair of Ray-Bans: Sterling was checking out a guitar that he'd seen for the first time.

The euphoria increased as Lou Reed played the first notes of "Heroin", rapidly submerged by a swell of noise. Everything was virginal, intact, more violent than any of the young kids today would dare to be: eight minutes of ecstasy, the audience in tears of emotion.

Three hours later, I kept bumping into people with dumbfounded expressions on their faces, still wondering what had happened. Some people were speechless. Cale, Reed, Morrison, and Tucker seemed even more ecstatic. At first they'd been forced together by the pressure of the event, now they seemed as inseparable as kids just having fun. Their legacy lives on.

Fifty years of Velvet Underground legacy. Collage by Christian Fevret & Rik Bas Backer.

Cat Power
JUNO
DANGEROUS
SUMMER 1987 No. 6
RHYTHMS
SLUT
NO NEW YORK
NEW YORK REVIEW OF SEX
NEW YORK'S GUIDE TO EROTIC EVENTS
The Toy Soldier EP
the riot squad
NEW YORK NOISE
DOMINATRIX SNATCH JUDY NYLON IMPLOG DARK DAY JAMES BLOOD ULMER IKE YARD MARTIN REV (SUICIDE) BORIS POLICEBAND UT
moe tucker
JOY DIVISION
POWER & SOUL
DANNY SAYS
SEPTEMBER 30
If I want to take a picture, I take it no matter what.
SCREW
UNTYPICAL GIRLS
the velvet underground
Club 57 Art Show
24 HOUR PARTY PEOPLE
FACTORY RECORDS / HACIENDA SPECIAL
A MAGNET PROMOTION
NIRVANA
NEVERMIND
CINDY SHERMAN
KUNSTHAUS ZÜRICH
More Women in Trees
the slits
TRASH
FRI JAN 24th
PHOENECIAN CLUB
SAT JAN 25th
BIG DAY OUT FESTIVAL
ARAKI
HOW MUSIC WORKS
DAVID BYRNE
beat PUNKS
Dazed and Confused
EXTREME CINEMA
DAVID BOWIE is
THE BALLAD OF SEXUAL DEPENDENCY
SLIDE SHOW BY NAN GOLDIN
i-D
DESPERATE LIVING A JOHN WATERS FILM
$2
Trainspotting
GERHARD RICHTER
NME
MAPPLETHORPE
FILE
O-P SCREENING
SUNDAY MAR 29
DEAD KENNEDYS
BUSH TETRAS
NICO
up
?uestlove.
PARADISO
JOHN CALE
COME OUT!!
SAGMEISTER
PUNK SHOWCASE
POSITIVE MENTAL ATTITUDE!
BAD BRAINS
In Person!
ALL AGES
MIRÓ
JEFF WALL
KENZO
HERE NOW
N.Y.C. ROCK
PSYCHIC TV
SCREW
RADIOHEAD
N.E.R.D
DAVID BOWIE - WITHOUT YOU
THE RATS
RUN RUN RUN
the CRAWdADDYS
there she goes again
LOU REED
New Scientist
vincent gallo
TEEN TURMOIL
Does growing up shrink your brain?
JOIN THE SISTERS & BROTHERS GAY LIBERATION
ANDY WARHOL
STEPHEN SHORE
ABEL FERRARA
"A GENUINE MASTERPIECE"
LILI TAYLOR
CHRISTOPHER WALKEN
ANNABELLA SCIORRA
THE ADDICTION
ALAN VEGA
100 000 WATTS OF FAT CITY
FAMOUS FOR 15 MINUTES ULTRA VIOLET
OUTSIDE THE LINES
BLONDIE
KATE WOMAN
EDIE FACTORY GIRL
RAMONES
ANARCHY PROTEST & REBELLION
DAVID BOWIE
BANKSY IN NEW YORK

PRIMITIVES
BLACK FLAG
Six Pack
NEW YORK
IS THIS FINALLY IT FOR THE STROKES?
USE HEARING PROTECTION
Time Out New York
New York kids
David Bowie on tour:
BOMB
24 HOUR PARTY PEOPLE
FAC 51 THE HAÇIENDA
ALL TOMORROW'S PARTIES
NICO
ROCK & ROLL JUST HAD A MINOR REVOLUTION
Chelsea HOTEL
nico and the faction
AUCKLAND Sat 22nd Feb, His Majesty's Theatre
Sun 23rd Feb, St James Theatre WELLINGTON
A VELVET REVOLUTION
VACLAV HAVEL
ELLEN WILLIS
BEGINNING TO SEE THE LIGHT
BAD
JOHN CALE
SCREW
ARAKI
ERASERHEAD
Gay Gotham
Bande à part
COURTNEY BARNETT & KURT VILE
CUT COOK COKE CRACK CRASH CROAK
BOY'S OWN STORY
EDMUND WHITE
DAZED
HISTORY IS MADE AT NIGHT
GODLIS
THE KILLS
THE OUTSIDERS
CBGB
Fall Fashion New York
Go-Betweens
HAPPY MONDAYS
NewOrder
THE FIRST POP AGE
HAL FOSTER
ANTON CORBIJN
SUTURE
YOU SAY YOU WANT A REVOLUTION?
V&A
the DOOM generation
URS LÜ
KUNSTHAUS
BECK
CLUB 57
Film, Performance, and Art in the EAST VILLAGE 1978–1983
PATTI SMITH
JOHN CALE
nico
CONTROL
TEST PRESSING
LAST DAYS
PUNKS, POETS & PROVOCATEURS
sonic youth
SWANS
KEVIN AYERS JOHN CALE ENO NICO AND THE SOPORIFICS
JUNE 1, 1974
IT'S NOT ONLY ROCK 'N' ROLL BABY!
MOJO
NICK CAVE
KLAUS NOMI
art sex music
BLONDIE
THE FEELIES
BAUHAUS
CBGB
...007...JOHN CALE...READY...FOR WA

LCD SOUNDSYSTEM
WITH SPECIAL GUEST
TV ON THE RADIO
2ND SHOW ADDED!
SATURDAY 28 APRIL
GREEK THEATRE
happy together
NAN GOLDIN
ROBERT PATTINSON
1000 LIVES
LCD SOUNDSYSTEM
LAST SHOW
with
LIQUID LIQUID
MADISON SQUARE GARDEN
APRIL 2
2011
JOHN CALE
WHAT'S WELSH FOR ZEN
STRANGER THAN PARADISE
ECHO & THE BUNNYMEN
Your body is a battleground
VIV ALBERTINE
THE CURE
STALKER
TARKOVSKI
PUNK
LOU REED
Time Out New York
PJ HARVEY
PUBLIC Image
HIGH & LOW
i-D
ARCHIE RAMONES
The Smiths
THE ALBUM
NICO 1988
WHY
VINYL
MATTERS
SEARCH & DESTROY
TEENAGE JESUS AND THE JERKS
DANIEL JOHNSTON
ROBERT MAPPLETHORPE
sally•can't•dance
New York Dolls
september 28 - 11pm
the bowery electric
327 bowery, nyc • tickets at TICKETFLY
Pervert your sense of decorum
KRAFTWERK
MAN
THE VELVET UNDERGROUND
Suicide
LOU REED BERLIN
SLACKER
MYSTERIOUS SKIN
LOU REED
ROCK
N
ROLL
ANIMAL
ALBUM SUICIDE BY SUICIDE
WIRE
JOHN CALE
Wonderland.
Kristen Stewart
THE WHITE STRIPES
INTERVIEW BY JIM JARMUSCH
DIGITALLY REMASTERED
JEAN MICHEL BASQUIA
DOWNTOWN 8
78-82
PRIMAL SCREAM
mixmag
Candy
ZIGZAG
The Slits
CHELSEA HOTEL NEW YORK 1965
"forget all that trip hop bullshit"
the return of
MASSIVE
Nan Goldin
VIVA FRANCO
So Yo
Issue Sixteen
STEPHEN SHORE
Sonic Youth
LOU REED
WANTED
LOU REED DEAD OR ALIVE
DOUGLAS GORDON
LITTLE CAESAR
The Peanuts
BLONDIE
1976-1980
ANGER
MAGICK LANTERN CYCLE
THE SAVILLE EXHIBITION
PSYCHOTIC REACTIONS AND CARBURETOR DUNG
BY LESTER BANGS
EDITED BY GREIL MARCUS
LESTER BANGS
THE JESUS AND MARY CHAIN
DIFFERENT TIMES
LOU REED IN THE 70S
NO WAVE
POST-PUNK.
UNDERGROUND.
NEW YORK.
1976-1980.
THURSTON MOORE
BYRON COLEY
Anton Corbijn
1-2-3-4
RIVER PHOENIX
KEANU REEVES
MY OWN PRIVATE IDAHO
A FILM BY GUS VAN SANT
LOU REED
TELEVISION
At Max's Kansas City
Wed. Aug. 28th-Mon. Sept. 2nd
Poison
A FILM BY TODD HAYNES
RAMONES
CBGB
RECORD COLLECTOR
PUNK
SIOUXSIE AND THE BANSHEES
LOU REED
METALLICA
NICO
SLOW DAZZLE
KNOW YOUR PHOTOGRAPHERS
NAN GOLDIN

WHITE LIGHT/WHITE HEAT, REVISITED

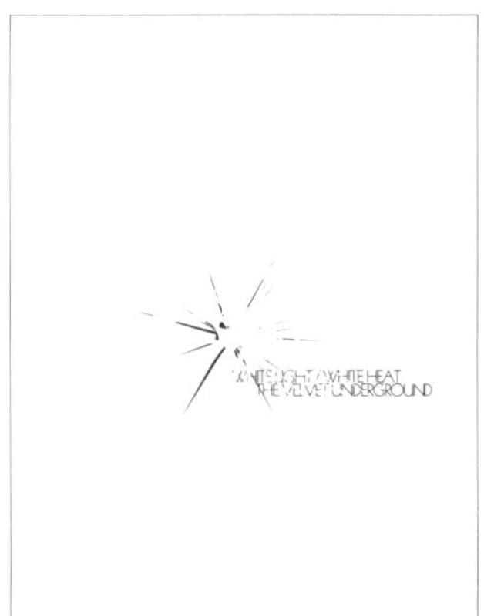

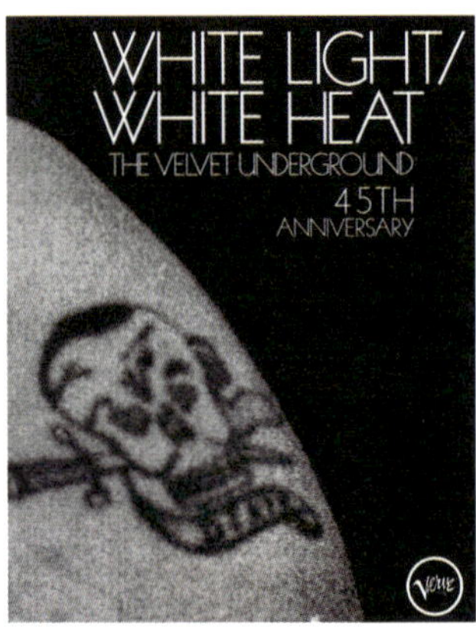

Posters designed, from left to right, by Thorsten Hoening; Keith Nickerson; Charlie Cruz; Jbeans; Mr Sinister; Nicholas Gagnon; Fitz Illitch; Ruru; Ana Virtuoso; Zingarina; Simon; Janderson; Oscar Daniel Montilla; Gigi Grà; Kris R.; I'm Sorry. Creative Allies Archives.

BIBLIOGRAPHY

"America" by Allen Ginsberg, from *Howl and Other Poems*, San Francisco, City Lights Books, 1956.
America/America by Jonathan Caouette: text written in November 2015 for the exhibition "The Velvet Underground New York Extravaganza," Cité de la musique-Philharmonie de Paris, 2016.
Excerpt from *What's Welsh for Zen? The Autobiography of John Cale* by John Cale and Victor Bockris, London, Bloomsbury Publishing PLC, 1999.
"A Family in Peril: Lou Reed's Sister Sets the Record Straight about his Childhood" by Merrill Reed Weiner. Excerpt from the text that appeared in *The Guardian*, April 2015.
"Letter to Delmore Schwartz," by Lou Reed: letter written in 1965, original typescript. Delmore Schwartz Papers, Beinecke Library, Yale University, collection of American Literature.
"Explosive Years," by Jonas Mekas: first-hand account in preparation for "The Velvet Underground New York Extravaganza" exhibition, 2015.
"How I discovered the Underground," John Cale: excerpt from an interview by Christian Fevret, published in the special edition of *The Velvet Underground and Andy Warhol, Les Inrockuptibles*, no.24, 1990.
"I Started Liking Rock 'n' Roll," Tony Conrad: interview by Christian Fevret in New York, November 2015.
"Chords and Words," Lou Reed: excerpts from an interview by Christian Fevret, published in the special edition of *The Velvet Underground and Andy Warhol, Les Inrockuptibles*, no.24, 1990.
"Why We Aren't Angry Young Men," by Jonas Mekas: *The Village Voice*, July 25, 1963.
"From the Diaries: On Barbara Rubin," Jonas Mekas, personal diary original typescript, December 18, 1980.
"Going Back in Time to Piero Heliczer," Sterling Morrison, *Little Caesar* no.9, 1979.
"The Velvet Underground Debuted at My High School," by Tony Jannelli: first-hand account recorded by Christian Fevret in New York, November, 2015.
"How I Was the First to Photograph the Velvet Underground," by Adam Ritchie: first-hand account recorded by Christian Fevret in January, 2016.
Excerpt from *Popism. The Warhol Sixties*, Andy Warhol & Pat Hackett, New York, Harcourt Brace Jovanovich, 1980.
"Andy Warhol and His Gang Meet the Psychiatrists," by Grace Glueck, © *The New York Times*, January 14, 1966.
"Nico by Ari" by Ari Boulogne : from *Cible mouvante, Nico* © Pauvert, département des éditions Fayard 2001
"Return to Rock," Lou Reed: excerpt from a 1969 interview for *Third Ear* magazine.
"Another Story of the Velvet Underground," Doug Yule: excerpt from an interview by Christian Fevret, published in the special edition of *The Velvet Underground, Les Inrockuptibles*, 1996.
"Last Concerts" by Richard Nusser. July 2, 1970, © Copyrighted 2013. Village Voice. 273452:0918JB.
"Fallen Knights And Fallen Ladies" by Lou Reed, from *No One Waved Good-bye: A Casualty Report on Rock and Roll*. Edited by Robert Somma. © *Fusion Magazine*, 1971.
"Dead Lie the Velvets Underground! R.I.P. Long Live Lou Reed!" by Lester Bangs. © Creem, 1971.
"The Velvet Revolution Rocks On" by Simmy Richman © *The Independent*, 2012.
"Please Kill Me," 12 original editions. Cover + prologue first page. From an idea by Danny Fields.
Thanks to Jonathan, Tommy, Gillian McCain.
"From the Velvet Underground to the Strokes" by Julian Casablancas © *Rolling Stone*, 2004.
"Nothing Compares to VU" by Christian Fevret, published in *The Velvet Underground and Andy Warhol, Les Inrockuptibles*, no.24, 1990.

CREDITS

© Cité de la Musique/Philharmonie de Paris–Un monde meilleur: AMERICA AMERICA a video mashup created by Jonathan Caouette–All rights reserved: 21, 26-27, 28-29.
© Collection John Cale: 31, 32, 34, 38, 39, 42.
© Collection Merrill Reed Weiner: 30, 32, 40.
© Collection Gerard Malanga: 14, 79, 92, 124, 130, 131, 174, 200, 222-223, 224.
© Collection Martha Morrison: 17, 18, 100, 101, 110, 120, 128, 160-161, 163, 172, 173, 176, 188, 189, 201
© Collection Jonas Mekas: 13, 25, 61, 63, 64, 66, 67, 69, 80, 81, 82, 83, 86-87, 99, 121, 125, 134, 144.
© Estate of Fred W. McDarrah: 1, 24, 25, 45, 46, 48, 49, 50-51, 52-53, 54-55, 56, 57, 58-59, 60, 62, 65, 70, 75, 77, 108-109, 129, 220-221, endpapers back.
© Estate of Nat Finkelstein: 6-7, 110,132-133, 152, 153, 154-155, 156, 157, 158-159, 166.
© Adam Ritchie Photography: endpapers front, 2-3, 4-5, 84, 94, 95, 96, 114-115, 116, 117, 118, 146, 147, 148, 149, 150, 151, 218-219, back cover.
© Stephen Shore, courtesy 303 Gallery, New York: 8, 136, 137, 138, 139, 140, 141, 142, 143.
© Fred Eberstadt/The Life Picture Collection: 135
© Hervé Gloaguen/Gamma Rapho: 126, 164, 165, 217.
© Bob Gruen: 205
© Ian Dickson@www.later20thcenturyboy.com: 205
© Steve Schapiro: 71, 168.
© Stephanie Chernikowski: 19. Used with her special authorization.
© Arturo Zavattini/Solares Fondazione delle Arti: 145.
© Henri ter Hall: 181, 183, 187, 195.
© Copyright & Courtesy of Anthology Film Archives, New York: 85.
© Don Snyder (Gerard Malanga Collection): 79.
© Diane Dorr Dorynek (Gerard Malanga Collection): 131.
© Ira Cohen Archives, LLC: 131
© Columbia University Division of Rare Book & Manuscript Butler Library: 78.
© Delmore Schwartz Papers, Yale Collection of American Literature, Beinecke Rare Book and Manuscript Library: 43, 44.
© Lynn Goldsmith/Corbis/Getty Images: 178-179.
© Donald Greenhaus: 98.
© 2018 Barbara Moore/Licensed by VAGA at Artists Rights Society (ARS), NY, Courtesy Paula Cooper Gallery, New York: 72.
© New York Outlaw Art Museum, the Clayton Patterson collection. Permission granted by Jeremiah Jay Newton: 175.
© Collection David Weisman: 135.
© National Youth Orchestra of Wales Collection: 36-37
© Steve Nelson: Poster design by Steve Nelson, copyright 1970, all rights reserved: 191.
© Everett Collection: 175.

Allan Rothschild Collection: 90-91, 113, 175.
Estate of Piero Heliczer for Marisabina Russo–Marisabina Russo Collection: 93, 103, 104, 105, 106.
Alfredo Garcia Collection: 65, 111, 122, 145, 170, 171, 184,
Posteritati Gallery, New York provided all film posters : 211, 212, 213.
Creative Allies Archives: 214
Private Collection: 16, 17, 25, 66, 76, 88, 89, 112, 162, 180.
Cornell University Library–Collection Division of Rare and Manuscript Collections: Cover

NEW YORK
The Velvet Underground
Experience exhibition
presented at
718 Broadway, New York
October 10th–December 30th,
2018

PARIS
The Velvet Underground
New York Extravaganza
presented at the
Philharmonie de Paris
March 30–August 21,
2016

NEW YORK EXHIBITION

Curators
Christian Fevret
Carole Mirabello

Scenography
Matali Crasset

Production Team
Summerlight Corp
Carole Mirabello
Christine Ponelle
Sylvie Sergent
Dominique Durand-Goldberg
Christian Fevret
Fabrice Sergent
Elad Azoulay

Assistant of the curators
Madeleine Olive

Production Manager
Invisible North
Rocky Ramniceanu
Tatyana Guzeva

Scenography Operations
Manager
Lionel Scharly Studio

Audiovisual Management
Matthias Abhervé
Rafaël Gubitsch

Audiovisual Technician
Rafaël Gubitsch

Graphic design
Nicolas Rouviere
Colin Ledoux
Robert O'Dowd

This exhibition is
presented by
BANDSINTOWN and CITI

Sponsored by
TIDAL (TBC)
SENNHEISER
JC DECAUX
NICE PROD

The curators gratefully acknowledge the following individuals for their contributions
Merrill Reed Weiner, Martha Morrison, John Cale, Nita Scott, Sebastian & Jonas Mekas, Gerard Malanga, Danny Fields, Stephen Shore & 303 Gallery NY, Marisabina Russo, Gloria & Timothy & Patrick McDarrah, Elisabeth Finkelstein, Jonathan Caouette, MM Serra, the Piero Heliczer Family, Adam Ritchie, David Weisman, Christopher Whent, Hervé Gloaguen, Esther Robinson, Allan Rothschild, Steve Nelson, Henri ter Hall, Bob Gruen, Geralyn Huxley & the Warhol Museum, Claude Ventura, Real Art Press, Frederic Eberstadt, Posteritati, MC Beaud, Dominique Wood Benneteau, Isabel Marant, Tony Jannelli & Robert Pietri, Sylvia Reed, Alfredo Garcia, and Fluxus friends.

Christian Fevret would like to extend a very special thanks to
Domi & famiglia + The Three Boys Gang, Simon, Kolja & Lucas, for their everlasting support.

Very special thanks from Carole Mirabello to
Patrick, Lou, Clara and Elio.

PARIS EXHIBITION

Director General
Laurent Bayle

Deputy Director General
Thibaud Malivoire de Camas

Secretary General
Hugues de Saint Simon

Director
Musée de la Musique
Marie-Pauline Martin

Deputy Director
Jade Bouchemit

Graphic Design
Nicolas Rouvière

Head of Exhibition
Department
Isabelle Lainé

Exhibition Project Manager
Julie Bénet

Production Manager
Christine Busset

Scenographic Operations
Manager
Olivia Berthon
Georgiana Savuta

Technical Manager
Dictino Ferrero

Audiovisual Manager
Matthias Abhervé

Audiovisual Technicians
Inès Saint-Cerin
Raphaël Gubitsch
Hugo Rouxel

FRENCH CATALOGUE

Project Management
Christian Fevret and
Carole Mirabello,
with the collaboration of
Bruno Juffin

Graphic Design
Change is good, Paris
Rik Bas Backer
José Albergaria

La Découverte/
Dominique Carré éditeur

Editorial Director
Rémy Toulouse

Editor
Nadège Baheux

Iconographer
Cécile Niesseron

Cité de la musique-
Philharmonie de Paris

Editorial Director
Stéphane Roth

Editor
Sabrina Valy
assisted by
Claire Martinet

"Long live the underground! The devil take the underground!"
—Dostoevsky

page 217: Velvet Underground shadow. Photograph: Hervé Gloaguen. pages 218-219: *Venus in Furs*. Photograph: Adam Ritchie. © Adam Ritchie Photography. pages 220-221: The Velvet Underground at the Film-Makers' Cinematheque, New York, February 1966. Photograph: Fred W. McDarrah. © Estate of Fred W. McDarrah. pages 222-223: Nico, Sterling Morrison, Moe Tucker, Lou Reed and John Cale at Castle, Los Angeles, May 1966. Photograph: Gerard Malanga. page 224: The Velvet Underground with their backs turned to the camera, May 1966. Photograph: Gerard Malanga. Endpapers back: MacDougal Street at night, Greenwich Village, New York, May 1966. Cafe Wha? is in the center. Photograph: Fred W. McDarrah. © Estate of Fred W. McDarrah.

CAFFE